INTERIOR FINISH MATERIALS FOR HEALTH CARE FACILITIES

INTERIOR FINISH MATERIALS FOR HEALTH CARE FACILITIES

A Reference Source For All Installations
Where Durable Surfaces Are Needed

By

VIRGINIA BEAMER WEINHOLD, IBD, IDEC

Department of Industrial Design
The Ohio State University
Columbus, Ohio

CHARLES C THOMAS • PUBLISHER
Springfield • Illinois • U.S.A.

Published and Distributed Throughout the World by
CHARLES C THOMAS • PUBLISHER
2600 South First Street
Springfield, Illinois 62794-9265

© *1988 by* CHARLES C THOMAS • PUBLISHER
ISBN 0-398-05397-9
Library of Congress Catalog Card Number: 87-17990

Printed in the United States of America
Q-R-3

Library of Congress Cataloging in Publication Data
Weinhold, Virginia Beamer.
  Interior finish materials for health care facilities.

  Includes bibliographies and index.
  1. Health facilities--Design and construction.
2. Finishes and finishing. I. Title. [DNLM: 1. Construction Materials. 2. Facility Design and Construction. 3. Health Facilities. WX 140 W423i]
RA967.W45   1987   690'.551   87-17990
ISBN 0-398-05397-9

FOREWORD

I AM ALWAYS looking for a good book.

Often, I am looking for a **good reference book.** Good reference books are both accessible and authoritative. *Interior Finish Materials for Health Care Facilities* succeeds in both respects. Analyzing it from my role as design practitioner, I see that it gives me information quickly, accurately and concisely. I understand the code of the book. I am not hesitant to open the book. Analyzing it from my role as academician, I see it gives me information thoroughly, accurately and precisely. I can open the book again and again.

The fact that this book is authoritative, and thus functions for the practitioner and academician, is not surprising; the author has, herself, played both roles. Through her experiences in design practice, the author understands the type of information that a designer, administrator, or facility manager is seeking. Introductory chapters are consistently formatted to outline fundamental principles and considerations. Charts and illustrations provide quick, accurate, and concise information for real needs.

Through her experience in academe, the author understands the value of rigorous research and well-structured information. The conceptual framework of the book is sound and the facts and references are complete.

Good reference books—those you will find worn, front and center on your shelf—are rare. References specific to interior design are even rarer. And yet, these types of books are badly needed. New finish materials with complicated specifications arrive on the market constantly. Demands on health care facilities made by users and code officials grow more complex. Anyone who has hunted through sample books for specific information, or who has pried it out of a product representative, or who has anxiously relied on someone else's "experience," knows frustrations can be ameliorated by better sources of information.

This is really a large problem. And just plain **good books** have much to do with speaking to a problem. While design may never be wholly scientific or quantifiable, better tools or methods to provide better information and to reduce error can be found. I believe this problem statement was at the heart of the conceptual context of this book. The author, because of her own personal experiences, wishes to improve the tools available to designers. Information that is applicable, accurate and accessible is a powerful tool.

Laura Zimmerman Rolfe, IBD
The Ohio State University

PREFACE

U NDERSTANDING the essence of a material enables one to use it
well. Beyond enabling excellence in implementation of the common uses of materials, comprehensive understanding gives one the ability to go beyond accepted uses. This book is about understanding
interior finish materials so that they can be used well and creatively.

The focus in on hardy materials. In hospitals, use often borders on
abuse and materials need to be hardy. The selection of materials to include in the book was based on current construction techniques, prevailing budgets and adaptability of a material to change as buildings are
reconfigured to accommodate changes in services.

On the other hand, the effective use of materials involves more than
satisfying the physical functions. Health care is about human beings
whose psychological and aesthetic senses are an important part of being.
Materials must be used to create an environment in which human sensitivity is recognized and nurtured.

If a material can be used to meet the demands of the health care environment, it will probably perform admirably in many other hard-use
situations. Therefore, this book is intended also as a reference to materials that perform well in many types of heavily used environments. It is
for the design professional and the design student as well as for the facility personnel involved in new building and renovation projects.

I would like to thank some special people from each of these groups
for inspiration and assistance in writing this book. Two administrators
with whom I worked on some of my first hospital design projects, Jack
Taylor and J. Rock Tonkel, were instrumental in making me aware of
the specific demands of health care design and attracting me to the chal-
lenge. Richard Miller, AIA introduced me to the critical evaluation and
careful specification of materials. These people played an important role
in the career path I have taken. It has been a rewarding one, and I thank
them.

For more current assistance, I want to thank three designers whose involvement with health care design is extensive and who have taken the time to read my drafts and contribute many valuable suggestions. These are Christina A. Johnson, AIA, IBD, partner in Design Collaborative, Seattle, Washington, Laura Rolfe, IBD, formerly a project designer with Design Collective, Inc., Columbus, Ohio and now assistant professor at The Ohio State University, and Mary Stringfield, AUID, IBD, who is Interior Designer for The Ohio State University Hospitals. I would also like to thank design students Marietta Hock and Susan Dewitt for assisting with the illustrations.

Finally, I want to express appreciation to the many manufacturer's representatives who have supplied current samples and information.

CONTENTS

Part V. Furniture and Casework

LIST OF FIGURES

CHAPTER SIX

CHAPTER SEVEN

CHAPTER EIGHT

CHAPTER NINE

CHAPTER TEN

CHAPTER ELEVEN

CHAPTER TWELVE

CHAPTER THIRTEEN

CHAPTER FOURTEEN

CHAPTER FIFTEEN

CHAPTER SIXTEEN

CHAPTER SEVENTEEN

LIST OF TABLES

CHAPTER SIX

CHAPTER SEVEN

CHAPTER EIGHT

CHAPTER NINE

CHAPTER TEN

CHAPTER ELEVEN

CHAPTER TWELVE

CHAPTER THIRTEEN

CHAPTER FOURTEEN

CHAPTER FIFTEEN

CHAPTER SIXTEEN

CHAPTER SEVENTEEN

INTERIOR FINISH MATERIALS FOR HEALTH CARE FACILITIES

INTRODUCTION

THE APPEARANCE of hospitals, nursing homes and other health care facilities has changed significantly in the last twenty years. Through the late sixties and early seventies, it was a rare hospital or nursing home where the interior spaces were visually appealing.

Historically, the hard, white "institutional look" was the preferred look for hospitals. Implications were of surfaces that had been scrubbed, disinfected with bleach, and made germ free. The need for durable and easily maintainable finish materials further contributed to the institutional appearance. Terrazzo and ceramic tile prevailed where affordable and corridors echoed with reflected sounds. For budget projects, vinyl asbestos tile and paint sufficed and, in areas of hard wear, looked dreary all too soon.

The color palette in these materials was limited but accepted. White predominated for many years and signified cleanliness. With the advent of the psychological and physiological studies of the effects of color, a wave of warm beige and restful green materials was selected but still with one predominant priority—to be as tough and durable as the budget would allow.

Tough and durable, for the most part, have meant cold, uninteresting and non-human. While the staff and services of most hospitals have been sensitive to human needs, the physical environment has often not conveyed this sensitivity. At one time this might not have been possible, but with the recent proliferation of technologies has come the availability of many finish materials that were not even imagined ten or fifteen years ago. In addition, vast improvements have been made to traditional materials. It is entirely possible to have a functional finish that is durable and easily maintainable and, at the same time, aesthetically pleasing and psychologically supportive.

A wide variety of materials is available in textures and colors that enable the designer to create an environment conducive to patient well-

3

being as well as one that endures under rugged conditions. But how does one determine which ones are appropriate for what situation? What predicates the choice of materials? Any or all of the following may be decisive factors:

1. Familiarity with the materials available in the marketplace
2. Experience with materials used on previous projects
3. Availability of specification guidelines
4. Budgeted time to devote to research and testing

Ideally, persons involved in the building and renovation of facilities would become thoroughly familar with the performance of all the materials in the marketplace. As a result of intensive investigation, each material specified would have consummate attributes for the particular application. Practically, this is impossible. There is never enough research time to fully realize the benefits of the vast array of materials available.

The purpose of this book is to provide a timesaving, initial resource for evaluating materials appropriate for specific health care facility needs. The needs of hospitals are the chief focus, as these are the most demanding. Recommendations are made for the selection of materials that will withstand such problems as cart traffic and spillage. Unusual uses for some materials are suggested. Special problems of other types of health care facilities are, also, specifically addressed.

While the focus is on health care facilities, the information is broadly applicable to other settings that receive hard use and are subject to heavy wear. The book is intended to serve as a resource for persons involved in the selection of interior finish materials in new building and renovation projects, particularly those buildings subjected to harsh treatment by the users.

In any evaluation of materials, many factors must be considered and the best solution implemented in accordance with the particular circumstances. For example, a degree of durability may need to be sacrificed to stay within the budget. **The best compromises can be made when the consequences of alternatives are recognized and the compromise is based on knowledge and balance.** So that objective decisions can be made, the following information is given for each finish material: structure and properties, health and safety considerations, types or classifications, maintenance needs, installation or fabrication procedures, and specification guidelines.

In addition, introductory chapters to the content chapters on flooring materials, wall finishes, window treatment and upholstery fabrics contain general information and material comparisons according to: health and safety factors, environmental factors, wear-life factors, maintenance factors, and cost effectiveness.

The final chapter focuses on the nursing station. The nursing station is the essence of the hospital; it is the functional and aesthetic core. Much creativity can be utilized here, putting rugged materials together in new ways that protect the surfaces and, at the same time, contribute to the distinctive image of the facility.

While much of this information is presently available, it is scattered among many resources, and some very creative and unusual uses of materials have not been published at all. A single resource is needed to expedite the finish material selection process.

The idea for this book began to take shape during the author's ten years of experience in the design of the interiors of health care facilities. It was prompted by three primary conditions.

1. It was time consuming to research the needs and possible solutions for each building area. Often, it was not possible within the allotted budget.
2. It was necessary to give each newly hired designer an introductory education as to specific facility requirements and available solutions.
3. The client, in many cases, wanted outside confirmation that design solutions would work.

This book is directed to both the designer and the client. This includes interior and architectural designers, administrators, facility managers and planners, maintenance engineers and others involved in making the decisions for the interior finishes of the facility.

From the Client's Point of View

When the time arrives for a new building or new renovation project, there are many managerial demands on the person in charge; research into appropriate finish materials is seldom a high priority. The tendency is towards conservatism (towards sticking with proven materials and suppliers) or to respond to a smooth and enthusiastic sales presentation. The selected material could be the best available, but most persons involved in a building project would prefer to have an efficient and systematic way to evaluate the alternatives.

From the Designer's Perspective

Once the contract is signed, meeting the schedule is of the essence. Again, efficiency in identifying and evaluating alternatives is mandatory. What materials can most effectively be used to meet the requirements of function and aesthetics? Here, also, designers have a tendency to specify what has been used before without performing time-consuming research for other materials that might better meet the needs of the particular project. Even when an "office expert" has done the necessary research, the expert may not be available for timely consultation with the designers working on the project. All too often the information and research results are in the expert's head rather than in a form readily available to the designer at the time most efficient for making a decision.

This book is intended to assist communication among designers and between designer and client. Health care facilities and especially hospitals are expensive building types with many unique design requirements. It is critical that the decision makers involved are able to use design time efficiently and to be confident of appropriate finish material decisions.

Part I

THE FLOOR

Chapter One

INTRODUCTION TO FLOORING MATERIALS

FLOORING MATERIALS can be divided into three broad categories: resilient flooring, hard surface flooring and carpet. Which type to install in which locations is highly controversial in many construction and renovation projects, particularly when carpet is being considered. In this chapter, attributes of these three categories are compared. Chapters Two, Three and Four contain an extensive analysis of each of the flooring types and explain the details which are the basis of Chapter One comparisons.

Resilient and hard surface floorings are the traditional materials used in health care facilities. They are still the best alternative in many situations. Only recently has carpet become a consideration. The first carpet installations were not notably successful and, in many cases, left others reluctant to install carpet. However, technical advances have made it a viable alternative. The advantages that prompted the first installations are the same today, and technology has overcome many of the initial limitations.

It is worthwhile to evaluate the advantages and limitations of each type of flooring material in the various environments found in the health care facility. Factors that assist in this evaluation divide readily into three categories. First are the health and safety factors. These are always important in a facility where many of the clients are elderly or handicapped. Some health and safety factors are mandated by code regulations. Second are the environmental factors which contribute to the physical and psychological well-being of the inhabitants. Third, the wear life of the materials must be considered.

Health and Safety Factors

Flame resistance, electrostatic propensity, biogenic factors and slip resistance are the most essential health and safety factors to be considered. **Flame resistance** codes are specified in regulatory districts and must be met. The **electrostatic propensity** of a material determines the static generation of that material. Static can be a mere annoyance, can cause malfunction of sensitive equipment or can cause an explosion under certain conditions. **Biogenic** factors may affect the control of growth and spread of organisms, and **slip resistance** is an important safety consideration.

Flame Resistance

Carpet that meets code requirements will not support combustion. However, nylon (the most appropriate fiber for health care facilities) will melt when exposed to a concentrated heat source about 350° F. A burning cigarette will melt and stain nylon carpet; it will create a permanent stain in vinyl resilient flooring. Rubber resilient flooring is affected less and ceramic tile not at all.

Electrostatic Propensity

For most people, 3.5 kV (kilovolts) is the threshold of sensitivity to static electricity. In a properly specified carpet for general use areas, the static electricity generated at 20° C and 70 percent relative humidity must be specified as less than 3.5 kV. At this threshold, one need not be concerned about static electricity generated by other floorings. For areas where sensitive electronic equipment such as computers or heart monitors is being used, the electrostatic propensity that can be tolerated is much less. Special static-resistance carpets must be specified. For some sensitive equipment, special, conductive resilient and hard surface floorings also must be specified.

Biogenic Factors

Published reports from the Centers for Disease Control in Atlanta, Georgia rate carpet at least as safe as resilient and hard surface flooring with regard to spreading bacteria and fungi. In fact, some informal studies conclude that vacuuming carpet actually reduces the number of bacteria present, which is not true for wet mopping floors.

Slip Resistance

Falls are a consideration in flooring decisions. Resilient and hard surface floorings, especially when polished or wet, are a contributing factor to falls. Carpet reduces the incidence of slips and falls and cushions them when they do occur, reducing severity of injury. On the other hand, older people wearing shoes with soft crepe soles can sometimes stumble more easily on carpet.

Environmental Factors

Environmental factors such as **acoustics, comfort** and the **ambience** of the space affect people in their everyday use of any facility. Another factor, especially important to hospital personnel, is **wheeled vehicle mobility.**

Acoustics

Moving equipment and voice noises are a source of annoyance to patients. Carpet lessens airborne sounds and virtually eliminates impact sounds. One hospital study reported an average difference of 15 decibels between carpeted and tiled areas (Graham and Berkman, 1978).

Maintenance sounds must also be considered. The vacuum cleaner is somewhat noisier than the buffer and, obviously, considerably noisier than the mop.

Impact sounds of dropped objects are less with carpet. The cushioning effect can also significantly reduce breakage of dropped objects.

Comfort

Carpet reduces foot and leg fatigue for nurses who spend a large part of the day walking. It relieves coldness at floor level for both patients and staff. With carpet, floors are physically warmer and the total environment is psychologically warmer. This is especially an advantage in a nursing home or other long-term care facilities where cold sensitive, elderly residents are encouraged to be up and about.

Ambience

The appearance of carpet suggests quality, warmth and a home-like atmosphere. Resilient and hard surface floorings suggest cleanliness and reinforce the institutional image. These are important considerations in view of the correlation between environment and morale.

Wheeled Vehicle Mobility

More effort is required to move carts, stretchers, radiology equipment and other wheeled vehicles on carpet than on resilient or hard surfaces. However, this can be mitigated with the use of large (5"-8") wheels and properly specified, low pile, dense carpet. Wheeled vehicle mobility is best over hard surface flooring. The degree of resilience in resilient flooring determines wheeled vehicle mobility, and there is a wide range as discussed in Chapter Three on resilient flooring.

Wear-Life Factors

The wear life of a material is dependent upon three essential factors: **durability, appearance retention** and **maintenance.** In assessing the potential specification of a material, one must look at the **initial cost** of obtaining appropriate durability and appearance-retention characteristics, and at the **maintenance cost** of properly sustaining them.

Durability

Durability refers to the ability to endure or not wear out. The chief cause of wear in a flooring material is abrasion from the constant traffic and the abrasive soil particles that are ground into the floor by this traffic. Some materials inherently resist abrasion better than others.

Overall, hard surface materials are the most resistant to abrasion, resilient floorings are less resistant and the textile fibers of which carpet is made are the least resistant. However, within each category, there are substantial variations in durability dependent on the specific materials used and the construction methods. Evaluation of contributors to these variations is an essential factor in the specification of any material, especially carpet. A complete discussion is included in each chapter on flooring. Proper specification can contribute greatly to durability.

Appearance Retention

A flooring material can have excellent wearing qualities and still appear worn if it is crushed, dirty, faded or otherwise disfigured. Appearance retention refers to the ability of the material to recover from deformation and to disguise blemishes until relief comes from scheduled maintenance. It is a function not only of materials and construction but also of color, texture and pattern. Again, these will be specifically discussed for each floor finish. These are extremely important factors, as a finish that looks worn will convey a poor image and may need to be replaced long before it actually is worn.

Maintenance and Cleaning

Proper and regular maintenance of any material will prolong its wear life. The shorter the time an abrasive particle remains, the less damage it can do. The shorter the time a spill remains, the less potential for permanent stain.

Equipment needs, cleaning solutions and personnel skills differ for different materials. An essential part of the floor finish selection is an assessment of the ability and commitment of the institution to acquire proper equipment, train the staff in proper procedures and monitor implementation.

Another maintenance issue is standardization of materials used, so that replacement inventory can be kept low and a minimum number of cleaning supplies need to be stocked. Also, with standardization, fewer procedures and idiosyncrasies of materials will need to be learned by maintenance and cleaning staffs.

Initial Cost and Maintenance Cost

A large number of studies have been conducted regarding a cost comparison between carpet and other flooring materials. In comparisons of carpet with resilient and hard surface floorings, substantial agreement exists that the initial cost of carpet is higher and carpet must be replaced more frequently, but that these higher costs are outweighed by the lower maintenance costs of carpet.

Tables 1.1 and 1.2 have been compiled based on tables and data in the *Carpet Specifier's Handbook* (Carpet and Rug Institute, 1980, 1987). Results of most of the studies in this subject have been published by entities associated with the carpet industry. While this could make the results suspect, it would seem that producers of competitive products would have been more active in conducting and publishing studies if carpet industry claims were faulty.

The tables compare the total cost of flooring, that is, the sum of the initial cost plus maintenance cost, on an annual and twenty-year basis. Materials used for the study include level loop, third-generation nylon carpet glued to the substrate, 0.090 sheet vinyl, 1/8" vinyl composition tile, and " terrazzo. Hard surface materials in addition to terrazzo were priced in the study. Among these was ceramic tile at $4.65 per square foot. It was assumed that the maintenance cost would be the same as for other resilient and hard surface floorings; however, this was not tested.

Table 1.1

COMPARISON OF ANNUAL COSTS OF 1000 SQ FT OF FLOORING

	Carpet	Vinyl	VCT	Terrazzo
Material Cost Basis				
Cost/sq ft	1.61	2.10	1.06	5.10
Life Expectancy	10 years	15 years	15 years	25 years
Annual cost/sq ft	.161	.140	.070	.204
Annual cost/1000 sq ft	161.00	140.00	70.60	204.00
Initial Cost				
Material Installed	161.00	140.00	70.60	204.00
Maintenance Cost				
Cleaning Labor	312.40	491.20	491.20	491.20
Capital Equipment	30.45	55.94	55.94	55.94
Expendable Supplies	26.90	192.15	192.15	192.15
Equipment Care	7.61	13.98	13.98	13.98
Total	$538.36	$893.27	$823.87	$957.27

Legend:

vinyl = sheet vinyl
VCT = vinyl composition title

Figures are from the *Carpet Specifiers Handbook,* 1987 edition, printed by The Carpet and Rug Institute.

Table 1.2

COMPARISON OF TWENTY YEAR COSTS OF 1000 SQ FT OF FLOORING

	Carpet	Vinyl	VCT	Terrazzo
Initial Cost				
Material Installed	$3220.00	$2800.00	$1412.00	$4080.00
Maintenance Cost				
Cleaning Labor	6248.00	9824.00	9824.00	9824.00
Capital Equipment	609.00	1118.80	1118.80	1118.80
Expendable Supplies	538.00	3843.00	3843.00	3843.00
Equipment Care	152.20	279.60	279.60	279.60
Total	$10,767.20	$17,865.40	$16,477.40	$19,145.00

Legend:

vinyl = sheet vinyl
VCT = vinyl composition title

Figures are from the *Carpet Specifier's Handbook,* 1987 edition, printed by The Carpet and Rug Institute.

Maintenance costs given in the tables are based on a work standard system and a maintenance level system developed by Industrial Sanitation Counselors, Inc. to provide a base of known values. The figures used are based on an appearance level of 90 on the maintenance level system scale of 100.

Transitions

Another factor, in addition to the characteristics of individual finishes, is the number of transitions from one to another. At most transitions between two materials, a transition strip must be used. This forms a bump which can cause difficulties with small-wheeled carts. Care must be taken to specify low profile strips, but problems can occur even with the lowest profile. Bumps can cause inconvenience in equipment transport and pain for severely injured patients.

It has also been found that some older people have perceptual problems with transitions. Because of differences in color and texture, there may appear to be a difference in height that does not actually exist. In passing from one surface onto another, an adjustment in walking must be made for each new surface. This can be troublesome for both older people and children.

Another transition consideration is housekeeping. A carpeted office in the midst of a large area of vinyl means that a vacuum cleaner must be brought into a space where mops and buffing equipment are used for the care of all other flooring in the area. For example, a carpeted dietician's office may appear to be the proper solution when considered as a single entity, but if the office is the only carpeted room in the center of a vinyl or ceramic floor area, accessibility to a vacuum cleaner can be a maintenance problem.

Two other problems having to do with maintenance must be addressed. When wax is being applied to resilient floors, the applicator can slip over onto the adjacent carpet, spoiling the appearance along the carpet edge. Also, dirt from shoes tends to be deposited on the first foot or two of carpet adjacent to hard surface floors. The dirt clinging to shoes tends to fall off a little at a time as a person walks over hard surface floors, but, due to friction, is deposited all at once as the person first steps onto carpet.

These problems do not preclude the use of any particular material but do suggest that each material be used in the widest possible contiguous area. Small isolated areas of materials should be avoided where possible.

Organization of Chapters on Flooring

For each functional area, advantages and limitations of various flooring alternatives must be weighed. The following chapters on carpet, resilient flooring and hard surface flooring are intended to help the reader make knowledgeable decisions. The information in each is organized under six major headings:

1. Structure and Properties
2. Health and Safety
3. Types
4. Maintenance
5. Installation
6. Specification Notes

Structure and Properties

Structure, as used here, includes both the components used and the construction methods. **Properties** are the characteristics or attributes of the material. Each finish has certain properties as a result of the components used and the way that they are put together. Understanding this structure will aid in understanding to what extent desirable properties are possible, help to judge the validity of glowing statements in the manufacturer's literature, and note omissions of vital facts in this literature. It should help define the critical questions to be asked for proper evaluation.

Health and Safety

With each finish, there are associated questions of health and safety. This section seeks to respond to those most frequently asked.

Types

Flooring materials are referenced by type. The type often defines critical functional qualities. For example, porcelain tile is non-porous by definition and quarry tile is semi-porous. Many times, however, the differences within a type are greater than the differences between types. For example, the fiber used in a carpet will make a greater difference in such properties as abrasion resistance and resilience than whether the carpet type is tufted or woven.

Maintenance

In this section, maintenance requirements are discussed. In evaluating any finish, it is essential to understand the equipment and labor that will be needed to maintain it. These will profoundly affect the total cost of the product. They must be added to the initial cost to make a valid assessment of the lifetime or life cycle cost.

Installation

First, it should be stated that this section is not a complete guide to installation. Most manufacturers give excellent installation instructions for their own products and these are typically found in the manufacturer's literature. Instead, the information presented here is intended to help in evaluating what type of installation will be most appropriate for the function of the space, problems that may arise with certain types of installations, and other key points that may assist in material selection.

Specification Notes

This is not a complete guide to specification. Rather, it identifies sources for complete specification guides and notes some special points that are often not given the attention they deserve. It also identifies frequently overlooked details and refinements.

Chapter Two

CARPET

CARPET IS floor covering that can be recommended for many locations if it is properly specified. Emphasis should be placed on the
words "properly specified." There are all too many installations where
carpet is performing poorly because the specification was inappropriate
for the function of the space.

The advantages of carpet that prompted its use for health care applications were principally the environmental factors of noise cushioning,
comfort and the ambience that could be achieved. Safety, specifically
slip resistance, was also a major factor. In the first installations, some of
the other health and safety factors and wear life factors such as durability
and appearance retention were marginal. Improvement in these properties has been the object of intensive research.

Great strides have been made in carpet technology. It is now possible
to specify a carpet that will meet the strictest health and safety criteria
and have excellent durability and appearance retention. Maintenance
procedure recommendations have been refined to achieve the greatest
potential in wear life. All of this means that carpet is the best choice for
many health care applications. It also means that the specifier must understand which carpet has the qualities that meet stringent health care
criteria. There is much carpet made that does not. The properties of any
carpet are highly dependent on the fibers used and the way they are put
together. To understand and specify carpet, one must understand its
structure.

Structure and Properties

The wear life and environmental factors of a carpet can be predicted
with reasonable accuracy when the important structural components
and their affect on the desired properties are understood.

In the "Introduction to Floor Coverings," wear-life factors were identified as durability, appearance retention and maintenance. Durability of carpet is chiefly a matter of abrasion resistance. Principle contributors to abrasion resistance are the **tuft density** or how tightly the face pile yarns are packed together, the **face weight** or weight of the face pile, the **tuft type** and the nature of the **fiber,** itself. Using a fiber for the face of the carpet that is naturally abrasion resistant is obviously important. A lot of these fibers packed closely together will resist dirt penetration. It is the embedded granules of dirt that wear away or abrade a carpet.

A carpet can have excellent wearing qualities, losing very little of its face fiber, and still appear worn if it is crushed, dirty, faded or otherwise disfigured. Appearance retention refers to the ability of the carpet to recover from deformation and to disguise blemishes until relief comes from scheduled maintenance. It is a function of the face **fiber** as well as **color, dye method, texture** and **pattern.**

As durability and appearance retention can be predicted using a knowledge of carpet structure, so can ease of maintenance, life cycle cost and the effects on the environment. Table 2.1 provides a quick reference

Table 2.1

PROPERTIES AFFECTED BY THE STRUCTURE OF CARPET

Property Affected	Structural Components						
	Tuft Density	Face Weight	Tuft Type	Face Fiber	Color	Dye Method	Texture Pattern
WEAR LIFE **Durability**							
Abrasion Res.	X	X	X	X			
Appearance Retention							
Resilience	X	X	X	X			
Soil Hiding				X	X		X
Color Change			X	X	X	X	
Maintenance							
Cleanability	X		X	X	X	X	X
ENVIRONMENTAL							
Acoustics	X	X	X				
Comfort	X	X					
Ambience	X	X	X		X		X
Wheeled Equip.	X	X	X				

to this section showing which properties are affected by the various components of the structure of the carpet.

Tuft Density

Fiber thickness and compactness prevent dirt from getting down into the carpet. Dirt is abrasive, and abrasion is the biggest deterrent to long wear. Also, the denser the pile, the less weight each tuft must support. Generally, the higher the density, the greater the resistance to crushing.

That the density of carpet is extremely important is confirmed by the number of density terms used. Commonly used terms are tuft density, density index or density factor, and average pile density value. Each of these terms has a different meaning, but all are directed toward defning just how dense the face pile of the carpet is.

Tuft density describes the number of tufts per unit area of carpet. It is measured in tufts per inch across the carpet and stitches or rows per inch along the length of the carpet. These are described differently for different types of carpet construction. (If the reader is unfamiliar with construction methods, it may be helpful to first read the section, "Types of Carpet.")

In **tufted carpet,** where each row of tufts is inserted by a row of needles, the tufts per inch are identified by the gauge or the distance between tufting needles. This distance is expressed in fractions of an inch. The satisfactory gauges for high traffic areas are 5/64", 1/10" or 1/8". The number of lengthwise tufts are determined by how many rows of tufts are stitched into each lengthwise inch of carpet. This is the stitch rate and is called stitches per inch. There should be at least 8 to 10 stitches per inch (see Fig. 2.1).

The tuft bind or measure of the force required to pull out the tufts is an important consideration in the specification of tufted carpet. Tuft bind is discussed in the section on carpet construction.

In **woven carpet,** the tufts per inch are measured by the pitch which is the number of warp yarns in a 27" width. For a velvet or an Axminster, 216 is the minimum pitch that should be used. In a woven carpet, another row is formed every time the weft yarn is woven through the warp yarns. The weft yarn is pulled through the warp by a wire over which loops are formed. The number of lengthwise tufts are called rows or wires per inch. For a velvet, 8 to 10 rows or wires is appropriate; for an Axminster, 9 to 12 (see Fig. 2.1).

A comparison between the two types can easily be made. In a tufted carpet, the number of tufts per inch is the reciprocal of the gauge, e.g.

Tufted Carpet

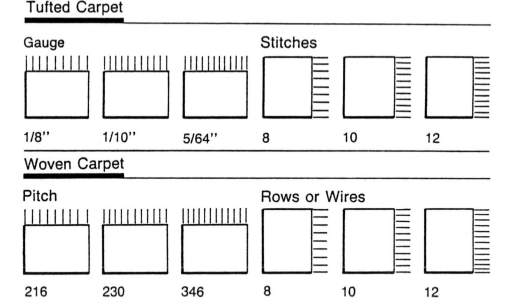

Gauge

Stitches

| 1/8" | 1/10" | 5/64" | 8 | 10 | 12 |

Woven Carpet

Pitch

Rows or Wires

| 216 | 230 | 346 | 8 | 10 | 12 |

Figure 2.1. TUFT DENSITY. While the physical density may be the same in tufted and woven carpets, the measures of density are expressed differently. A comparison of closeness of warp yarns, in particular, is apt to be confusing. The figure illustrates that similar distances are identified by different names and numbers. The mathematical comparison is $1/\text{gauge} = \text{pitch}/27$.

1/8 gauge = 8 tufts per inch. In a woven carpet, the number of tufts per inch is the pitch divided by 27, e.g., $216/27 = 8$ tufts per inch.

Assuming the carpets in the above examples have 9 stitches or rows per inch, the tuft density or quantity of tufts per square inch, in each case, is:

$$8 \text{ tufts/in} \times 9 \text{ stitches or rows/in} = 72 \text{ tufts/sq in}$$

For best performance in all types of carpet, there should be balanced tuft placement, that is, tufts/inch equal stitches or rows per inch. For health care use, a **minimum** of 64–72 tufts per square inch is recommended.

However, having an adequate number of tufts per square inch is not enough to assure a sufficiently dense carpet face. The size of the tuft yarn will also make a difference in the overall density of the face pile. If the number of tufts remains constant, an increase in yarn size will increase the density of the carpet.

The expression for density that takes into account tuft density plus tuft size is density index. This is sometimes called the density factor. In computing the density index, yarn size is measured in denier. (For more about denier and how to convert other fiber size measurements to denier, read about fiber coarseness in the subsection, "Fiber Properties.")

The density index is found by multiplying denier times tuft density. Assuming a denier of 1800 and using the above example of 8 tufts per inch and 9 stitches or rows per inch, the following is an example of computing the density index.

Density Index = denier (tufts/in × stitches or rows/in)
Density Index = 1800 (8 × 9)
Density Index = 129,600

Increasing the density index will increase the performance, but the relationship is not constant. Allied Corporation has prepared a graph to show this relationship. Figure 2.2 is taken from this graph. As can be

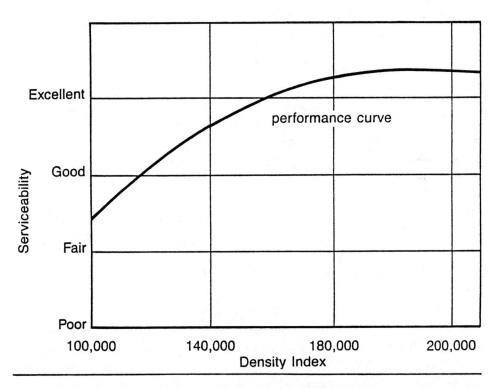

Figure 2.2. PERFORMANCE CURVE FOR FILAMENT NYLON. For a filament nylon carpet, a minimum density index of 176,000 is desirable. Performance improvement gained by further increasing the density index is negligible. The comparable minimum, desirable density index for a staple nylon carpet is 256,000. (Graph adopted from Allied Corporation, Anso[R] IV Guide to Commercial Carpet, p. 13.)

seen, the performance improvement increment lessens as the density index or density factor becomes higher. Beyond a certain point, improvement gained from increasing the density index becomes negligible. The curve would differ somewhat for different types of carpet with different types of tuft. This chart illustrates a tufted, looped pile, filament nylon carpet.

Face Weight

Face weight (also called pile weight) refers to the amount of pile yarn in a given area of carpet face. Because the cost of the pile yarn is a major cost element in production, heavier carpets cost more. **For any given face weight, lower pile and higher tuft density give the best performance for the money.**

The relationship of face weight to pile height is called average pile density value, weight density or simply density. Here is yet another use of the term, density. This density is defined as the weight of pile yarn in a unit volume of carpet. It is generally given as ounces per cubic yard.

$$\text{Density (oz/cu yd)} = \frac{\text{Face Weight (oz/sq yd)} \times 36}{\text{Pile Height (inches)}}$$

Minimum densities and face weights suggested for health care facilities vary according to the tuft type, loop or cut. Table 2.2 shows these minimums along with the maximum pile height that would maintain the minimum density at the given face weight. Decreasing this pile height or increasing the face weight would increase the density value with a probable increase in performance.

An increase in face weight will increase performance up to a point of diminishing returns. After 30 ounces per square yard in loop and 40 ounces per square yard in cut, there are no real returns.

Noise reduction bears a relationship to pile height. This is an area where compromise may be necessary. While any carpet will substantially reduce noise, a higher pile carpet will reduce it more than a lower pile carpet. There is a wide variation in the NRC (noise reduction coefficient) rating of carpet in any particular thickness, but a good approximation is 1/8" thick carpet would have an NRC of 0.15, while a 7/16" thick carpet could have an NRC of 0.40.

Another consideration in selecting pile height is cart traffic. The lower the pile height, the less effort is required to move a cart over the carpet. A high density would also contribute to a firmer surface and less effort.

Table 2.2

MINIMUM DENSITY RECOMMENDATIONS

Tuft Type	Minimum Density	Minimum Face Weight (oz/sq yd)		Maximum Pile Height (inches)
Level Loop	4600		22	.176
Multi-level Loop or Cut and Loop	4800		26	.195
Cut	3800	BCF	28	.265
		staple	34	.322

Tuft Type

Tufts can be cut, loop, or a combination of cut and loop. They can be all of one level or multi-level. A loop pile carpet is the longest wearing and a single-level loop the longest of all. However, a multi-level loop while giving slightly less wear has more texture which tends to hide seams and provide some camouflage for soil.

A cut-and-loop pile gives somewhat less wear but provides more pattern which may conceal the wear. However, a pattern that is dependent on cut and loop can tend to disappear, as the cut pile flattens out more than the loop. The greater the density, the less this effect will occur. High density is of great importance in cut-and-loop as well as cut pile constructions.

Cut pile has the shortest wear life. As the pile flattens, sides of the yarn are exposed. These are a different color from the ends and the color appearance of the carpet changes as wear occurs. Yarn twist adds resilience which helps combat this tendency to flatten out. A frieze with its highly twisted yarn has excellent appearance retention, the best of the cut piles.

The degree of twist and twist stability which are achieved by heat setting are most important for cut pile. In general, the tighter the twist, the better the carpet performance. One way to judge the twist level is to look closely at the cut tips of individual tufts. They should be neat, well defined and not flare open.

The exception to this is a velour plush (a very smooth-appearing cut pile carpet) where the smooth surface is achieved by using very little yarn twist. In selecting a plush, a high density and low pile become very important for satisfactory performance. This type of carpet should not be chosen for high traffic areas.

Cut pile carpets are typically better sound absorbers than loop pile. In cut pile carpets, NRC (noise reduction coefficient) values increase as either pile height or pile weight are increased. In loop pile, however, the NRC value increases as pile height is increased but shows little change if only the weight is increased. Loose, less dense carpets are superior to tight construction for sound control. This opposes the criteria for wear resistance. Designers need to take this trade-off into consideration.

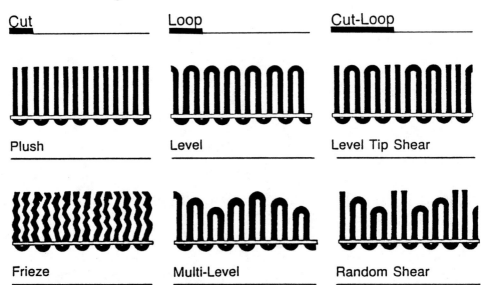

Figure 2.3. TYPES OF CARPET TUFTS. The dual options of cut or loop and level or multi-level tufts provide the opportunity for many variations in appearance and a wide range of appearance-retention attributes. In general, a loop pile will retain its appearance much longer than a cut pile, but differences in pile height, tuft density and yarn twist cause considerable variation.

Face Fibers

Within the United States, almost all commercial carpet is manufactured from five pile fibers: the natural fiber; wool, and the synthetics; acrylic, nylon, olefin and polyester. (For a more complete description of fiber classification, see Chapter 11 on "Drapery.") It was the development of synthetic fibers that made carpet possible in health care facilities. While two of these fibers can be considered for use in public and hard use areas, nylon is the fiber of choice. It is the most durable and has the best appearance-retention attributes. Olefin is a durable second choice, but its lower resiliency means a shorter appearance life. Acrylic does not have sufficient durability nor does polyester which also lacks the necessary resiliency. For a summary comparison of performance characteristics of carpet fibers, see Table 2.3.

Table 2.3

EVALUATION GUIDE: PERFORMANCE CHARACTERISTICS OF CARPET FIBERS

Property	Fiber					
	Nylon 6,6	Nylon 6	Acryl	Olefin	Poly	Wool
HEALTH & SAFETY						
Flame Resistance	4	3	1	3	2	3
Static Resistance	3	3	3	3	3	2
Mildew Resistance	3	3	3	3	3	1
WEAR LIFE						
Durability						
Abrasion Resistance	4	4	2	3	2	2
Appearance Retention						
Resiliency	4	3	3	1	2	3
Soil Resistance	4	4	2	4	2	3
Stain Resistance	3	3	2	4	3	2
Fade Resistance	3	1	3	4	3	3
Maintenance						
Cleanability	4	4	2	4	2	3
ENVIRONMENTAL						
Dying Flexibility	4	4	3	2	2	3
Styling Versatility	4	4	2	2	2	3

Legend:

Poly = polyester

4 = excellent

3 = good

2 = fair

1 = poor

OLEFIN: Olefin, most commonly the polypropylene type, is being made into carpets for institutional applications. Less expensive than nylon, olefin could be considered in cases of critical budgetary problems and for temporary renovations and other cases of short-term use. It is chemically related to nylon and has many of the same properties. Wear is comparable, but nylon has better appearance retention, is more resilient and more easily cleaned. Olefin, which has a lower melting point, will acquire scorch marks from the heat of friction generated when furniture or equipment is dragged over it. With the frequency of moving large items in most health care institutions, this is a severe handicap.

While olefin is second best in overall performance, there are some locations where it may be the best solution. It is highly moisture and stain resistant and fairly resistant to fading and deterioration from sunlight. It is the fiber from which "indoor-outdoor" carpet is made. Areas where it might be considered preferable to nylon are those where sunlight is a problem. Some olefin carpets are constructed for poolside use. These can be advantageously used in hydrotherapy spaces.

NYLON: First introduced for carpeting by Dupont in 1947, nylon offered the best combination of qualities for performance in heavy traffic areas and rapidly became the predominant fiber. Its natural attributes are outstanding strength, abrasion resistance and resilience. It is soil, mildew and rot resistant, non-absorbent, and has good cleaning characteristics.

These natural attributes have been enhanced by ongoing research to the point where the life of a properly constructed nylon carpet is primarily a function of its surface appearance. Pile wear itself is so slight that it is a minor factor in determining the effective life. According to one estimate, wear in a nylon carpet of 24 oz/sq yd is less than 1 percent per five million traffics.* Two thousand people entering and leaving every day, seven days a week, would generate about 1.5 million traffics per year.

Development continues as fiber manufacturers pursue techniques to modify the characteristics of nylon for improved performance. The improvements that have been made in the initial nylon fiber can best be comprehended after gaining an initial understanding of how a nylon fiber is made.

In making a nylon fiber, a liquid polymeric material is forced through tiny holes in a spinneret to form a filament. Filaments solidify and are wound together. A stretching process enables the producer to build in the correct strength and stretching properties for the intended use of the fiber. The straight smooth fiber is then bulked and crimped under high heat.

At this stage the continuous length of fiber is called BCF (bulked continuous filament). It can be directly processed into yarn or chopped into short lengths called staple. Staple is spun into yarn in the same way that natural wool and cotton fibers are. BCF is generally used for loop or cut-and-loop pile construction. The advantage of BCF is that there are no short lengths to pull out of the carpet. Staple yarns with greater bulk and texture are generally used for cut pile construction.

The improved qualities of nylon have been developed in a series of generations and nylon fibers are commonly classified by generation. Each generation signifies a major breakthrough or advancement.

---

*Dupont Company: "Specification Guide for Carpets of Antron Nylon—Health Care."

Solution to Fiber

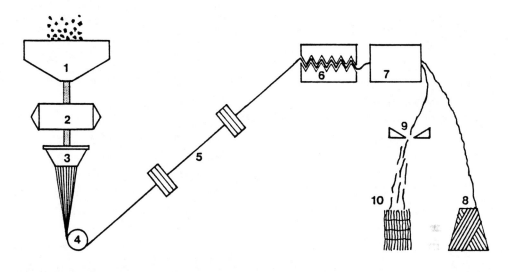

Figure 2.4. PRODUCTION OF A SYNTHETIC POLYMER FIBER. To make nylon fiber, nylon polymer chips are melted and blended (1), heated (2), and forced through holes in a spinneret (3) to form filaments. The filaments are gathered (4), stretched (5), crimped or bulked (6), and heat-set (7). At this stage, the continuous fiber is referred to as BCF or bulked continuous filament. It can be wound and later processed directly into yarn (8), or cut for staple (9), and baled (10) to later be spun into yarn.

First-generation nylon was a round cross-section fiber with chemical modification of the polymer to reduce its transparency. This was a soil hiding measure based on the theory that if you could not see through the fiber, you could not see the accumulated soil. It worked well at low soil levels, but at high soil levels the quantity of additive needed reduced color clarity.

Second-generation improvements were directed toward a method of soil hiding in which transparency could be reduced without adding opaque additives. By changing the shape of the cross section, light was deflected or scattered from the fiber surface. Of various experimental cross sections, two stood out: a trilobal solid fiber and a modified square with four hollow tubes within the fiber. The trilobal and hollow tube shapes are still the standard with various refinements by different fiber producers.

Third-generation nylons have all the attributes of the second generation along with static shock protection. Static control was a major breakthrough. This was achieved by integrating into the carpet silver-coated filaments, carbon-coated filaments or nylon-coated carbon filaments.

The fourth generation is less clearly defined than preceding generations. Manufacturers continue to refine and improve the fiber; features which make the fiber even more soil and stain resistant are sometimes called fourth-generation features. Their use will allow the designer to broaden the acceptable range of pattern and color as the need to camouflage soil lessens.

Fourth-generation features include heavy deniers which have less surface area for the accumulation of soil, and fluorocarbon treatment for soil and stain release. Regarding fluorocarbon treatment, there is some disagreement among manufacturers as to whether there must be a chemical modification of the fiber to qualify as fourth generation or whether a coating will suffice.

Fiber and Yarn Characteristics

In the fiber and yarn making process, many characteristics important to the performance of the carpet are determined: the shape of the cross section of the fiber, fiber chemistry, the crimp and twist, the coarseness of the fiber and the yarn. These, along with further chemicals which may be added, affect properties such as soil hiding, absorbency, resilience, and resistance to soil penetration.

The names of a manufacturer's fibers are indicative of the characteristics of the fiber such as fiber coarseness and soil resisting or antibacterial additives. For a summary of characteristics of nylon fibers by brand, see Table 2.4.

SHAPE: Soil-hiding properties were improved in second-generation nylon by changing the fiber shape. Modification of the trilobal and hollow tube shapes continues.

CHEMISTRY: Nylon fibers are of two basic chemistries: Nylon 6 and Nylon 6,6. Each has advantages. Nylon 6 has a reactive structure that allows bonding of some other substances. This makes it advantageous for bonding fluorocarbons and antimicrobial substances. It also has a more open molecular structure which may enhance deep diffusion of dyestuffs.

Nylon 6,6 has a tighter molecular structure; it may be more resistant to stains and has greater resistance to atmospheric and solar fading.

Table 2.4

SUMMARY OF CHARACTERISTICS OF NYLON FIBERS BY BRAND

Brand names given to their products by the fiber manufacturers define certain characteristics of the fiber. The following chart organizes this information for fibers produced by four manufacturers of nylon fibers for carpet.

| Fiber | Generation | | | Flourocarbon | | Denier | | Dye Stage | | | | Antimicrobial | Yarn Type | | Fiber Cross Section | | | | Fiber Chemistry | |
	Second	Third	Fourth	In Fiber	Applied	Standard	Heavy	Solution	Fiber	Yarn	Carpet		BCF	Staple/Spun	Circular	Trilobal	Square w/ Voids	Pentagonal w/ Voids	6	6,6
Allied																				
Anso	X						X		X	X	X		X	X		X				X
Anso X	X						X		X	X	X		X	X		X				X
Anso IV		X		X		X			X	X	X		X	X		X			X	
Anso IV HP		X		X			X		X	X	X		X	X		X				X
Anso IV Halofresh		X		X		X			X	X	X	X	X	X		X				X
Anso IV HP Halofresh		X		X			X		X	X	X	X	X	X		X				X
BASF																				
Zeftron Nylon	X	X					X		X	X	X		X	X		X				X
Zeftron, Stock Dyed	X						X	X					X			X				X
Zeftron 500 staple	X						X	X						X	X					X
Zeftron 500 ZX BCF	X		X				X	X				X	X					X		X
Zeftron ATX	X					X	X		X	X			X					X		X
Dupont																				
Antron	X						X			X	X		X			X				X
Antron cf	X						X			X	X		X				X			X
Antron XL		X					X			X	X		X			X				X
Antron XL BCF		X					X			X	X		X				X			X
Antron Precedent		X		X	X					X	X		X				X(w/voids)			X
Antron Precedent BCF		X		X	X					X	X		X				X			X
XTI nylon	X				X	X				X	X		X		X					X
SDN nylon	X				X	X		X					X		X					X
Monsanto																				
Ultron	X						X			X	X					X				X
Ultron Z	X						X			X	X					X				X
Ultron 3D		X					X			X	X		X			X				X

Hollow Tube
Square

Hollow Tube
Pentagonal

Trilobal

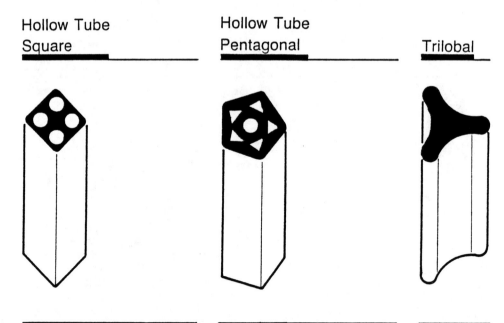

Figure 2.5. SHAPES OF NYLON FIBERS. Soil-hiding characteristics of the initial nylon fibers have been improved by changing the shape of the cross section. Variations of hollow tube shapes (most often for filament yarns) and trilobal shapes (most often for staple yarns) have been the most successful.

CRIMP AND TWIST: Resilience is the ability to spring back or regain original form after deformation by bending or compressing. Crimping of fibers during the fiber-making process and twisting of the fibers as they are formed into yarns enhances resilience.

Just as fibers are brought together to form a single yarn, most BCF and staple yarns are made by twisting the individual singles yarns or ends together. These twists, heat set to insure permanency, positively affect appearance retention. Twist also affects the textural appearance of the carpet.

Appearance of carpet is highly dependent on the resilience of the fiber. The natural resilience of nylon fiber has been enhanced by reshaping the filament, crimping the filament and twisting the yarn. Fiber resiliency is enhanced by a high tuft density as the yarns support one another.

COARSENESS: Weight is the indication of the relative coarseness of the fiber or yarn. It is expressed as denier for BCF and as cotton count (cc) for staple. Some manufacturers are making BCF in heavier weights, increasing the denier from the standard 15–18 to 24–36. These larger filaments are claimed to increase appearance retention due to better resistance to crushing, less exposed surface area in any given area of carpet and closer packing. Any given number of fibers packs closer together allowing less dirt to penetrate the carpet.

Denier is defined as the weight, in grams, of 9000 meters of fiber or yarn. Weight is directly related to the coarseness. An 18 denier fiber refers to 9000 meters of a fiber that weighs 18 grams. It is heavier and thicker than a 10 denier fiber. A yarn of BCF fiber may consist of 88–120 filament ends. If there were 100 ends of 18 denier fibers, the yarn would be 1800 denier (100×18).

A cotton count (cc) is the number of 840 yard skeins necessary to total one pound. It has an inverse relationship to the coarseness of the yarn. A cc of 4 indicates that four standard skeins weigh one pound. This yarn would be coarser than one with a cc of 6.

When a choice is to be made between spun and filament products, there may be a need to visualize the size relationship between spun yarns designated in cotton count and filament yarns designated in denier. Dividing either cotton count or denier into the number 5315 yields the yarn size in the other system. For example, an 1800 denier yarn is a 2.95 cc yarn (5315/1800).

Conversion to the metric system will bring a new unit of measure, already common outside the United States. The basic unit of the metric system is the tex. A tex is the weight, in grams, of one kilometer of yarn.

When singles yarns are plied; two-, three- and four-ply yarns can be formed. The ply construction of a filament yarn is usually expressed by stating the number of plies followed by a slash and the denier, e.g. 2/1950 denier. The deniers of singles are multiplied by the number of plies so that a 2/1950 denier yarn has a total denier of 3900. The ply construction of a spun yarn is usually expressed by the cc followed by a slash and the number of plies, e.g. 3.50 cc/2. Because of the different relationships in the measures of yarn coarseness, units are divided by the number of plies. A 3.50 cc/2 yarn would have a total cc of 1.75.

The number of plies in the yarn is primarily a matter of appearance, not performance. Performance is affected by the denier of the plied yarn. Performance improves as the density is increased. When the tuft density remains the same, a larger denier should improve performance as the density index is increased. If tufts are moved further apart, decreasing the density index, a larger denier yarn would not necessarily improve performance. Performance would only improve if the density index (denier $\times$ tuft density) were increased.

The number of singles yarns or ends in a yarn can have a significant effect on the appearance. With more ends, more opportunities exist for variations in color and shading. This is well demonstrated in the heather-tone carpets.

Color

Color, texture and pattern play a primary role in disguising and hiding soil. Uniformity is perceived as cleanliness, contrast as soiling. Appearance features that cause soil to visually blend with the carpet will reduce contrast between soil and carpet, disguising soil until scheduled maintenance can occur.

Color is composed of three elements: (1) hue, that element commonly known as color, i.e. red, green, blue, (2) value or the relative darkness or lightness, and (3) intensity or the degree of purity. All three elements must be considered and balanced in accordance with the functions that will take place and the nature of the soil that is apt to occur.

Color must also be selected in accordance with the lighting to be used as color appearance will differ under different light sources.

HUE: Dirt has distinctive colors, although most people become insensitive to them. Its hue may be black, brown, red, sand and various mixtures of these. **Carpets and, in fact, all flooring near entryways should be in the same part of the color wheel as the local dirt.** This way it will show a lot less when the walk-off mats don't catch all the dirt or when the local cattle rancher comes to the emergency room with half the ranch on his shoes.

Redder, warmer hues can be used when red clay soils predominate such as in the southeastern portion of the United States. Browns and blacks are effective in the farmbelts where soils are rich and dark. In shore and desert areas, the large sand content blends with beige and sand colors. In large metropolitan areas, the colors of grease and tar must be considered.

If these colors are not what is desired for the entire building, consider using them at entrances, elevator access points and adjacent high traffic areas combined with a complementary color in other areas. Design adjoining shapes for function in the space and compatibility with the building form. Place the seams so that the carpet in areas of highest use can be replaced on a different schedule from the main portion of the carpet.

VALUE: Both very light and very dark colors tend to show soil to a greater degree than medium value colors. Again, keep in mind the function of the space and the type of soil anticipated. In a patient bed area, where lint can be expected, the soil will have a lighter value than elsewhere. If there is doubt about the color value of the soil, look at the contents of vacuum cleaner bags from similar areas.

Luster level affects color appearance. Luster or the relative brightness of the fibers determines how much light is reflected off the fibers. Any hue will assume a visually lighter value as the luster level becomes brighter. High luster levels tend to show more soiling. However, fibers that are too dull may result in a drab appearance.

INTENSITY: Very little soil is of a pure, clear, highly saturated color such as fire engine red. It is typically weakly saturated or greyed such as brick red. There will be more difficulty in maintaining the appearance of a pure, bright color carpet than one of a somewhat less intense color.

EFFECTS OF LIGHTS: Both sunlight and artificial light have effects on the color of carpet.

Colors should always be selected under the anticipated light conditions, as any color will appear different under each of the different light sources: sunlight, incandescent, fluorescent, or high intensity discharge (HID). Fluorescent sources come in a number of colors, and there are several HID sources, each with its own color spectrum. Light source color will strongly affect the appearance of the finish material colors.

Some colors have less resistance to solar radiation than others. Reds and rusts are particularly vulnerable to sun fading and should not be selected for areas where they will be constantly exposed to the sun. Nylon, itself, is also affected by the sun, and if exposed to long hours of sunlight, the fiber will deteriorate. A constantly sunny exposure may dictate the use of another fiber, at least in the immediate area.

Dye Methods

Consistency of color and its lasting qualities are functions of the dye method used. Some methods of dyeing are more resistant than others to sun fading and to staining. Some have more consistency between dyelots and throughout one dyelot, an important consideration when carpeting large open areas. Dye methods can be categorized by the stage at which dyeing takes place. Dyeing can occur at the solution, fiber, yarn or piece good stages. Nylon can be dyed at any of these stages.

SOLUTION DYEING: During manufacture of a synthetic fiber, dye is mixed with the raw chemicals in liquid form. The dye becomes an integral part of the fiber. It is an excellent method for colorfastness and color matching. The resistance to fading and to bleaches and other chemicals is outstanding. Olefins are typically solution dyed. Some nylon is solution dyed. However, the open structure of Type 6 nylon used for solution dyeing may tend to absorb stain more readiliy than the less open Type 6,6.

When large open spaces such as lobbies are carpeted, color match of adjacent carpet strips can be a problem. Solution dyeing is one good way to assure consistent color throughout the carpet with resulting good, side-to-side match from strip to strip of carpet. Very good color match is also achieved when dyeing takes place at the fiber stage.

FIBER DYEING: This is also known as stock dyeing. It is the first stage at which a natural fiber could be dyed and is often used for the staple form of synthetic fibers. Before the fiber is spun into yarn, large batches are placed in pressurized vats of heated dyestuff. Dyed batches are mixed to gain uniformity of color. After the fibers are cleaned and dried, they are spun into yarn.

YARN DYEING: Yarn dyeing is done in a variety of ways such as skein and package dyeing for solid colors and space and differential or cross dyeing for multicolors. Every effort is made to ensure even coloration throughout the lot and between lots. However, at each later stage there is less consistency between lots. This may or may not be important, depending on the size of the spaces to be carpeted and the openness of the plan.

CARPET DYEING: This refers to dyeing the fabricated carpet. Processes for carpet dyeing are piece, continuous, foam and printing.

Probably, the most popular is piece dyeing in which carpet rolls are dyed in large vats called becks, sometimes called beck dyeing. Cross dyeing is a method used to obtain more than one color in a piece-dyed carpet. The carpet is constructed of yarns with differing color affinities. That which appears uniform before dyeing emerges from the dye bath in two or more colors.

There are several methods of continuous dyeing. TAK dyeing selectively positions drops of dye onto the carpet pile producing multicolored effects. Gum TAK is a variation whereby a dye-resistant chemical applied to the carpet pile permits only part of the pile to accept the dye. TAK is an acronym of the name of the German equipment producer. In gum resistant dyeing, a dye-resistant gum is applied to the upper pile surface, selectively preventing heavy dye penetration and resulting in a light to dark gradation from top to bottom of the pile. Computerized placement of dye through air jets is another innovation in continuous dyeing as is foam dyeing which distributes the dye over the carpet surface in an air/water medium.

Printing can also be used to color carpet. Most often used are flat bed and rotary printing which use equipment similar to a printing press. In rotary printing the carpet passes against cylinders embossed with a pattern and coated with dye. The pattern is transferred to the carpet. It usually requires large-run sizes per color and design. Flat bed or screen printing can be used on relatively short yardages. In this method, dyes are forced through a screen on which the pattern has been outlined. Another system of printing is jet printing in which computer-controlled jets inject dye onto the carpet roll.

It is more difficult to get good side-to-side color match with carpet dyeing than with a method utilized earlier in the construction process. However, this is the most economical and flexible method; it is often satisfactory unless large open areas are to be carpeted.

Table 2.5

COMPARISON OF DYE SYSTEMS

| Dye Method | Lot Size | Attributes | | | |
		Streak Resist	Color Match	Color Fastness	Color Clarity
Solution	Extra Large	High	Very Good	Excellent	Very Good
Fiber	Very Large	High	Very Good	Very Good	Excellent
Yarn	Moderate	Moderate	Good	Very Good	Excellent
Piece	Small	Low	Fair-Good	Good	Excellent
Continuous	Very Large	Low	Poor-Fair	Good	Very Good
Printing	Very Large	High	Good	Good	Very Good

REFERENCE STANDARDS: Carpet dyes are subject to attack from chemicals, sunlight and atmospheric contaminants. It is important that dyes be properly fixed in the yarn to resist fading and crocking when dry or wet. They should be unaffected by standard cleaning methods.

The following are reference standards and suggested minimum requirements: (Numbers refer to the international grey scale, where 5 = no change, 4 = slight change, 3 = moderate change, 2 = considerable change and 1 = severe change).

1. *Lightfastness:* AATCC Test Method 16E. This test measures color-fastness to light in an xenon arc fadeometer. Shade change after 80 standard fading hours should not be less than 3.
2. *Atmospheric Fading:* AATCC Test Method 129, Ozone/AATCC Test Method 23, Burnt Gas. These tests measure the color change of carpet when exposed to gas in the atmosphere under high humidity. Minimum shade change after 2 cycles in each test should be no less than 3.
3. *Crockfastness:* AATCC Test Method 8. This test measures the degree of color transfer from the carpet to a white cloth rubbed across the face of the carpet. Minimum standard ratings should be wet = 4, dry = 4.
4. *Shampooing:* AATCC Test Method 138. The color change caused by severe shampooing is measured. Results should not be below 4.

Texture and Pattern

Whatever color carpet is chosen, its effectiveness in concealing soil will be greater if an appropriate texture or pattern is also used.

TEXTURE: Texture is concerned with the visual and tactile qualities of the carpet. Webster defines it as the characteristic disposition or connection of threads in a woven fabric. In a carpet, it is affected by tuft density and type, face weight and pile height, fiber crimp and twist, yarn twist, fiber coarseness, yarn piles and the type of construction.

The advantages and disadvantages of variations in each of these factors are discussed in the relevant sections. Also, an appearance of texture can be achieved with very small dots of color. The combination resulting from the sum of the choices gives a carpet its particular texture. In general, if it is smooth and regular, soil will contrast and show more than if it is rough and irregular. Multi-level loop carpets have an irregular texture that will conceal some soil and are excellent at concealing seams.

There are some beautiful textures available in double heddle and staggered stitches. Approach these with caution, as they do not seam well.

PATTERN: Pattern is a structural or applied configuration that has a particular shape or form. The pattern may be repeated or several patterns may be repeated to make up a larger pattern. Pattern can be formed by color or texture or both. A pattern using texture is usually formed during carpet construction. A few texture patterns are made by applying a chemical which changes the density of the fibers in selected locations. Color patterns can be formed during construction using colored yarns or by printing the completed carpet.

The most subtle patterns are heathers and tweeds. These serve admirably for some soiling conditions. For example, a light tweed fleck is excellent for concealing lint. Another subtle but effective pattern is one constructed from cut-and-loop tufts of the same yarn. This can form a series of stripes or checks in a velvet woven carpet. The cut ends will appear darker than the loops. This construction must have a high tuft density or the pattern will change in use; the cut pile spreads out more than the loop.

In other cases such as dining areas, more complex patterns are needed. A very complex pattern can be achieved in an Axminster construction with its ability to be woven in many different color yarns. If an Axminster is not in the budget range, a printed carpet can be used. All types of carpet can be printed. In good quality printing, the dyes penetrate deeply into the face pile. They do not just lie on the surface where they will quickly wear off. Line definition will vary with the yarn weight, the tuft form and the type of printing method. Printing on loop pile is often less successful than printing on cut pile.

A random pattern will disguise more than a regular geometric. When choosing the pattern, know what you want to hide: mustard and ketchup spills, blood stains, cigarette burns or lint. Select color, texture, shapes and complexity accordingly.

Pattern is an excellent camouflage. When choosing a pattern, observe some precautions:

1. A linear pattern is difficult to lay in long stretches. Even when laid straight, it may appear wavy or bent.
2. Certain strong contrasts or small bold patterns can cause eye fatigue as the pattern perceptually "jumps" off the carpet.
3. Be sure a pattern match can be achieved. There is more tolerance in an "over-pad" than in a "glue-down" method of installation. Better yet, select a random pattern or a tweed or small geometric that does not need to be matched in installation.
4. In large expanses of space, patterns can do strange things that are not perceptible when looking at a small sample. Tweeds may form a chevroning effect; a geometric may begin to look like flowers. Visit an installation of the same carpet if possible. If not, use a mirror box to get an idea of the effect. A mirror box is simply a

box with an open top and one open side. Three sides are mirrored to reflect the carpet that is laid on the bottom of the box. The illusion is of a broad field of carpet (see Fig. 2.6).

5. Cut-and-loop construction can experience pattern loss as the cut pile mats at a different rate from the loop.

Carpet Reflected

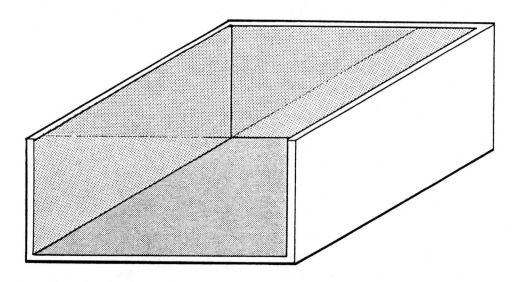

Figure 2.6. MIRROR BOX. Using a mirror box is a helpful technique for envisioning a large expanse of carpet when only a small sample is available.

Health and Safety

Flammability

The purpose of interior finish regulations is to prevent the rapid spread of fire. What level of flame resistance must a material have to satisfy this purpose? Fire codes pertinent to carpet as a flooring material address two situations: (1) ignition and initial growth, and (2) full involvement or "flashover" and the time after flashover when fire spreads beyond the room of origin into corridors and beyond.

The methanamine "pill test," Federal Flammability Standard DOC FF-1-70, tests materials for resistance to ignition by a small incendiary source and resistance to spread in the absence of an external radiation field. The "pill," or ignition source tablet, is placed in the center of an eight-inch diameter exposure of carpet and ignited. If two or more of eight carpet specimens burn three inches in any direction, the carpet fails the test. Carpet systems passing this test will not spread flame during the ignition and initial growth stage of a fire. "Carpet systems, used in rooms, will not normally spread fire provided they meet the requirements of the DOC FF-1-70" (the pill test).* All carpets and rugs made or imported for sale in the United States must pass this test.

But it is the tests for carpets exposed to a major fire source with which health care facility specifiers must be most concerned. This is the testing to which carpet intended for corridors and public spaces must be submitted. This testing is now in a state of transition. Most regulatory bodies are evaluating and many have accepted the ASTM E-648, Flooring Radiant Panel Test, as the test of choice. This is replacing the ASTM E-84 Steiner Tunnel Test and the UL 992 Smoke Chamber Test.

In the Radiant Panel Test, a test carpet sample is exposed to radiant heat energy from a sloped panel mounted above the sample. Due to the slope, the exposure varies, decreasing along the length of the sample. The sample is ignited and allowed to burn until it self-extinguishes. The radiant energy exposure at the point where burning ceases is identified as the critical radiant flux. It represents, in watts/sq cm, the minimum radiant energy required to sustain flame propagation. **The higher the number, the more resistant is the material to flame propagation. The minimum critical radiant flux recommended by the National Bureau of Standards is 0.45 watts/sq cm within corridors and exitways of hospitals and nursing homes.**

The Steiner Tunnel Test, used for many years and still in effect in some regulatory districts, uses a comparative rating based on the progress of flame along a test sample. The sample is mounted, pile down, on the ceiling of a test tunnel and subjected to a heavy flame source. Test duration is ten minutes or until the sample has burned up completely, whichever is first. The flame-spread rating is then calculated from the greatest distance of flame spread. A flame-spread rating of 75 or less is generally required for carpet used in hospital corridors, although 25 or less is required in some regulatory districts. Note that this is an inverse relationship; the lower the number, the greater the flame resistance.

Most government regulatory agencies now approve the use of the Flooring Radiant Panel Test for non-sprinkled corridors and primary

---

*"Flammability Testing for Carpets," U.S. Department of Commerce National Bureau of Standards, April 1978, p. 4.

exitways. The methenamine pill test would then be used for room carpet and sprinkled corridors.

Smoke, and more particularly toxic smoke, is probably the major cause of death from fire. At present, there is no standard which relates to the measurement of toxicity in smoke from flooring materials. The NBS Smoke Density Chamber Test measures smoke obscuration. This test is described in NFPA standard 258. It measures the amount and density of smoke emitted from a burning specimen expressed as maximum specific optical density. Some regulatory authorities require a maximum specific optical density of 450 as measured by the NBS smoke chamber.

Electrostatic Propensity

The standard procedure used to measure static electricity levels in carpet is AATCC Test Method 134, Electrostatic Buildup in Carpets. This test simulates use conditions and measures the peak charge generated by walking across the carpet sample. The normal threshold of human sensitivity to static electricity, the point at which shock is experienced, is commonly accepted as 3.5 kilovolts at 20° C and 70 percent relative humidity.

Shock is the discharge of built-up static electricity. If static electricity is not allowed to accumulate, there is no shock. Good conductors allow electrons to move about easily, and static charges tend to dissipate as they are generated. Therefore, a technique to prevent shock is the use of conductive fibers. Nylon carpets with a static propensity of less than 3.5 kV were achieved with the use of conductive fibers in third-generation nylons.

Digital electronic devices are more sensitive, typically to 2 kV. Not only is the sensitivity greater, but the consequences are more costly. The old problem of static was personal discomfort due to the discharge of static accumulation when a charged person touched an object. The new problem is the cost of malfunction when that object is a piece of electronic equipment.

Virtually every hospital today has digital electronic devices in the form of computers, word processors, calculators, medical monitors and other specialized equipment. These digital devices are controlled by a series of electronic pulses. Not only will the purposeful punching of a key activate this electrical pulse, but a discharge of static electricity will do likewise. The machine may malfunction if it mistakes a static-induced pulse for a command pulse.

It is usually impractical to give the equipment the special protection of a closed environment. In an open environment, the equipment is exposed to an aware operator and also to unaware passers-by. The entire environment must be planned to be machine compatible. Accumulated charges must be dissipated upon entering the electronic environment, and any further accumulation must be kept below the critical 2 kV. Is this possible with a carpeted floor?

Producing a carpet with a static propensity below 2 kV is a part of the solution. Another key factor is dissipating excessive charges accumulated in a previous environment before equipment is touched by the person entering the electronic environment.

An approach to the problem taken by Allied Corporation has been to determine the amount of time during which the carpet must dissipate the charge. Motion studies were conducted (Industry in Depth, April 1984). They showed that people entering a room typically took three or more steps before touching an object. These three steps took 1.4 seconds; an effective carpet would need to reduce static accumulation to the harmless level in less than 1.4 seconds.

Typical third-generation nylons often take a minute or more to reduce the accumulated charge. For the electronic environment, more stringent criteria are necessary, as follows:

1. Any excessive static charge a person may have accumulated elsewhere (must be reduced) to the critical 2 kV level of machine sensitivity within three steps, or 1.4 seconds, after stepping onto the control carpet.
2. It must achieve this rapid control with little or no current flow that might generate electromagnetic waves, causing the same problem it is trying to eliminate.
3. It must continually reduce the static electricity which could be accumulated by the person, from all sources and all activities in addition to any carpet-generated charge, never permitting it to approach the level of machine sensitivity.

   It must achieve this control without increasing the conductivity of the carpet to the point where it would be a safety hazard in the event of a short circuit.*

The test for static propensity, AATCC Test Method 134, is not adequate to test the new criteria, suppression of an initial charge to 2 kV

---

*Allied Corporation: "Carpet and Computers in Conflict; Electrostatic Disruption of Electronic Equipment."

within 1.4 seconds and maintenance of this level of control as the subject continues movement. Therefore, fiber processors, such as Allied, have designed the test equipment as well as the carpet. The carpet system Allied has created to meet the criteria is called TEC (total electronic compatability). It is a refinement of prior methods of control using highly conductive fibers linked to a special latex backing material. It is available in BCF and staple yarns in many constructions including carpet tile. Doubtless, fiber producers and manufacturers will continue to improve electronic equipment compatible systems.

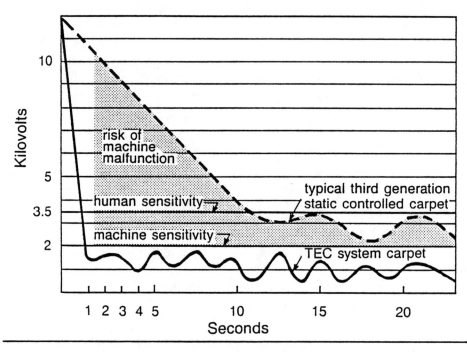

Figure 2.7. COMPARISON OF METHODS OF STATIC CONTROL. The figure illustrates a comparison of static generated in a TEC system carpet versus static generated in a carpet meeting third-generation standards. When a person carrying a 12 kV static charge steps on this electronic compatible carpet, the charge is suppressed in less than a second to a level of 2 kV or less. (Adapted from Allied Corporation, *Industry in Depth*, Vol. 8. Printed with permission of the Institute of Business Designers.)

Keeping in mind the above criteria should enable specification of carpet suitable for the electronic environment. A warranty should be required with the producer responsible for performance of the system for the life of the carpet.

Biogenic Factors

The well-being of patients and staff depends on having a sanitary environment. Ever since carpet was first suggested for hospitals, the sanitation aspect has provoked apprehension. During the 1970s much exhaustive testing was done by hospital staffs themselves to determine if carpet could become a bacteriological nesting place: could carpet introduce infectious bacteria, accelerate its spread or nurture pathogenic growth?

As early as 1974, the Carpet and Rug Institute (1980) was compiling a record of these studies and publishing results.

> Significantly, every one of the many published test findings confirmed that carpet is at least as safe bacteriologically as hard surface floorings. In fact many of the studies conceded that vacuuming carpet actually reduces the number of bacteria present in it — a point lost by wet-mopped tile floors. . . .
>
> The conclusions drawn by the studies are shown in the following report prepared for Carlisle Hospital in Carlisle, Pennsylvania by Dr. James M. Smith, Pathologist and Chairman of the hospital's Infections Committee. . . . Conclusion: There is no apparent increase in total bacteria in rooms which have carpeted floors. The reverse is probably true. There is a decrease in pathogenic bacteria harbored in carpet as compared to vinyl tile (p. 40).

For copies of the most significant of these independent studies, contact the Carpet and Rug Institute in Dalton, Georgia. Later studies have continued to confirm these early studies. The following appears in the publication of a 1978 study by P. G. H. Bakker, *The Influence of Carpets on Hospital Hygienics:*

> Does carpeting pose more of a risk to the patient than hard floors? It has been maintained that there is a correlation between bacteria in the air and the number of nosocomial infections (wound infections). There is sufficient evidence to show that local environment, traffic patterns, and cleaning procedures affect airborne microbial populations. However, no distinction can be made between the number of germs in the air above carpet versus hard floor areas. Consequently, carpets would not adversely affect the hygienic requirements of hospital wards.

In a summary of a study conducted by Bakker and Faoagali (1977) in New Zealand, they say, "Airborne bacteria were found to be present in similar numbers in two blind corridors whether the floors were carpeted or covered with sheet vinyl."

As far as this author has been able to discover, there is no published information of a scientifically designed test that contradicts these findings.

In guidelines prepared for the Centers for Disease Control (1985), Garner and Favero report the following:

> There is no epidemiological evidence to show that carpets influence the nosocomial infection rate in hospitals. Carpets, however, may contain much higher levels of microbial contamination than hard surface flooring and can be difficult to keep clean in areas of heavy soiling or spillage; therefore, appropriate cleaning and maintenance procedures are indicated (p. 242).

While a variety of studies leading to acceptance of carpet in health care installations have shown carpet to be no more conducive to the growth and spread of bacteria and fungi than resilient and hard flooring, fiber manufacturers have nonetheless endeavored to improve this characteristic. To date, at least two manufacturers have introduced to the nylon fiber antimicrobial components which will inhibit the growth of mold, mildew, fungi, algae and yeast. Others say that antimicrobial solutions added to the fiber by the manufacturer are negatively affected by the carpet finishing procedures and argue for topical application.

Still others argue that antimicrobial agents may reduce carpet performance due to affinity for soil and for atmospheric oxidizing agents. These persons claim that the treated carpet will have poorer soil resistance, dye lightfastness and NO_2 and ozone fastness. Some people advise caution, as it is not yet fully understood whether the inclusion of these chemical components may have a toxic effect on humans.

In testing by Bakker and Faoagali (1977), they found that, "None of the carpet bactericides showed any diffusible activity, but some had a certain degree of effectiveness in suppressing odours" (p. 132).

The one conclusion that can be reached, regarding the effect of the addition of antimicrobial agents, is that this is still an area of uncertainty and controversy.

Types — Carpet Construction

Carpet is commonly classified according to type of construction. Four types of construction are important to the health care facility specifier: woven, tufted, knitted and fusion bonded. Attributes of a certain type may be functionally appropriate for a given situation. However, considerations listed under the section "Structure and Properties" are, in most cases, more important to performance than type of construction.

Weaving is the oldest method of carpet construction and still offers the greatest styling latitude. However, technical innovations have resulted in the ability to produce tufted carpet twenty-five times faster than woven carpet. The cost implications of the fabrication time comparison are obvious. Ninety percent of the contract carpet used today is of tufted construction.

Tufted Carpet

In the tufting process, ends of yarn are punched through a primary backing and returned, forming tufts or loops on the face side of the carpet. To make cut pile carpet, a knife slices through these loops. At this stage in construction, the tufts can easily be pulled out. A layer of liquid latex or thermoset plastic is applied to the back to hold the tufts in place. Without this latex or plastic, pulling one tuft can easily pull out a whole row of tufts. Over this coating, a secondary fabric backing is laminated to further increase tuft bind and dimensional stability. (see Fig. 2.8).

Tuft bind is the measure of force needed to pull one tuft out of the pile of the carpet. In the early days of tufted carpets, coatings and secondary backings were not so well developed. Tuft bind was weak and tufted carpets were subject to long rows of tufts being pulled out. These empty rows are sometimes called runners.

Note that a tufted carpet typically has two backings, the primary backing into which the tufts are inserted and the applied, secondary finishing backing. In any area where moisture may be present, these should be of synthetic materials which are resistant to shrinkage, rot and mildew. Specify primary backings of woven or spunbonded olefin at a minimum weight of 3.5 oz/sq yd and secondary backings of woven olefin with a minimum weight of 4.0 oz/sq yd. For dry locations, stainless jute at 7.0 oz/sq yd is an acceptable backing, and a jute-backed carpet is somewhat easier to install.

Sometimes, a tufted carpet backing consists of just a coating. This is called a unitary backing. This coating is applied to the back of the tufted primary backing and becomes an integral part of the carpet. Unitary-backed carpets are most appropriate for glue-down installations. They are difficult to lay over pad.

Both coatings and laminating compounds secure tufts and add antifray qualities and dimensional stability. Synthetic rubber latexes are the most frequently used laminating compounds. Some hot-melt adhesives are also used for laminating secondary backings. Latex is also used for a back coating as is polyvinyl chloride. Secondary backings further enhance dimensional stability, contributing resistance to stretching and wrinkling.

Good tuft bind and a properly applied secondary backing that does not delaminate are important considerations in the choice of tufted car-

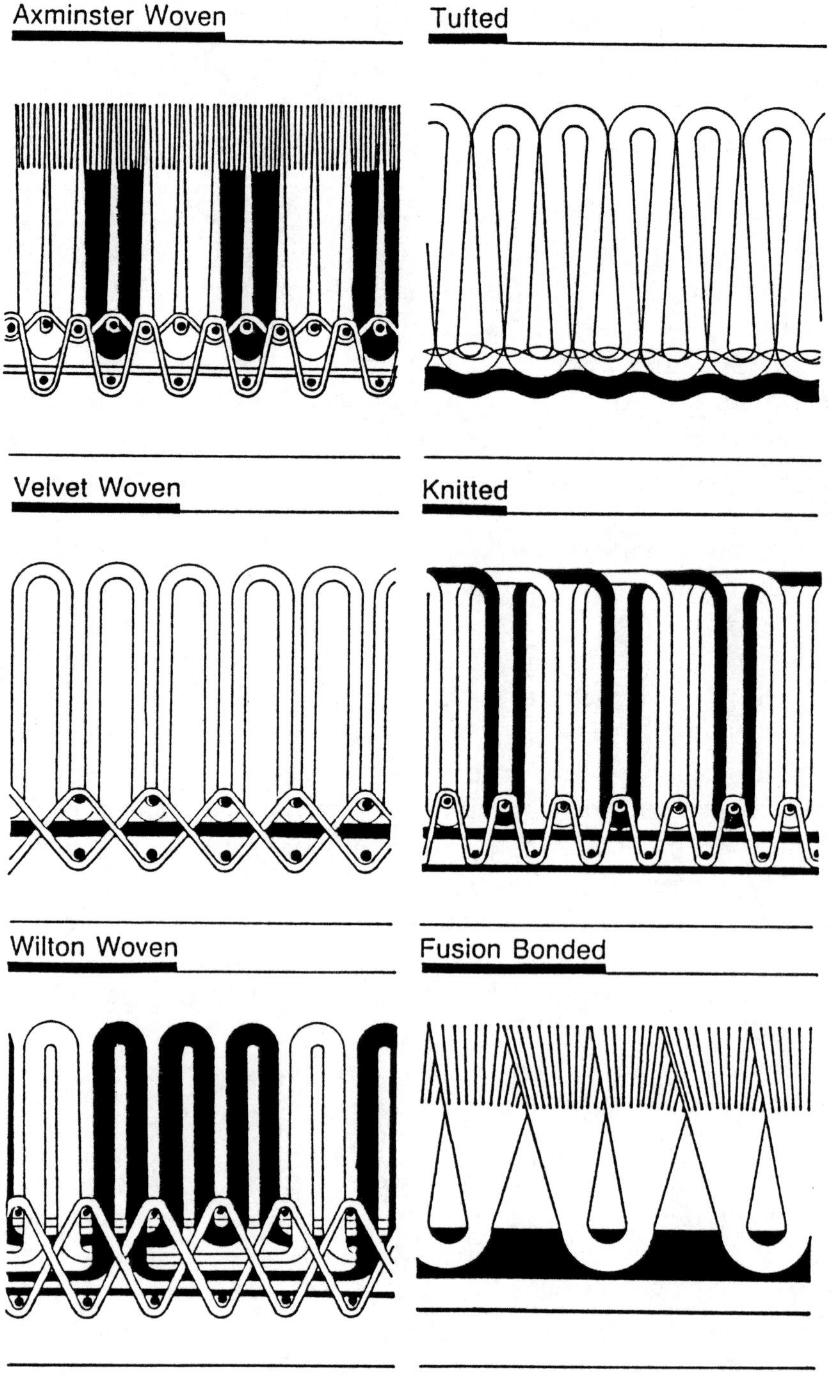

Axminster Woven

Tufted

Velvet Woven

Knitted

Wilton Woven

Fusion Bonded

Figure 2.8. TYPES OF CARPET CONSTRUCTION. In woven carpets, both face and back are constructed by the weaving process. Pile yarns plus chain and stuffer yarns make up the warp. Weft yarns are shot through the warp yarns to simultaneously bind in the face

→

pet. The strength of the lamination is especially relevant where there is wheeled traffic. The horizontal pressure exerted by wheeled carts and chairs is considerable. Relevant tests and standards are:

1. *Tuft Bind:* ASTM Test Method D-1335, Tuft Bind of Pile Floor Coverings. Minimum tuft lock should be 13 pounds (57.9 Newtons) on any single pull and 15 pounds (66.8 Newtons) average for eight pulls. Many mills offer lines with tuft binds that exceed 20 pounds. These would be an excellent choice.

2. *Peel Strength of Secondary Backing:* Federal Test Method Standard 191, Textile Test Method 5950. These measure the force required to delaminate or separate the two backings. Minimum acceptable peel strength is 3.35 pounds per inch (5.9 Newtons per centimeter).

Carpets with more permeable backings have superior sound-cushioning qualities. This is in conflict with requirements in many health care areas where an impermeable backing is desired so that liquid spills do not penetrate the carpet.

Woven Carpet

While there have been many improvements in weaving machinery, the process still reflects the basic weaving techniques: weft or filler yarns

---

pile and weave in the stuffer and chain yarns that form the back. Velvet is the simplest carpet weave and is used to produce many variations of cut or loop carpets; patterns are limited to rectilinear geometrics. The Axminster carpet can be produced in an almost infinite number of patterns and colors, limited ony by the number of tufts in the carpet; the pile is always cut and level. Wilton carpets can be made in a variety of textures with up to six colors or frames. One color at a time forms the pile and the others are buried beneath the surface resulting in a strong and resilient carpet.

In the tufting operation, yarns are threaded through hundreds of individual needles contained in a bar that extends the full width of the loom. The needles force the yarns through the primary backing material. As the needles are withdrawn, yarn loops are formed and held in the fabric. A coating and secondary backing hold the loops in place. The loops can be cut if desired and many loop, cut or combination textures are available. Striped patterns are possible.

In knitted carpets as in woven carpets, the face and back are formed simultaneously. Machines with three sets of needles are used to loop together backing and pile yarns with a stitching yarn. Knitted carpets usually have a level loop pile texture and are solid or tweed in coloration.

In fusion bonding, pile yarns are embedded in a viscous vinyl plastisol. A backing is also adhered to the vinyl which hardens as it is cured. The carpet has an impermeable back. The tuft bind is superior to any other type of cut pile carpet, and 90 percent of the yarn is in the face. Level, cut pile is the only pile option with this process. Patterns are not possible within the process and are applied by printing or other means to the finished carpet.

are woven through the warp yarns. There are three major types of woven carpet: velvet, Axminster and Wilton. Prior to discussing these different weaves, a brief word about backing for woven carpets may avoid confusion.

In woven carpets, there is no separate primary backing. Filler and stuffer yarns which serve the stabilizing purposes of a tufted carpet backing are woven into the carpet simultaneously with the weaving of the face yarns. To eliminate the possibility of shrinkage from moisture caused by spills, wet cleaning, or on-grade installation, all fibers should be specified as 100 percent moisture resistant.

Often, a latex or vinyl coating is applied to the finished carpet back to provide better body and greater dimensional stability. There is no need for a coating to provide tuft bind as yarns are interlaced in the weaving process and do not pull out. Only along the edges can woven carpet be unraveled. Infrequently, a fabric backing is applied.

VELVET: In this simplest and most common of weaves, row after row of weft yarns is woven through the pile and warp yarns. Wires inserted between the pile and warp yarns form the pile. The nature of the velvet-weaving process limits patterns to variations of stripes and checks. These patterns can be achieved with color, cut-and-loop pile and multi-level pile heights. A velvet woven is the least expensive of the woven carpets.

AXMINSTER: An Axminster is more expensive than a velvet but has the advantage of limitless patterns. Produced on a modified Jacquard loom, which draws pile yarns from large spools bound with various color yarns, each tuft is inserted individually into the pile. Almost any conceivable color pattern can be produced, since each tuft can be a different color. Because of the construction method, Axminsters always have a cut pile surface and usually an even pile height. They can be distinguished by their heavily ribbed back. Axminsters are an excellent choice for dining areas, as the complex patterns chosen in the proper colors excel in concealing food stains until they can be removed.

WILTONS: These are woven on a Jacquard loom where a punch card system similar to that in early computers is used. (In fact, historians trace this development to the Jacquard loom.) All colors are woven throughout the carpet, with the cards controlling which ones appear on the face and which are buried under the surface. Because of the abundance of pile fiber, Wilton carpets are thick and resilient. They can be produced in intricate patterns, as many as five colors or frames, various pile heights and cut or loop pile. They are luxuriously thick, sturdy and wear well but tend to be too costly for use in most health care facilities.

Knitted Carpet

A technique similar to hand knitting, but using three sets of needles to loop the backing, stitching, and pile yarns together, is used to produce knitted carpet. As in woven carpet, the face and back are formed simultaneously, with filler and stuffer yarns included in the carpet construction. The finished back may be coated with latex or vinyl to provide stability and body. Sometimes a fabric backing is applied for greater stability.

Solid colors and tweeds predominate, although new techniques make free-form patterns possible. Knitted carpet is produced in cut piles, loop piles and in single- and multi-level piles. It can be constructed in any width or shape which makes it possible to control seams and waste in projects large enough for custom runs. For example, knitted carpet could be produced in corridor widths allowing practically seamless corridors with little waste. Its cost is, in general, higher than tufted and lower than woven carpet.

Fusion-Bonded Carpet

A very small but important percentage of the carpet made is produced by fusion bonding. It is an excellent method for producing carpet tile. In the fusion-bonding process, a multifold web of fibers is inserted between two adhesive-coated backing sheets and adhered to each. A blade then slices through the middle of the fiber web forming two identical carpets.

The major advantage is the exceptional tuft bind created between surface fiber and backing. The fusion-bonded construction process also offers the most yarn fiber above the backing of any process. The pile is very dense and is always cut and level. The primary fusion layer acts as an impregnable barrier, preventing spills from soaking through the carpet. Pattern cannot be achieved in the manufacturing process itself but can be applied using various printing methods.

Maintenance

In addition to durability and appearance retention, the third essential in obtaining maximum life from a carpet is maintenance. The carpet can be appropriately selected, but no matter how excellent the selection, durability and appearance retention will be enhanced with proper maintenance.

Soil Occurrence

A maintenance program should be planned prior to installation and begun immediately after installation. Understanding how soil occurs simplifies the design of the maintenance program. Normally, soil enters the carpet in three ways: (1) tracked in, (2) deposited from the air and (3) spilled. This soil exists in three basic forms: dry, wet and oily.

TRACKED-IN SOIL: This normally represents 85 percent of the soil deposited in the carpet. Much tracked-in soil is dry, consisting of particulate matter in various sizes. There may be a significant portion of oily matter, and on rainy or snowy days much of it is wet. In winter, it may also be salty.

With tracked-in soil, there is an equilibrium phenomenon that occurs. Soil from shoes tends to be deposited on the carpet in the first two or three steps where there is less soil on the carpet than on the shoes. When the carpet becomes very soiled at the point of entry, it becomes ineffective as a catcher of dirt and, in fact, may release soil to be redeposited at the next clean carpet. **Understanding this makes it immediately apparent where maintenance efforts must be concentrated: at building entries and at any location where people step onto carpet from another material, especially at high traffic locations.**

Entrance mats collect soil from shoe soles before it is deposited on the carpet. To do this, mats must be large enough to receive at least four steps before a person reaches the carpet. Once they become soiled, effectiveness declines. They must be cleaned and exchanged regularly.

For new construction, recessed entry mats are effective, as there are no edges to trip people or impede opening of doors. Types selected should allow removal or some method to regularly clean under the mat.

Regular vacuum cleaning is essential. For maximum effectiveness and efficiency, the major effort should be expended at entrance points such as exterior doors and elevators and in high traffic areas, especially main corridors, doorways and pivot points. If these are kept clean, little soil remains on shoes to be deposited elsewhere. Regular use of a power pile lifter opens up carpet pile, breaks up soil complexes and results in more efficient vacuum cleaning.

AIRBORNE SOIL: This usually represents 15 percent or less of the soil deposited on the carpet. It consists of dust and various air pollutants. Many of these pollutants are oily and, along with oily tracked-in soil, will bond with dry soils to form sticky soil complexes. These do not come up with vacuum cleaning but can be removed with absorbent powders, dry foam cleaning and absorbent pad cleaning.

SPILLS: Spills are a very small proportion of the soil deposited but may be visually the most offensive because of their typically high contrast with the carpet. Most spills are easy to remove if treated promptly. As the spill sets, removal of the resulting stain becomes more difficult and sometimes impossible. Many hospitals have discovered that informing nurses of the importance of the immediate notification of housekeeping helps tremendously in the time required for stain removal and its completeness.

Major Cleaning

A regular program of vacuum cleaning, touch-up cleaning with an absorbent, and spill removal is the basis of maintaining carpet appearance. Eventually, all carpets, no matter how resistant to soil and stains, will build up a layer of soil. This is usually the oily or sticky type which does not respond to vacuum cleaning. If allowed to remain, it will cause matting and show as a traffic lane. Do not wait until the carpet is badly soiled to begin periodic shampooing.

There are a number of methods for major cleaning. Debate reigns, but none has proven to be the best. Selection should be based on the manufacturer's recommendation for your particular carpet and on your staff's training and equipment. New equipment can be expensive. A decision to invest in new equipment should be a deliberate choice in the selection of carpet and not an unforeseen result.

Chemicals

The major functions of a spotting chemical are to dilute, dissolve, or neutralize the material causing the spot or stain. The major functions of a cleaning chemical are to displace soil from carpet fibers, to emulsify oils, to suspend soil particles and prevent reattachment to carpet fibers. Various chemicals will perform these functions.

There are two precautions: (1) Do not use chemicals that leave a sticky or oily residue. To test, pour a small amount of the solution in a saucer and allow it to evaporate. Residue should be crisp and powdery or flaky. If it is sticky, find another chemical. (2) Cleaning solutions should have a pH between 6 and 10. Most carpet dyes are stable in this range. For spotting, a stronger solution may be needed to neutralize the stain. The solution, itself, must then be neutralized and thoroughly rinsed.

It is essential to have trained maintenance personnel, whether facility staff or outside persons, who understand the basic principles of carpet soiling, carpet construction and cleaning chemicals. Understanding the requirements of maintenance, the specifier can select carpet with positive maintenance features and the user can commit to an effective and efficient maintenance program.

Installation

There are three types of installation to be considered in the health care environment: (1) over pad, (2) glue down and (3) free lay or carpet tiles. Each has advantages and disadvantages and is appropriate in certain locations.

Over Pad

A good grade of pad can increase the appearance retention of carpet by 30–50 percent, as it enhances the resilience of the carpet. It can substantially increase the noise-absorbing characteristics and has a luxurious feel underfoot. It is suitable for conference rooms, small offices, some lobbies and waiting rooms, some dining facilities and other areas where acoustics and comfort are high priorities.

It is not suitable for large open offices or dining facilities where there is not sufficient perimeter space to properly anchor the carpet. Rolling traffic of any kind does not perform properly when there is padding under the carpet. This makes it unsuitable for hospital corridors where carts and other rolling equipment are found and also for office spaces where chairs with casters will be used.

Glue Down

Glue-down installation is recommended for any areas where there will be cart traffic. It should also be used in large open areas where an over-pad installation could result in ripples because of improper stretching.

Most of the advantages of glue-down carpet can be favorably compared to a resilient or hard surface flooring. While it does require somewhat more effort to push stretchers, wheelchairs, dietary carts, and x-ray equipment over glue-down carpet, this differential can be quite small. The carpet specification should be for a low pile, high tuft density carpet so that rolling vehicles ride on top of the carpet rather than sink into it. The other important factor is large wheels on the equipment. Hospitals deciding on carpeted corridors should be sure that all new wheeled equipment have wheels of a least 5" diameter and that larger wheels be retrofitted on most existing equipment.

Glue-down installation is also preferable to over-pad installations in offices where chairs with casters will be used. Hard surface mats under desk chairs can then be eliminated. It should be emphasized that office chairs are available with different types of casters selected for use on carpeted or hard surface floors; small, soft casters for hard surfaces and large, hard casters for carpet.

A chair with casters for hard surfaces will be difficult to move on carpet, while a chair with casters for carpet will slide almost dangerously over resilient or hard surface floorings. The type of caster must be properly specified for the floor finish. If existing chairs are to be used on a different surface, appropriate casters should be installed.

Free Lay

Carpet tiles are an installation type especially appropriate for hospitals. They can be removed, replaced and rearranged individually. This means flexibility to accommodate change in spatial organization. It also means that difficult stains can be treated off site and that permanent disfigurations such as cigarette burns can be removed with the replacement of one tile.

Carpet tile can be an ideal solution for the maternity patient room which is, in general, quite clean but where a large urine or blood spill can cause an unsolvable problem with broadloom. Tiles are also a good solution for laboratories where severe stains, though infrequent, could preclude carpet. Advantages of carpet in the laboratory are acoustical cushioning and lessening of breakage.

Although the cost of tiles is greater than that of broadloom carpet, labor and handling costs are generally less and there is less waste. Boxes of tile eliminate the problems involved in handling large rolls of carpet in elevators.

Carpet tile can be moved in the same way as furniture if use of a building is discontinued or changed. In renovation, downtime is less than with any other carpet; revenue gains may make up the difference in cost.

Carpet tile gives easy access to underfloor utilities and is mandated by the National Electrical Code where flat conductor cable is used. (Most regulatory districts do not allow flat wire cable in patient areas, but many allow it in administrative and office areas, where it is proving its value in enhancing office flexibility.)

Flat wire cable for power, telephone and data line wiring used with carpet tiles is a system that offers cost savings and flexibility in office planning. The flat wire cables distribute power in the same way as conventional round wire systems; the only difference is that the cables are very thin. The cable is laid directly over the floor, carpet squares are laid on top and outlets are placed where needed. As requirements change, outlets can be relocated anywhere along the wire and the carpet squares adjusted accordingly.

Flat wire manufacturers claim that initial installation can be accomplished for about 20 percent and relocations for about thirty percent of the cost of traditional cable. Additional savings can be realized by taking an investment credit on the required carpet tiles and depreciating the tiles as part of the furnishings and equipment.

However, the focus of this book is on finishes, and the advantages and disadvantages of flat wire should be further investigated elsewhere. If flat wire is selected, carpet squares are mandatory.

The modular flexibility of carpet tiles is not limited to access, exchange and replacement. It also provides opportunities for color variation such as bands and blocks of color.

The success of carpet tile depends heavily on the specification. Tiles are not simply cutup squares of broadloom carpet. They are highly dependent on the backing to provide dimensional stability, anti-curling and non-slip properties, superior tuft bind and resistance to edge ravel. Tiles must not move under foot or wheeled traffic but must be quickly movable for exchange or reconfiguration.

Interface and Milliken companies have each pioneered carpet tile systems which have demonstrated success. Interface uses a fusion-bonded surface pile with a five-layer backing sandwich of alternating PVC and fiberglass fused together. Most of the tiles are free laid with glue-down tiles in strategic spots. Typical for large areas is gluing around the perimeter and on a fifteen-foot grid. The manufacturer's recommendations for gluing should be investigated prior to specification.

Specification Notes

Selecting and documenting the materials to be used or performance standards to be met is a major portion of specification. For preparing the complete specification, both AIA (The American Institute of Architects) and CSI (The Construction Specifications Institute) have prepared good guidelines.

The following are some particular points to note.

When determining the location of floor finishes, make as few material changes as possible. This simplifies maintenance, in that equipment will not need to be transported to isolated areas. It is also at points of change from resilient or hard surface flooring to carpet that carpet collects soil. A third reason to avoid change as much as possible is that edge moldings are needed at transition points. These cause a bumpy path for wheeled equipment. In selecting edge moldings, choose the lowest profile available.

Shop drawings should always be required. These should identify seam layout, pile direction, location of all edge moldings and any dyelot changes if the job is large enough to require a change.

Avoid cross seaming wherever possible; where required, locate in low traffic areas. Cross seaming refers to seaming lengths of carpet together along the weft yarns (see Fig. 2.9). Cross seaming is not acceptable at doorways.

Maintain a consistent pile direction, color will appear different if the direction is changed. Carpet tiles have an arrow on the back of each tile.

Corridor Seam

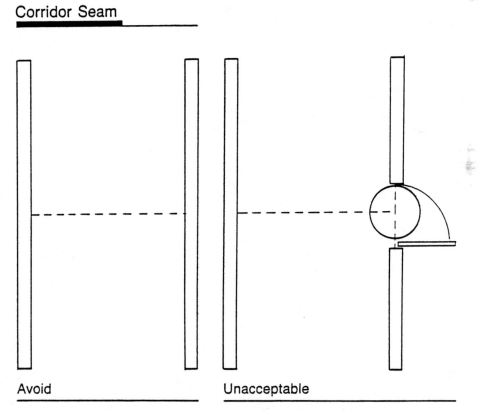

Avoid   Unacceptable

Figure 2.9. CROSS SEAMING. Seaming carpet along weft yarns is known as cross seaming. It should be avoided whenever possible and never used in high-traffic areas.

These should be run in the same direction to avoid the checkerboard look, unless that is the look desired.

Specify one dyelot when obtainable in the quantity needed. In any case, do not use more than one dyelot in a single space.

Generally, do not specify release adhesives. Less work may be required to prepare the substrate for carpet replacement, but release is more expensive than permanent and may cause problems in conjunction with casters, files and cleaning equipment. The exception to this is adhesive for carpet tiles.

Require copies of the manufacturer's maintenance data and, if appropriate, maintenance training for the cleaning staff.

Specify extra carpet from the same dyelot for maintenance and for use in refurbishing adjacent spaces.

Chapter Three

RESILIENT FLOOR COVERINGS

RESILIENT floor coverings are those which have a smooth surface and recover from impact or pressure. Common materials for resilient floors are vinyl (backed or full thickness), vinyl composition, asphalt and rubber. Their resiliency ranges from limited, as in asphalt, to good, as in rubber. An adhesive is usually used to bond resilient flooring to a subfloor.

Resilient floorings are produced in two forms: sheet goods and tiles. All are manufactured in the form of tiles of various sizes. Vinyl and rubber are also made in sheet goods. Sheet goods are an important consideration in hospitals and other health care facilities where spillage is prevalent. The flooring materials, themselves, are resistant to water; it is the seams that are vulnerable. With sheet goods there are many fewer seams than with tile and the potential of damage due to water is greatly lessened. To further insure against water leakage, the seams of many of the sheet goods on the market can be chemically or heat welded.

Structure and Properties

Unlike carpet, where structural variations are almost limitless and determine the properties, resilient floorings are all constructed in essentially the same way. Ingredients are mixed at a high temperature, then hydraulically pressed or calendered into homogenous sheets of the desired thickness. The ingredients, themselves, are the main determinant of the different properties of the various types of resilient flooring.

This section on structure and properties will, therefore, emphasize properties common to all resilient floorings and the impact of these properties on the selection process. It is in the section on types of flooring that the essential differences in flooring derived from the composition will be indicated.

59

Durability

The durability of the flooring is a function of the thickness of the wear layer and its resistance to wear. The material used for the surface of the flooring can extend the full depth, making a full depth wear layer, or it can be a wear layer over a backing of another material.

Wear is deterioration from the cumulative action of injurious mechanical influences. These include abrasion, scratching, scuffing, burning and gouging. While all of these mar the appearance of the floor, it is abrasion that has the greatest effect on long-term wear of the total surface. Abrasion resistance is a major factor in durability of resilient flooring. There are several recognized tests for abrasion of resilient flooring. Most use a Taber abrader. In the Taber Abrasion Tests, a specimen is placed on a rotating platform. As it turns, the specimen is rubbed by two abrasive wheels.

One test of abrasion resistance is ASTM F-510, Test Method for Resistance to Abrasion of Resilient Floor Covering Using an Abrader With a Grit Feed Method. The grit feeding device feeds 240 mesh aluminum oxide grit onto a specimen before it passes under leather-clad rollers. Weights with a 1000-gram load are used. The abrasive wheels of the special Taber abrader have an action similar to the twisting action between shoe and floor that occurs when a person turns. Results may be given as loss of weight or loss of thickness of the specimen.

Another standard laboratory test using the Taber abrader is the one most frequently cited by manufacturers in their literature. Caliber H-18 wheels are used with either a 500- or 1000-gram load. Results may be expressed in gram weight loss/100 cycles or as a measure of the number of cycles to loss of pattern. Materials that withstand 15,000 or more cycles should give good wear. Some vinyl products sustain many more cycles. TekStil Concepts has figures of 71,000 cycles and more for its solid vinyl Unifloor materials.

A high and uniform density contributes to abrasion resistance. Calendering produces the densest product with the most uniform density throughout the depth. The very durable Unifloor is produced by calendering. Calendered products can be recognized by the lengthwise elongation of the marbleizing. This elongation is not as pronounced in pressed products.

Vinyl resins are very resistant to abrasion. **The greater the proportion of vinyl resins in the flooring material, the greater will be the abrasion resistance.** Likewise, the greater will be the resistance to scuffing, chemicals and bacteria. Vinyl resins are expensive and the use of mineral fibers and inert fillers can help bring down the cost of the material.

Resilience

Resilience is the capability of a strained body to recover its size and shape after deformation, especially when the strain is caused by compressive forces. In the case of resilient flooring, resilience refers more specifically to the capability to recover from indentation. It is very important in the appearance retention of resilience floorings. The three main sources of indentation are impact, static loads and rolling loads.

IMPACT: Momentary indentation caused by people walking is the most frequent impact occurrence. This impact pressure can be high, as much as several thousand pounds. The smaller the impact area, the more pounds per square inch and the more damaging is the indentation. Thus, very tiny-heeled shoes can be extremely damaging if the flooring is not sufficiently resilient. Rubber and full thickness vinyl are most resistant to impact loads.

STATIC LOADS: The second type of indentation occurs in those situations where a concentrated load remains in a stationary position for an extended period of time, such as with stationary furniture and equipment. Recommended load limits in the manufacturer's literature refer to static load limits. These are expressed in pounds per square inch (PSI). The standard test method for indentation of resilient flooring is ASTM F-142, sometimes known as the McBurney Test.

Furniture legs are often fitted with bearing surfaces that are too small, resulting in excessive load concentration. Indentations will occur unless proper protective devices are provided. For very heavy stationary furniture or equipment, the load can be distributed with the use of flat composition furniture cups. Light chairs and furniture should have glides with a flexible shank, and a smooth flat base (1 1/4"–2 1/4" diameter) with rounded edges.

ROLLING LOADS: The third source of indentation is rolling loads. Carts, wheelchairs, gurneys and other wheeled vehicles are present in most areas of a hospital. Chairs with casters are ubiquitous. Wheels and casters must have widths and diameters commensurate with the loads to be carried, or grooved indentations may occur.

Office chairs and small rolling equipment should be equipped with casters at least 2" diameter, with soft treads 3/4" wide. These should

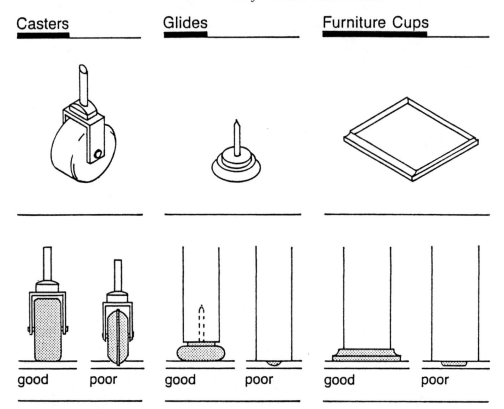

Figure 3.1. FLOORING PROTECTION. Flooring indentations caused by furniture and equipment can be prevented or lessened by distribution of loads over a broad area. For furniture and equipment, this translates into proper diameter and tread width for casters and wheels, and appropriate cups and glides under narrow legs. In all cases, rounded edges are needed to prevent cutting into the flooring material.

swivel easily. Wheels on dietary carts, linen carts, patient beds and other heavy equipment should be a minimum of 5" diameter. Edges on all should be slightly rounded to prevent cutting.

The degree of resilience is also directly related to the degree of sound absorption and to slip resistance. Rubber, the most resilient of this group of floorings, has the best sound-absorbing qualities and the best coefficient of friction.

Sunlight Resistance

Strong exposure to sunlight may affect the performance and appearance of some types of resilient flooring by causing shrinking, brittleness, blisters and fading. Red pigments are the most vulnerable to solar fading. Neutral pigments have the most resistance.

Resistance to Staining

Resistance to staining is dependent on moisture resistance and chemical resistance. A non-porous material that does not allow moisture penetration means spills can be wiped off the surface and stains are unlikely. Polishes are used on many of the resilient floorings to seal surface pores and enhance resistance to staining.

Chemicals attack the actual composition of the material. The result of spilled chemicals may be not only stain but brittleness, softening or other changes in the material's properties. Chemical attack affects durability as well as appearance.

The greater the proportion of vinyl resins, the less the chance of permanent stain damage. Vinyl resins are resistant to most chemicals, including oils and grease, acids and alkalis, blood, most food stains and most of the reagents, antiseptics and other chemicals used in hospitals. Rubber is more vulnerable to several of these substances.

The major manufacturers have run tests for staining on their various products. Results of these tests are available upon request. These should certainly be requested whenever flooring for areas subject to chemical spillage is being evaluated. Whatever material is selected, all spills should be immediately wiped up to lessen the chance of staining.

One place of particular concern is the operating room. Betadine or methylene blue may be used copiously, and just about every material is stained by these chemicals. Eventually, a circle of yellow brown or blue is established under the operating table. Claims for superior resistance to staining are made for some materials such as Armstrong's Medintech.® These should be investigated with regard to the specific chemicals planned for use.

Resistance to Cigarette Burns

Despite their excellent resistance to staining, vinyl resins are not resistant to cigarette burns. In this instance, the more resistant resilient flooring is rubber.

Color

Color is imparted in two main ways. In most resilient floorings, the pigments are added to the resin solution prior to forming the resilient sheet; color is homogenous throughout the face material. In some vinyl sheet goods, color is printed on the backing material.

Resilient flooring is produced chiefly in muted or weakly saturated colors. The clearest, purest colors are found in solid vinyl. Some rubber is made in intense, deep colors.

In resilient flooring as in all other finish materials, one of the functions of color is to conceal soil. Choose the material in the same color family as the chemicals being used. If the surgeons are using betadine, select a brown or yellow-brown flooring; if they are using methylene blue, select a blue flooring. This is backup protection. At least, if there is staining, it will show less.

In any case, do not use white. It may appear to indicate a sterile atmosphere when it is new, but any staining will give the appearance of uncleanliness. Also, reflections from the white floor into the surgeon's eyes are tiring and possibly dangerous.

Another function of color is to enhance performance of tasks that take place in the space. The operating room is a good example of this. The task field is the red of human blood and tissue. Its complement, blue-green is the optimal environmental color. It provides contrast to the operating field, thus aiding acuity of the surgeon's eyes. It also eliminates distracting afterimages.

Afterimages occur when the eye concentrates on one color and then looks at a white or very light value surface where it will see the complement of the color. In surgery, the eye is concentrated on the predominantly red center of attention. Blue-green images will appear on white clothes and walls when the surgeon looks up from the task. If the direct environment is blue-green the afterimages will be neutralized.

Texture and Pattern

While color is important, its camouflaging function will be much more powerful if texture or pattern are added. This is especially true on horizontal surfaces such as floors. Solid colors, if used at all, should be limited to small feature strips in low traffic areas.

Scratches, scuff marks, indentations and gouges, while not being serious overall wear problems, will spoil the appearance. Many of the resilient floorings appropriate for health care use have a textural quality achieved with large or small dots of color scattered in a random pattern. This type of textural pattern reflects the vinyl chips used in the fabrication process. As a natural outgrowth of the materials and process, this type of pattern can be very pleasing as well as being functional.

Patterns are achieved in several ways. Striations such as those in a marble pattern are formed by veins of color in the material. Using this linear element, tiles can be laid in a checkered, striped or other pattern. In some vinyls, patterns are printed on a backing underneath a transparent vinyl wear layer.

Acoustics

In comparison with wood, concrete or terrazzo, resilient flooring will reduce impact noises. It will not reduce impact sound as effectively as carpet, nor will it subdue reverberant sounds originating from such sources as conversation or the clatter of carts as will carpet. Cushioned resilient floorings developed for sound-cushioning characteristics as well as for foot comfort are not durable enough to be used in high traffic situations. They are more vulnerable to gouging and indentation damage than non-cushioned floorings.

In hospital corridors, a cushioned resilient flooring would also lose a major advantage usually attributed to resilient flooring materials: the ease with which a cart is pushed. For cart traffic, cushioned resilient flooring has no advantage over low, dense, loop pile carpet, and the carpet would generally have better sound-deadening properties.

Health and Safety

Flammability

Building code and other regulatory bodies have flammability requirements for flooring materials. Two tests are commonly used. These are discussed more fully under carpet and briefly reviewed here. The test used for many years to test the flammability of resilient floor coverings has been the ASTM E-84 Tunnel Test. This is still the most frequently required test for resilient flooring. Flooring materials for hospitals and many other health care facilities must generally have a flame spread rating of not more than 75 when tested in accordance with this test.

The Flooring Radiant Panel Test, NFPA Standard 253 and ASTM E-648, is the test used in many regulatory districts. A CRF (critical radiant flux) of 0.45 w/sq cm or more is usually required for flooring materials installed in corridors and exits of critical health care occupancies. Most resilient floorings have little trouble meeting these flame test standards or the requirements of the NBS Smoke Density Chamber Test.

Other applicable regulations concern the use of flammable gases. These are NFPA 56A Standard for the Use of Inhalation Anesthetics and the Underwriters Laboratory's hazardous location equipment list, guide number 120W0, "Flooring, Electrically Conductive."

Light Reflectance

Polishes are used to properly maintain most resilient floorings. This intensifies the light reflectance of whatever color is used. Light-colored floorings that are highly polished can be especially troublesome. Flooring materials should not exceed a light reflectance value of over 50 percent, and 30 percent or less is better.

Critical visual tasks performed where the background reflectance is high can cause glare with resultant eye discomfort and headaches. This is a factor when people are working at desks or lab tops with a light floor as a secondary background.

Another area of concern is long corridors where high reflectance and glare can distort the shape of the space and cause disorientation for the ill and the elderly. A window at the end of the corridor aggravates the problem with additional reflections and images. A corridor with a white floor, white walls and white ceiling can cause extreme orientation problems for some people.

Mid to dark value floors can almost always be recommended for the above reasons and because they visually establish a stabilizing base upon which all else rests. This is especially important when the floor surface is also glossy. If a floor is too dark, however, soil that is light in color will become unduly evident. As with carpet, the prevailing soil color should be considered in the selection of resilient flooring.

Slipperiness

Falls are the cause of many injuries. Slippery floors are a leading contributor to falls. This is an important factor in health care facilities where patients are not always steady on their feet and emergency conditions requiring quick staff response occur. Polished resilient floors are slippery; when wet from spills or mopping, they are even more slippery.

In some cases, this is a no-win situation. In areas where there is much spillage, a water-resistant flooring material must be specified and resilient flooring may be the only possibility within the budget. A limited number of slip-resistant floorings have been developed. One device used to increase slip resistance is the raised disk or strip.

The standard test for slip resistance is ASTM D-2047, known as the James Test Method. Results are recorded as an "index of slipperiness" or "static coefficient of friction." A surface having a static coefficient of friction of 0.5 or greater as measured in accordance with this test method is considered to be a slip-resistant flooring.

In general, rubber is the most slip resistant of the resilient flooring materials. Some rubber floorings have a slip-resistant coefficient as high as 1.09. Vinyls commonly vary from 0.5 to 0.9. However, it is difficult to establish a scale of slip resistance by materials, as there is considerable variation depending on the surface finish and whether or not the floor is waxed. Also, the James Machine is not suitable for use on wet, rough or corrugated surfaces.

Types of Resilient Flooring — Composition

Resilient flooring types are classified according to ingredients as vinyl, vinyl composition, asphalt and rubber. These ingredients determine the extent to which certain properties exist. They give rise to the advantages and limitations of the different types. Table 3.1 is a summary comparison of properties among the different types of resilient flooring.

Vinyl Flooring

Vinyl flooring is composed of vinyl resins, plasticizers, fillers, stabilizers and pigments pressed or calendered into sheets. Polyvinyl chloride (PVC) resin is the major ingredient. Plasticizers furnish flexibility; stabilizers enhance color uniformity and stability. Vinyl goods may be homogeneous throughout or may be backed by other materials, such as organic felts, asbestos-flex felt or scrap vinyls.

Sheet goods come in 6', 6'-6", 9' and 12' widths. The material can be cut into tiles which are available in 9" and 12" squares. It is an excellent material with many advantages. One aesthetic advantage is that vinyl has no inherent color, so that clear coats, bright accents and opaque whites can be made. Its most serious limitation is that it is somewhat more expensive than many of the other resilient flooring materials.

Advantages
Excellent abrasion resistance
Good to very good resilience
Excellent acid and alkali resistance
Excellent oil and grease resistance
Excellent moisture resistance
Easy to install, especially tiles
Very flexible, can flash cove
Clear, bright colors

Table 3.1

EVALUATION GUIDE: RESILIENT FLOORINGS

This table compares resilient floorings with one another. It does not compare the properties of resilient floorings with those of carpet or hard surface floorings.

Property	Types of Resilient Floorings				
	Vinyl Backed	Vinyl Solid	Vinyl Comp	Asphalt	Rubber
HEALTH & SAFETY					
Slip Resistance	2*	2*	1*	1*	3*
WEAR LIFE **Durability**					
Abrasion Resistance	4	4	3	1	3
Appearance Retention					
Resilience	3	4	2	1	4
Static Load Resistance	2	3	2	1	4
Moisture Resistance	4	4	3	2	4
Chemical Resistance					
Acids and Alkalis	4	4	3	3	2
Oil and Grease	4	4	3	1	2
Cigarette Burn Resistance	1	1	2	1	4
Maintenance					
Ease of Maintenance	3	3	2	1	4
ENVIRONMENTAL					
Comfort Underfoot	2	4	2	1	4
Sound Absorption	2	3	2	1	4
INSTALLATION					
Ease of Installation#	3,4	3,4	4	2	3,4
Flexibility	3	4	2	1	4
Cost	High	High	Medium	Low	High

* Varies considerably according to surface finish or polish.
# Tiles of any given material are easier to install than sheet goods.

Legend:
    4 = Excellent
    3 = Very Good
    2 = Good
    1 = Fair

Limitations

Not resistant to cigarette burns
Relatively expensive
Not a very good sound absorber, especially backed vinyls
Dulls under heavy traffic

Sheet vinyl flooring is of particular relevance to health care facilities. With large sheets, there are many fewer seams than with tiles. This makes it appropriate for use where spillage is a problem, as seams where liquid can penetrate the flooring and bacteria multiply are considerably reduced.

It is also advantageous where large amounts of water are flushed over the floor in cleaning. Excessive surface moisture can adversely affect the adhesive backing or underlayment. Not only are there many fewer seams, but with some sheet flooring the seams can be chemically bonded or heat bonded, making what is essentially a monolithic floor covering.

Being flexible, sheet vinyl can also be "flash coved"; that is, the sheet is coved up the wall to form a base that is integral with the floor, sometimes called an integral base. A coved base means no sharp corners where dirt can hide at the wall/floor juncture. The edge can be finished with a vinyl or metal molding. An even better edge finish solution is to construct the wall so that the base is slightly indented from the plane of the wall. The base can then butt up to the lip formed by the wall overhang. This gives a clean finished appearance and simplifies maintenance.

Molding   Overhang

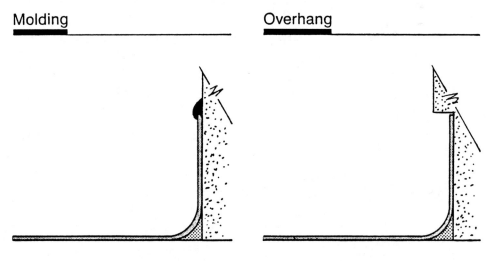

Figure 3.2. TERMINATION OF FLASH COVING. "Flash coved" vinyl sheet flooring can be terminated with a molding or can butt into a wall or cabinet overhang.

Each manufacturer makes a version of vinyl flooring that is somewhat different from the others. Some manufacturers have several versions in their line. These fall into three main categories. Table 3.2 is a comparison of sheet floorings produced by several manufacturers.

Table 3.2

SHEET FLOORING COMPARISON

Type	Manufacturer and Pattern	Use	Taber Cycles	PSI	Wear/ Total	Width	FR	*
Opaque vinyl over backing	**Armstrong**							
	Classic Corlon	General	15-21,000	100	.050/.085	6'	1,B	a
	Custom Corlon	General		100	.050/.085	6'	1,B	
	Crosswalk	Slip Res.		125	.035/.100	6'	1,B	b,e
	Tajima							
	Permaleum	General	27,000		.016/.080	6'	1	
	Permaleum	General	27,000		.016/.100	6'	1	
Translucent vinyl over printed backing	**Armstrong**							
	New Era	General	24,000	125	.025/.060	9,12'	1,B	
	Congoleum							
	Flor Ever	General	28,000	75	.025/.090	9,12'	B	
	Pavillion	General		75	.020/.085	6,12'	B	
	Royal Gallery	General		75	.025/.090	6'	B	
	Mannington							
	Arch. Choice	General	17,000	75	.025/.089	6,12'		
	Aristicon	General	17,000	75	.020/.095	6,12'		
	Tarkett							
	Ekstra	General		75	.024/.088	6'-6"	1,B	c
	Rillet	Slip Res.		75	.024/.088	6'-6"	1,B	c
	Contracfloor	Acoustic	16,000	75	.024/.086	6,12'	1,B	h
	Futur 2000	Chem. Res.		100	.032/.080	6'-6"	1,B	c,g
	Response	General		75	.025/.090	6,12'	1,B	h
Solid Vinyl	**Armstrong**							
	Medintech	Stain Res.	40,000	125	.080	6'	1,B	
	Tarkett							
	Multiflor							
	Granit	General	33,000	125	.080	6'	1,B	
	Marble	General	33,000	125	.080	6'-6"	1,B	
	Relief	Slip Res.		125	.106	6'	1,B	e
	Conductiflor	Conductive	20,000	125	.080	6'-6"	1,B	d
	Antistat	Antistatic	20,000	125	.080	6'-6"	1,B	
	Multisafe	Slip Res.		125	.106	6'	1,A	e
	Optima	General		125	.080	6'-6"	1,A	

Table 3.2 *(continued)*

Type	Manufacturer and Pattern	Use	Taber Cycles	PSI	Wear/ Total	Width	FR	*
	TekStil Concepts Unifloor							
	Select Super	General	71,000		.080	5'	1,A	
	Heavy Duty	Heavy Duty	71,000+		.100	5'	1,A	f
	Conductive	Conductive	71,000	125	.080,.100	5'	1,A	f
	Static Dissipative	Static Dissipative	71,000	125	.080,.100	4'	1,A	f
Opaque vinyl over foam interlayer or backing	**Tajima**							
	Fantasy	General	36,000		.052/.118	6'	1	
	U-Manity 28	General	27,000		.040/.110	6'	1	
	U-Manity 35	General	27,000		.040/.138	6'	1	
	U-Manity 55	Heavy Duty	55,000		.080/.217	6'	1	
	Tarkett Acoustiflor							
	Granit	Acoustic		150	.060/.157	6'	1,B	
	Marble	Acoustic		100	.040/.137	6'-6"	1,B	
	Salute	Conductive		150	.080/.125	3'	m	
	TekStil Unifloor							
	Silent Cushion	Acoustic			0.50/.120	5'	1,B	
Rubber	**Flexco**							
	Sheet rubber	General		200	.094,.125, .188	3'	A&B	
	RCA Rubber							
	Flexi-Flor	General		200	.094,.125, .188	3'	A	

All vinyls can be used below grade or higher.

Rubbers must be used on or above grade; consult manufacturer's literature.

When matrix space is left blank, information is not available in the manufacturer's literature.

Legend:

PSI = Recommended load limits in pounds per square inch

Wear/Total = Wear layer thickness/Total thickness

FR = Flammability rating

1 = Class 1 in when tested by ASTM E-648, Flooring Radiant Panel Test

A = Class A when tested by NFPA or 25 or less when tested by ASTM E-84

B = Class B when tested by NFPA or 75 or less when tested by ASTM E-84

m = Meets military standard, MIL-ST-1623

*Notes:

a. Consists of vinyl composition chips in an unfilled vinyl matrix.

b. Mineral aggregate gives a rough surface on raised disks.

c. Glass reinforced intermediary or backing layer.

d. Black only; conductor is carbon black.

e. Has a high and a low surface.

f. .080 materials tested at 71,000 cycles, .100 materials would be more.

g. Stain resistant polyurethane coating.

h. Foam interlayer.

OPAQUE VINYL OVER A BACKING: (often called inlaid) This type of sheet flooring is composed of an opaque wear layer of vinyl affixed to a backing of another material. The pattern extends through the full depth of the wear layer. This wear layer is constructed in a variety of ways: an unfilled vinyl matrix with inlaid vinyl composition chips, a filled vinyl, or a vinyl with mineral aggregate particles. In the latter, a version manufactured by Armstrong contains the mineral grit in raised disks to give a highly slip-resistant surface.

With inlaid vinyl, a two-part epoxy adhesive can be used in the seams to achieve a functionally seamless installation. This adhesive is extremely resistant to moisture and stronger than the flooring material itself.

TRANSLUCENT VINYL OVER A PRINTED BACKING: In these materials an unfilled vinyl wear layer is poured over a backing, the surface of which has been printed, usually by a rotogravure process. There may be a core between the wear layer and the backing, in which case the surface of the core would be printed. For example, Tarkett's Ekstra® and Rillet® have a vinyl core containing glass fibers for strength and dimensional stability.

Tarkett also has a special use material in this category; Contracfloor® has a core of PVC foam for sound control. **Materials with foam cores are not recommended for heavy-duty traffic areas, where heavy wheeled equipment will be used, or where heavy furniture or equipment may be dragged across the floor.**

In fact, this type of sheet vinyl is recommended only for light commercial applications. Because the vinyl wear layer is required to be only 20 mils, contrasted with 50 mils for inlaid vinyl, its resistance to damage from cuts and gouges is much less than that of inlaid. An advantage of this vinyl is that the pattern potential is unlimited.

FULL THICKNESS VINYL: In this solid vinyl flooring, the full depth of the flooring is the vinyl, itself. It is often called PVC flooring. There are a number of special-use materials in this category such as slip-resistant, conductive and antistatic floorings.

Solid vinyl floors are usually seamed by means of heat welding a vinyl rod into a routed seam. Some are seamed by chemical bonding or solvent welding. Primary applications for these vinyl floors are in operating rooms, cast rooms, dialysis, emergency and constant care units.

Vinyl tiles fall mainly in this last category of full-thickness vinyl. One advantage of tile is that a variety of patterns is possible through the use of contrasting tiles in various configurations. Another advantage is the possible savings in materials when installation in irregular spaces is involved. In some spaces, cutting waste with sheet goods can be considerable.

Only those materials specifically made for commercial use should be used in the hospital environment. Residential vinyls will not stand up in institutional use. The wear layer is thinner than in commercial goods and will wear through. Many have a "no wax" finish which will wear off with heavy use. Repair can be difficult and unsatisfactory. Embossed patterns, common in residential flooring materials, can collect dirt in the small indentations.

Vinyl Composition Tile

Vinyl composition tiles (VCT) are composed of the same ingredients as vinyl flooring materials with the addition of mineral fibers. Originally, these fibers were asbestos. Hence, the familiar name, VAT (vinyl asbestos tile). Today, a number of minerals including asbestos are used.

Asbestos, encapsulated within the tile, is believed to be safe, provided that the tile is properly used. The Consumer Product Safety Commission has ruled that 10 percent of a tile product can contain asbestos, but it must be totally encapsulated within the tile. VAT should never be sanded preparatory to laying another layer of flooring material; this would expose the asbestos fibers. While VAT appears to be safe when properly used, environmental concerns in the manufacturing process are driving manufacturers to seek non-toxic alternatives.

Vinyl composition is not flexible enough to be used in sheet goods and is used only in tile form. Tiles are 9", 12" and sometimes 16" square. The thickness or gauge appropriate for institutional use is 1/8". Sometimes, 3/32" is used. It may be satisfactory in low- or medium-traffic areas. When using 3/32" gauge, there is substantially more risk that any regularity in the subfloor may "telegraph" through. For this reason, 1/8" gauge is the safer choice.

In good quality VCT tiles, the vinyl composition material extends the full depth of the material, making the wear surface the full thickness of the tile. When specifying, it is important to select through grain tiles. Of all the recommended resilient flooring products, VCT has the lowest intrinsic resistance to abrasive wear; however, this is compensated for by its relative thickness.

The properties of vinyl composition tiles are similar to those of solid vinyl tiles but somewhat diminished. They are less resistant to chemicals and abrasion. They are less resilient than vinyl tiles and, therefore, more subject to indentation. PSI values range from 50 to 75. Vinyl composition tiles are considered semi-porous, whereas solid vinyl is non-porous. A non-porous characteristic contributes to easier maintenance. However, this material is more resistant to cigarette scorch and is less expensive than solid vinyl.

Advantages
Good abrasion resistance
Resistant to acids and alkalis
Resistant to oils and grease
Easy to install
Relatively inexpensive

Limitations
Low resilience
Semi-porous as compared to solid vinyl or rubber
Poor noise absorption

Vinyl composition tile for commercial use comes in limited patterns, a variety of textures, and in solids. Solids are often called feature tiles indicating their intended use as feature strips. The solid surface shows scuffing, scratching and soiling much more readily than a patterened or textured surface and should not be used in field areas where it will present a housekeeping problem.

Slip-resistant, heat-resistant and conductive types are available.

Asphalt Tile

Asphalt is very inexpensive. Its performance as an institutional flooring material is in line with its cost. In fact, its performance is such that it is difficult to recommend it for almost any application. Asphalt is slowly being phased out by new developments in technology. If it is used, be sure to specify a tile in which the pattern penetrates the entire thickness.

Advantages
Least initial cost of any

Limitations
Low resistance to abrasion
Low resilience/poor recovery from indentation
Softened by mineral oils and animal fats
Poor sound absorption
Low resistance to stains
Must be carefully installed and repaired
Not flexible/brittle when cold

Rubber Flooring

Rubber flooring is made of vulcanized compounds of rubber, mainly butadiene styrene rubber. Reclaimed rubber may be added. Other ingredients include stabilizers, mineral fibers providing reinforcement, oils and resins as plasticizers and stiffening agents, and pigments for color.

Rubber is very sound absorbent, more comfortable to walk on and less slippery than vinyl and vinyl composition. These properties may predicate its use in areas where staining is not a problem.

Staining of rubber is a problem when its use is being evaluated. Researchers have been working to increase its stain resistance. Nora Flooring has developed Noraplan® which it claims has better chemical resistance than other rubber floorings. Noraplan is also antistatic for use in computer rooms.

Advantages

Wears well, not as durable as vinyl or vinyl composition
Very resilient/good walking comfort
Good acoustic properties for resilient flooring
Resists cigarette burns
Easy to install
Very flexible
Less slippery than most resilient flooring
Static resistant

Limitations

Susceptible to deterioration from cleaning compounds, solvents, oil, grease, fatty acids and ultraviolent light
Relatively high initial cost

Rubber is available in tiles of 9" and 12" squares and in sheets 36 3/4" wide. Rubber flooring by European manufacturers is widely used. The tiles are generally larger than those produced by American manufacturers at 50-cm (19.69"), 60-cm (23.62"), and 100-cm (39.37") squares. Sheet goods are typically 1.2 meters (3.94') wide. Marble and travertine patterns and solids are the most common. As with most flooring, solids will appear most soiled. However, rubber shows scuff marks somewhat less than vinyl.

An interesting, functional and increasingly popular rubber flooring has been developed. This is a solid color flooring molded with raised disks or squares with rounded corners. These raised areas allow soil and grit to drop down below the wear surface; this lowers abrasion on the wear surface. Likewise, they allow water to flow below the wear surface, increasing slip resistance. This tile could serve admirably in hydrotherapy rooms. The same tile is available in stair treads where it provides increased safety.

Cleaning of this two-level tile is easiest when the disk or square profile is low and the bevel is gradual. Very light or dark colors are not recommended, as soiling is exaggerated due to the difference between raised and depressed surfaces. Where there is heavy soiling, this product quickly loses its pleasing appearance.

Maintenance

Asphalt, Vinyl Composition and Vinyl

Maintenance of asphalt, vinyl composition and vinyl consists of three essential components: daily care, washing, and polishing and stripping. The following is in accordance with the maintenance recommended by the Resilient Floor Covering Institute.

DAILY CARE: Sweep or damp mop regularly. A treated dust mop or soft-hair push broom can be used for sweeping. Use wax-based compounds. Never use oils. Spray buff as needed in scuff-marked and traffic-worn areas. The spray-buff solution is prepared by mixing equal parts of floor finish and water. Spraying is followed by machine buffing.

WASHING: Floors must be washed periodically. Thorough sweeping should precede washing to remove grit. Use the flooring manufacturer's recommended pads or brushes and cleaners. Do not use soap-based or other alkaline cleaners, as they will leave a dulling film. With tiles the amount of water must be controlled, as excess water can penetrate joints and soak the subfloor.

Remove gummy matter with a putty knife or plastic blade. Remove stubborn spots using a nylon scrubber or very fine steel wool dipped in detergent. Rinse the area thoroughly with clear water. Remove rinse water with a wet vacuum or clean mops.

POLISHING AND STRIPPING: Polish should be applied to clean dry floors. In corridors, it should be applied in the center of traffic lanes and spread to the outside. Allow the polish to dry thoroughly. When completely dry, it can be buffed to a higher gloss.

Periodic stripping of polish from floors is necessary to prevent excess finish buildup. The old finish is scrubbed off after being softened with an approved finish remover. The dirty solution is removed with a wet vacuum cleaner or clean mops. The surface is then rinsed thoroughly and allowed to dry before applying new polish.

Various types of machines are available for all of the above operations, depending on the size of the facility and the sizes of the areas to be maintained.

Use the manufacturer's recommended polish. Do not use paste waxes or liquid-solvent waxes. Do not use lacquers or varnishes.

The Resilient Floor Covering Institute (1975) suggests water-resistant (resin or polymer) polishes. When these are used on tile floors, it is especially important to strip the floors at recommended intervals.

> Some of the new water-resistant finishes build up impermeable films that are so strong they can curl or lift corners or edges of tile. Floors maintained with these must be stripped every three or four applications. Use a strong stripping solution of 8 oz (1 cup) household ammonia to 10 qts (1 bucket) of water with the recommended floor cleaner. Rinse floor thoroughly with clean water.

Most manufacturers do not recommend the "no wax" method of maintenance that heats the vinyl to soften it so that a high-speed buffer can smooth out the scratches and nicks. Softening the vinyl causes detergent residue and dirt to become permanently embedded in the floor.

Rubber

The maintenance of some rubber flooring is very similar to that of vinyl. The maintenance of others is simpler, as they do not need to be polished and periodically stripped. These rubber floorings contain integral waxes; the surface sheen can be renewed with simple buffing. This is a great advantage, as the cost of staff time spent in polishing and stripping resilient flooring is considerable.

For those rubber floorings that do not require polishing, the maintenance routine would be:

1. Sweep or damp mop daily, or as required to remove loose dirt from the floor.
2. Wet mop with a mild detergent solution or with the flooring manufacturer's recommended cleaning solution as needed. Rinse with clear water.
3. Buff with soft bristle or lamb's wool buffer.

All spills should be removed immediately to avoid staining problems, and all dirt should be removed on a regular basis to prevent abrasive particles being ground into the floor.

No oil-treated mops or oil-sweeping compounds should be used. No petroleum-based, naptha or similar solvent cleaners should be used.

Rubber flooring can be waxed with standard non-slip rubber floor wax. For rubber that must be polished, a liquid emulsion wax as recommended by the flooring manufacturer should be used. Stripping must be done periodically.

Installation

Detailed installation information has been compiled by the Resilient Floor Covering Institute. Nevertheless, installation specifications are not standard but are issued by the various manufacturers for their own products. The manufacturer's installation instructions for the specific item should also be carefully read. Installation involves two major factors: the condition of the substrate and the type of adhesive used. When the material is to be used below grade, the proper adhesive and preparation of substrate are of particular importance. Adhesives are an important factor in the life of a resilient floor. Selection is based on the type of flooring, the type of underlayment, the type of subfloor, location with regard to subsurface moisture and the probability of surface moisture. It is advisable to use the manufacturer's recommended adhesive for the prevailing conditions.

Resilient flooring will mold itself to the substrate over which it is laid, showing any irregularities that exist. A smooth underlayment, either mastic or board, must be installed over the structural subfloor. Mastic-type underlayments are generally used to level concrete floors. Board-type underlayments are used for wood floors. Particle board is generally not recommended. Careful preparation of the underlayment is necessary, as irregularities will "telegraph" right through the resilient flooring. The higher the gloss, the greater the visibility of underlayment irregularities.

All rooms, flooring and adhesive should be maintained at a minimum temperature of 70° F for at least 48 hours before, during, and 48 hours after application of the flooring.

Vinyl composition, solid vinyl and asphalt tiles may be installed over radiant-heat concrete floors, provided the heating system is properly controlled to give a maximum temperature of 85° F measured directly over the heating pipes. Equipping all furniture and equipment with proper load-bearing devices is especially important when radient heating is used. Do not use rubber over radiant-heated floors. Its excellent insulation properties will cause problems.

Specification Notes

Standard AIA and CSI specifications are available for editing.

Instructions for layout of pattern must be included in the specification of resilient flooring. Detail drawings should be shown for all but the most basic linear or checkerboard layouts.

Edge moldings, base moldings and other treatments used where resilient flooring terminates or joins other materials must be clearly specified. Detail drawings may be required to show floor/base intersections, termination of resilient flooring and intersections with other materials.

Edge moldings are made of extruded metal or vinyl. Vinyl is visually more compatible with the flooring and softer underfoot.

Type, location and extent of base trim materials and flash coving should be identified. Details of flash coving must appear in the drawings.

A level substrate is of the utmost importance for a smooth resilient flooring installation. For all projects, and especially for remodelling projects, instructions for underlayment requirements should be specific and the contractor's responsibilities clearly stated. Blanket specification, such as "Repair the old floor to provide a suitable base for resilient flooring," invites the least expensive method of substrate preparation. This is seldom of the quality desired.

Instructions for cleaning and application of a light coat of wax, where applicable, immediately after installation, should be included in the specification.

Whenever possible, it is advisable to specify flooring, adhesive and underlayment from the same manufacturer.

Samples should be submitted to confirm understanding of the selection and to serve as a standard for the project.

Shop drawings need be required only for special layouts or unique conditions.

Certificates of compliance are usually necessary only for special products such as conductive flooring.

Chapter Four

HARD SURFACE FLOOR COVERINGS

HARD SURFACE floorings, properly specified, are very durable and easy to maintain. They should certainly be considered where extra heavy-duty floor coverings are needed.

The cost of materials and installation, however, is generally higher than for most resilient flooring or carpet. Hard surface floorings lessen flexibility when alterations occur, when walls are moved or function changes. Some are very heavy and extra structural support is needed. Some are difficult to patch, and all are expensive enough so that there is a reluctance to ever replace or cover them with a different material. Another limitation with some is the lack of sound-deadening qualities. Impact noise reverberates and airborne sounds are reflected.

There are locations where the durability, strength and ease of maintenance of these materials outweigh any limitations they may have. Of particular interest to health care facilities are ceramic tile and acrylic-impregnated wood.

CERAMIC TILE

In general, ceramic tiles are durable, non-fading and easy to maintain. They are hard, strong, impervious to heat, and resistant to chemical attack and to moisture. Design flexibility is excellent, as the floor is built unit by unit. There is a rich color range. Ceramic materials, especially the dark colors, absorb and retain heat, making this a good choice for use with solar heating. Ceramic materials have also become more price competitive as the cost of petroleum-based finish materials has increased.

Limitations are that ceramic is a poor sound-cushioning material, it can be slippery, and its hardness increases the probability of breakage of dropped objects.

Structure and Properties

The properties of the various kinds of tiles are determined principally by the following structural variables: body composition, method of forming, degree of vitrification, and glazed or unglazed.

Body Composition

Ceramic tiles are made of clay which is shaped, dried and fired. Pure clays are composed of alumina, silica and water. Kaolin, also called China clay, is a pure, white, fine-grained clay. It is the basis of porcelain. Natural clays contain various impurities which give them their characteristic properties. For example, the impurities in ball clays give them greater plasticity than kaolin. All ceramic bodies contain:

1. Clays of varying plasticities in various proportions
2. Non-plastic ingredients, e.g. flint which reduces shrinkage and talc which lessens expansion when water is absorbed
3. Mineral fluxes, e.g. feldspar which is a vitrification agent
4. Minerals, e.g. iron oxide which imparts color and may affect porosity

Method of Forming

Most commercial tiles are formed by either extrusion or dust pressing. The extrusion process is a method by which the damp clay is forced through a die in a continuous column and a wire is used to cut the extruded material into tiles. Dust pressing is a process by which ground clay is compressed in a mold box. The density of the tile is partially dependent on the intensity of the pressure exerted.

Both methods can produce glazed or unglazed tiles. Dust pressing tends to produce a denser tile with less shrinkage than extruded tile. Because of less shrinkage, dust-pressed tiles typically accept the glazing process better. Most unglazed tiles are made by the extrusion process and have consistency of color throughout.

Degree of Vitrification

Vitrification refers to the change into a glass or glassy substance by heat and fusion. During firing, mineral fluxes in the clay body vitrify when a sufficiently high temperature is reached. When vitrification occurs, the clay particles become embedded in a glass matrix. A vitreous body is non-porous. Ceramic bodies are classified as vitreous and non-vitreous. Vitreous bodies are further classified as impervious, vitreous and semi-vitreous. This classification relates directly to the porosity and absorptive properties of the ceramic tile.

Type	Water Absorption Rate
Vitreous	0.5% to 7.0%
Impervious	0.5% or less
Vitreous	0.5% to 3.0%
Semi-vitreous	3.0% to 7.0%
Non-vitreous	More than 7.0%

To control water absorption, the tile can be fired to a temperature at which it becomes vitrified. A second way to control water absorption is to glaze the tile surface.

Glazed or Unglazed

A glaze is a mixture of materials that, when heated sufficiently, forms a permanently hard layer of glass over the surface of the tile. It renders a porous body impermeable or adds brilliance and smoothness to a body that is already virtually non-porous and impermeable. A glaze may be colored or colorless, transparent or opaque.

Various oxides and other mineral compounds impart color and sheen to the glaze. These may also contribute non-visible properties to the tile surface. For instance, the color of the glaze can affect abrasion resistance. Beware! Tiles in the same line may differ in abrasion resistance and durability due to the coloring materials. Colors in the same line may also vary in cost. Some colors are considerably more expensive than others due to the value of the mineral colorant.

Most glazes are glasses which are wholly amorphous, supercooled liquids imparting a smooth gloss sheen to the surface. Some, however, contain substances that crystallize out as the glaze cools. Some of these give matte, semi-matte or crystalline effects.

While glazes can add depth and brilliance of color and impart a sheen to a vitreous tile, they are not as durable as the hard and dense bodied tile itself. Wearing and scratching do occur, and glazed tiles should be avoided in areas of hard wear. Glazes can also be quite slippery when wet. Advances in glazing technology include the development of slip-resistant glazes containing abrasives and of more durable glazes containing quartz and other minerals fired to very high temperatures.

Glazes serve a valuable function in making the surface of a soft-bodied tile impermeable to moisture. However, these soft-bodied tiles are not durable enough for institutional floors and their use should be confined to walls. (Glazed wall tile will be discussed in Chapter Eight, "Heavy-Duty Wall Coverings.")

Health and Safety

Flammability

Ceramic tile is fireproof and will meet the strictest fire codes. The cementitious mortars and grouts are also fireproof. It is when some of the organic grouts are used that problems can develop. Mastic is flammable and gives off toxic fumes. It also exudes fumes when curing and so should not be used in renovation projects that are occupied while under construction. Urethane and silicone grouts can also give off toxic fumes.

If ceramic tile is to be installed where flammable gases are used, an applicable regulation is NFPA 56A, Standard for the Use of Inhalation Anesthetics.

Biogenic Factors

Only the vitreous tiles are recommended for floor installation in most health care facilities. Therefore, they are by definition moisture resistant and will not support growth of fungi or bacteria. Again, any problems encountered will be with the grout. In locations where moisture is present, the grout must be specified as moisture resistant.

Slipperiness

Slipping and falling is a serious source of hospital and nursing home injuries. Ceramic tile can be very slippery. If ceramic materials are to be used, great care must be taken to insure selection of a slip-resistant product. Abrasives such as silicon carbide in the tile body or raised patterns on the tile surface reduce slipperiness. However, these solutions can make cleaning slightly more difficult.

Types of Tile

Vitreous ceramic tile types can be classified in two broad categories. The first category contains the impervious and vitreous types: porcelain, ceramic mosaic and paver tiles. There is some overlap within this broad category, as both ceramic mosaics and pavers are sometimes made of porcelain. A second category contains the semi-vitreous quarry and packinghouse tiles. While each of these tiles has its own particular properties, all have a high degree of structural strength and abrasion resistance. The color extends throughout the tile; whatever abrasion does occur will not score through the color.

Porcelain Tile

These tiles have a high kaolin content and are generally formed by the dust-pressed method, giving them a hard, fine-grained, dense body. They have an absorption rate of 0.5 percent of less. Being impermeable, their resistance to moisture and staining is excellent. Resistance to the abrasive wear of foot traffic is also excellent. They are usually unglazed and the color is the same throughout the tile. Colors are clear and luminous. The surface may be plain, mottled or textured. Although some manufacturers are making larger procelain tiles, many are the size of ceramic mosaics.

Ceramic Mosaic Tile

Ceramic mosaics are the most common of the vitreous tiles. They are usually 1/4"–3/8" thick and have a surface area of six square inches or less. Common sizes are 1"×1", 2"×2" and 1"×2". Hexagons of comparable size are also available. These are dust pressed of porcelain clays or natural clays. The natural clay colors are strong and dense.

With a water absorption rate of 3 percent or less, the non-porous character and stain resistance of ceramic mosaic tile makes it an excellent choice for public rest rooms. However, slipping can be a problem. The use of tile with a slight cushion edge and concave grout areas will give slip resistance by breaking up the smooth surface. Abrasive grain, available in some tiles, will also improve slip resistance but may make housekeeping slightly more difficult.

Conductive Tile

Sometimes, ceramic mosaics are produced as conductive tiles. In conductive tiles, carbon black, iron oxides or other conductive materials are added to the tile body to dissipate static buildup. These tiles are used where sparks from static electricity could cause an explosion. Conductive flooring is required in special procedures rooms and in operating rooms if explosive gases are used. This is becoming uncommon in modern operating rooms. Today, it is more apt to be used in the computer room where static electricity can cause mistakes as severe as the loss of irreplaceable records.

Paver Tile

Pavers are usually dust pressed, vitreous tiles very similar to ceramic mosaics but larger, with a face surface of more than six square inches. They are also somewhat thicker than ceramic mosaics, because increased stability is required during the firing process.

Porcelain, ceramic mosaic and paver tiles are also available as glazed accent tiles. These should never be used in a broad field area, nor even as an accent in areas subject to abrasive wear. Sometimes, porcelain tiles are polished. This gives an appealing sheen to the surface but lessens slip resistance.

Quarry Tile

Natural clays and shale with a high proportion of ball clays are used in making quarry tile. Natural clays are usually buff, brown, red-brown, grey or blue-grey and impart to quarry tiles their naturalistic colors. Colors other than those occurring naturally in the clay are seldom used. Sometimes, a flashing is sprayed on a portion of the tile to obtain shading or a deeper color.

The clay is extruded in a column of about 1/2"–3/4" thick. The extrusion is cut off in increments to form the tiles which may have a surface area as large as twelve inches square. In the extrusion process, the body, while quite dense, can never be compressed to the density obtainable in the dust-pressed process. Quarry tile is semi-vitreous at a 3–7 percent absorption rate. It is generally considered stain resistant but not stain-proof. Due to the slight absorption, a patina is developed over the years. This patina is often adjudged to be one of the beauties of quarry tile.

Quarry tile is tough, durable and can be recommended for high traffic areas such as entries and for kitchens, where heavy traffic and grease spills are factors. Again, slipping can be a problem. The tiles are often made with a scored or rippled surface for added traction. Carborundum chips or a grit of pre-fired tile can be added for slip resistance. This is highly recommended for areas such as kitchens, where spills are common, but it does make mopping the floors slightly more difficult.

Packinghouse Tile

Packinghouse tiles, often called brick pavers, are semi-vitreous and similar to quarry tile but of greater thickness, to about 1 1/4". These tiles are rarely tinted and never glazed. They are suitable for heavy loads and highly trafficked surfaces.

Maintenance

Maintenance of ceramic tile floors is simple. It does not require waxes or other recurrent treatments. Use a damp mop for light soil. If soil is heavy, mop with a detergent and water. It is also a simple procedure to repair a damaged surface by replacing individual tile units.

While maintenance of the tiles is simple, the grout between tiles can cause problems. Tile and grout are two different materials, with the grout being more porous and less resistant to soil and staining. Some grouts are more stain resistant than others, and sometimes stains in the grout can be removed with a strong bleach solution. Colorant added to the grout will help conceal stains. Grout sealants will help prevent them.

In areas of grease buildup, unglazed ceramic tile may be sealed prior to use with a commercial tile sealer. Grease and oil stains can be removed with a special eradicator developed by the Tile Council of America.

If care is not taken in the selection, tile can be slippery when wet. This can be a maintenance concern and an inconvenience when traffic must detour around wet ceramic floors.

Installation

There are many ways to install ceramic tile. It is always wise to consult with the manufacturer of the tile. Reasons for failures range from today's greater building movement due to lighter-weight construction to the complex variety of mortars and grouts.

Tile is set in a bed of mortar. Grout is then applied to fill the narrow spaces between the tiles. The grout protects from water and lateral movement. There are several ways to set and bond the tile. Various grouting methods are associated with each. The two basic methods of installation are full mortar bed and thin bed. Within the thin bed techniques, there are a number of methods developed to achieve specific properties.

Full Mortar Bed Method

A bed of Portland cement mortar is floated over a prepared backing surface. The setting bed is up to 1 1/4" thick. While it is still plastic, a bond coat of neat cement is applied over the mortar and tiles are pressed into place. Alternatively, the mortar bed may be allowed to cure and one of the thin bed methods used to bond the tile.

Advantages to this method are that it is structurally sound for heavy-duty surfaces, a level surface can easily be produced over work done by other trades and accurate slopes can be achieved.

Limitations are its weight, the long curing time, the need to be wet down during the curing process and the compatibility of depth with other flooring systems unless special constructions are used to obtain a level finish surface.

Thin Bed Methods

Thin bed methods are used where minimal finish thicknesses are desired and speed of installation is critical. They are compatible in thickness with other flooring surfaces such as carpet and resilient flooring. These thin layers are not effective for hiding or leveling subsurface irregularities.

Both cementitious (made of cement) and non-cementitious materials are used. Non-cementitious materials were developed for chemical resistance and environments where unusual heat or water conditions are present. They require special skills to install and are generally more expensive than cementitious materials.

Cementitious mortars are based on Portland cement. Various additives give characteristic properties to each.

DRY-SET MORTAR. Dry-set mortar is basically Portland cement and sand. Additives enhance the water-retention characteristics of the mix. This means that it does not have to be wet down during the curing process as does a wet-cured mortar. It can be used over a cured full mortar bed and over most properly prepared surfaces. It is not affected by prolonged contact with water, but neither does it form a water barrier.

LATEX-PORTLAND CEMENT MIXTURE. This mixture is similar to dry-set mortar with special latex additives. It has greater adhesion, is somewhat more flexible and less permeable. It can be used for showers and other areas that do not thoroughly dry out in use.

CONDUCTIVE DRY-SET MORTAR. Conductive dry-set mortar is a special formulation used as the bond coat for ceramic conductive tile. An epoxy grout is utilized for moderate-use floors, a wet-cured grout for heavy-duty floors.

Non-cementitious mortars include epoxy and furan mortars. There are also mastics which have good bond strength and flexibility at an economic price but have little resistance to wet conditions or heavy traffic. Mastics are not recommended for hospitals or other heavy-traffic situations.

Epoxy Mortar. Epoxy mortar is a two-part system using epoxy resins plus catalytic hardening agents. It is suitable for use where resistance to acid or alkaline environments, high bond strength and high impact resistance are important considerations. Heat-resistant formulas are also available.

Epoxy adhesive mortars and modified epoxy emulsion mortars do not have the strength of an epoxy mortar and are suitable only for light commercial use.

Furan Mortar. The highest level of chemical resistance is achieved with furan mortars. They resist all inorganic chemicals and most organic corrosives and solvents. Like epoxies, they are a two-part system of resin and hardener, require special installation skills and cost a premium.

Grouts

Unglazed vitreous, ceramic tiles are an extremely durable, stain-resistant, attractive floor covering. Most of the problems arise with the grout used between the tiles. Staining and chipping of grout can spoil the floor even when the tiles retain their original appearance.

Portland Cement and Latex-Portland Cement Grouts. Portland cement grouts, both wet-cured and dry-set, are the most commonly used grouts. They must be properly cured to develop strength. If this is not done, there will undoubtedly be staining and chipping problems. Portland cement grouts are, in general, more absorbent than ceramic tiles. If a medium or medium dark color is selected, stains will be less obvious. The use of latex additives in the grout helps the curing process and the grout is less absorptive than regular Portland cement grout.

Epoxy and Furan Grouts. Like the mortars, epoxy and furan grouts are especially formulated for chemical resistance. Epoxy grouts also provide high bond strength and impact resistance. Furan grouts are resistant to high temperatures. Their use involves extra cost and special installation skills.

An advantage of these two-part epoxy and furan systems is that an area where they are utilized can be used soon after the tile is laid, eliminating the waiting time needed for cementitious systems to cure. With the correct combination of epoxy mortar and furan grout, waiting time is eliminated. Certain epoxy systems can be applied to a green concrete slab or a damp surface. Grouting can commence immediately. If a furan grout is used, the surface is ready for use right after completion.

Specification Notes

The most complete specification information for installation of ceramic tile is put out by the Tile Council of America in their annual publication *Handbook for Ceramic Tile Installation*. All methods in the handbook have been researched and tested. A detailed description of each and appropriate specification information is given. Charts showing recommended applications are included. It is a must for the person who is actually writing the specification.

Tile selection and proposed setting and grouting methods should be confirmed with the manufacturer's representative as to appropriateness for function and substrate. Condition of the floor is extremely important. Any floor preparation should be done by the tile setter or done under his or her supervision.

Beyond selection of the tile and installation information, the specifier should keep in mind the following points.

Ceramic tile floors are often finished with a ceramic base mold tile. This trim tile has a cove at the bottom and a bull nose at the top, or it may be simply a cove to round the corner if walls also are to be of ceramic tile. If a base mold is desired, be sure it is available. Many ceramic tiles, especially European products, do not have matching trim tiles.

Specify the layout of the tile. Detail it on the drawings. Written instructions such as "herringbone" are open to misinterpretation. The contractor will do it the way he thinks best; very likely, it will not be the way the designer intended. Draw it!

Quantities should be specified with 2 percent extra of each color and size. This will facilitate quick replacement of any damaged tiles and assure color match. Unlike color in many materials, ceramic colors remain true. Tiles stored for many years will match previously installed tiles, provided they were originally from the same lot.

Remember to specify the color of the grout. Darker grouts show less soiling.

Remember to specify a grout sealant if this is desired.

At the junction between tile and another floor covering, trims are usually not necessary. A butt joint is preferred. This means that it is important to verify all flooring heights so the joint will be flush.

ACRYLIC WOOD

Standard wood floors are rarely appropriate for health care facilities. To keep them attractive requires extensive maintenance. Natural wood floors are vulnerable to staining, abrasion and scratching, burning, contraction and expansion and chemical deterioration. It is difficult to rationalize the use of natural wood, even though it has a warmth and beauty to which almost everyone responds, has good acoustic properties and is resilient and comfortable underfoot.

Acrylic-impregnated wood is a wood that has been treated to mitigate the limitations of natural wood and enhance its advantages.

Structure and Properties

The treatment process for producing acrylic wood begins with the sealing of the wood in a chamber where a vacuum is produced and the air removed from the cells of the wood. Then a liquid containing acrylics, fire retardants and dyes is forced, under pressure, into the voids. After the wood is fully impregnated, it is irradiated by controlled exposure to a cobalt 60 gamma ray source. Radiation causes polymerization of the liquid into a solid resulting in a treated wood that is dense and hard. The wood is trimmed and fabricated into modules for flooring. The end product is a floor that is durable and easy to maintain.

Specific effects of this treatment are:

1. Resistance to abrasion is greatly increased.
2. Density of the wood is increased to as much as twice the density of the natural wood.
3. Compression strength is increased resulting in decreased expansion and contraction.
4. Indentation resistance is increased.
5. The wood gains fire resistance and can meet the requirements of most regulatory bodies.
6. Resistance to bacterial growth is gained.
7. Sound-cushioning properties of the wood are improved.
8. Color is uniform throughout the thickness of the wood and will not wear away over time.
9. Depth of color and clarity of figure are gained.

This very durable product comes in several sizes and shapes such as twelve-inch squares, pickets, planks, and tongue-and-groove strips. Acrylic wood made and tested by Perma Grain Products, Inc. is hard enough to sustain only an 8 mm loss of surface depth after 4000 wear cycles with the coarse H-22 wheel in ASTM D-1044 surface flooring tests. This compares to 40 mm for surface-finished oak. Test results of acrylic woods made by Applied Radiant Energy Corporation show them to be three times as abrasion resistant as unconverted oak. Acrylic wood is proving to be durable in the elevators of busy hospitals.

Health and Safety

Health and safety concerns appear to be well met with acrylic woods. Flame spread ratings are under 75 when tested in accordance with ASTM E-84. Resistance to bacterial growth is greater than that in untreated woods and has not been identified as a problem. Concerning slip resistance, typical test results show a coefficient of friction of 0.55–0.65 (dry) and 0.62–0.80 (wet). This compares with vinyl which ranges from 0.5 to 0.9.

Maintenance

Soil is removed with a spray mist and buffing. The wood is extremely stain resistant and should never require refinishing. Cigarette burns can be removed with light sanding.

Installation and Specification Notes

As with any floor finish, the condition of the substrate is of vital importance. It must be level, free of all dirt, oil and grease, and properly dry. In the case of acrylic wood, curing compounds and surface sealers should not be used.

The manufacturer's installation instructions should, as always, be scrupulously followed. An important point to keep in mind is that all materials should be stored at the job site long enough to come into equilibrium with the site conditions before installation.

The layout of the acrylic wood modules should always be detailed in the drawings.

Part II

THE WALLS

Chapter Five

INTRODUCTION TO WALL FINISHES

WALLS ARE a major proportion of the visual field in just about every interior. Fortunately, on the vertical surface, the wear life requirements for finish materials are not as stringent as they are for floors. The prime requisite is protecting the wall from destructive impact by the ever-present cart. Abrasion from furniture and vandalism may be problems in some locations.

With wall finishes having fewer physical restrictions than floor finishes, greater attention can be paid to psychological and aesthetic needs. Wall treatments can do much to establish and reinforce the ambience of the space. Mathematically, the wall is often the largest proportion of the architectural envelope; perceptually, it is even larger. It is the portion at eye level; therefore, it is the portion that visually attracts greatest attention and psychologically has the greatest significance.

As with carpet, it is worthwhile to evaluate the advantages and limitations of each type of finish in the various environments found in the health care facility. These are presented in the same three categories as carpet: health and safety factors, environmental factors and wear-life factors.

Health and Safety Factors

Flame resistance codes are specified in regulatory districts and must be met. **Biogenic** factors may affect the control of growth and spread of microorganisms.

Heat and Flame Resistance

Requirements for wall finishes are usually stricter than those for floor finishes when it comes to fire code regulations. For example, materials used on walls of public exit corridors must be class A or class 1 in most regulatory districts. Optical smoke density must be under 50.

As strict as these requirements are, they are not difficult to meet. Most manufacturers producing institutional wall finishes have managed to create a wide variety of finishes within the specified limit. In fact, there is sufficient variety that consideration should be given to maintaining this standard throughout the facility, even in areas where the legally required standard is less restrictive. This approach can only increase the safety of the total facility.

Of all the finishes discussed in the next four chapters, carpet is the only one where choices may be somewhat limited by codes. Even here, more products are coming on the market, especially the new carpets being developed especially for walls by some fabric and wall-covering manufacturers. Wall carpet is no longer restricted to what is produced by the established carpet mills.

Biogenic

With vertical surfaces, cleanliness is not the problem that it is with horizontal surfaces; it is harder for things to settle on the surface and stick to it. Except in locations such as surgery where a sterile environment is mandatory, only occasional scrubbing or washing is required. Many materials are sufficiently durable to withstand this.

Where moisture is present in such locations as bathrooms and hydrotherapy, moisture-resistant finishes are available in a price range from epoxy coatings to vitreous ceramic tiles.

Many manufacturers specializing in health care facility products add antimicrobial agents to their products. This is of questionable value in a non-porous, non-absorbent material in a dry environment. It may not hurt, but it probably won't help much either. On the other hand, these antimicrobial agents may have some positive effect where moisture is present or on a product that is constantly handled such as a handrail. Questions remain to be answered regarding the overall environmental impact of introducing large quantities of these toxic antimicrobial agents into the human environment.

Enviromental Factors

Environmental factors such as **acoustics** and the overall ambience of the space affect the attitudes of patients, visitors and staff toward the facility. Because the area covered by the wall finishes is large, their part in establishing the overall ambience of the interior is of particular significance. The ambience of the space is particularly affected by **texture** and **pattern, color** and **lighting.** The decided trend toward a more pleasant environment in health care facilities as in interiors, in general, supports this significance.

Acoustics

The sound-reflectance properties of materials are of greater-than-ordinary significance in a health care facility where the client is most often physiologically or psychologically disturbed. Much less noise and chaos can be tolerated than when a person is physically and emotionally well.

Corridor spaces generate high activity and much noise, from the clanging of carts to the chattering of people. A sound-absorbent wall covering should be considered if the budget allows, especially for patient floor corridors in a hospital. Sound-reflective materials such as ceramic tile should not be used in patient corridors.

Texture and Pattern

Texture can be smooth or rough. In some cases, it must be smooth so that the surface can be kept hygienically clean. More often, some irregularity of texture is psychologically desirable and visually pleasurable. It is still possible to keep scrupulously clean as long as the indentations are not too deep or too narrow.

Many of the vinyl wall coverings and semirigid PVC wall coverings have textures that add visual interest and help conceal slight blemishes that may occur. These materials are easily cleaned with standard cleaning solutions or with special solvents as necessary.

Carpet, of course, brings welcome textural relief in addition to its acoustical qualities and can be used where washing walls is not a recurring maintenance requirement. Textile wall fabrics can add subtle or bold texture to walls. The warp lay or string constructions are rich and contemporary. Those that are firmly constructed and cleanable are pleasant and suitable for light to medium traffic areas. However, they are not suitable for heavy traffic areas, as they are apt to snag and are not washable.

Texture can also refer to sheen which may be matte or gloss. Paint will most often need to be gloss or semi-gloss, as flat paint does not withstand washing. However, ceramic tile can be used in a full range of sheens. Some care must be taken in using high-gloss, glazed tiles, as the reflections generated can be bothersome and disorienting, especially to the elderly.

Texture at a larger scale becomes pattern. As with texture, pattern adds visual interest and is pleasing to most people. Ceramic tile naturally forms a pattern as it is set. Many vinyl wall coverings have printed and embossed patterns.

The variety of patterns in Type II vinyl is limited. However, there are many appropriate patterns in Type I vinyls. These are satisfactory for low traffic locations and add important visual interest in places where people stay for extended periods. Birthing rooms and linear acceleration exam/treatment rooms are locations where a patterned Type I vinyl can be effectively used.

The nursery is a place where color and pattern are psychologically desirable but functionally inappropriate for full walls because of color reflection on the babies. Here, a patterened vinyl border can add a cheerful note and, being proportionally small, avoid the color-reflection problem.

Color

The materials discussed in Part II have a wide range of color availability, from paint which is available in almost any color one can imagine to some moldings and protective guards which can be had "to match any decor" as long as one of six neutrals will do it.

Despite the opinion of some that neutrals will blend with anything, they won't. Most of the colors commonly called neutral are a weak chroma (low intensity) of a hue. To achieve good color harmony, this must be recognized. The color of the neutral must enhance the bolder colors in the scheme.

In wall finishes and wall protection systems, the toughest and most easily maintained have, in general, the most limited color range. While many more colors are available than just a few years ago, this is still largely true. An exception to this is ceramic tile which is available in a wide variety of colors.

It should also be noted that very deep and very bright colors are usually the most expensive. Pigments are expensive and more pigment is required for these intense colors. Some color pigments are also more expensive than others; strong reds and strong blues are among the most expensive.

These statements of limitation are not meant to stifle the imagination but to suggest an efficient approach to developing color schemes. Begin with the materials having the most limited color range such as plastic laminates or PVC wall coverings. The scheme can then be developed with materials available in a wider color range. The subtle gradations needed to complete and tie together the scheme can almost always be achieved with paint.

On the other hand, starting with paint can be very inefficient when one has to start over, because a PVC cannot be obtained in a color that will work with the concept developed. Too often, 90 percent of the material colors are selected before it is discovered that the specified corner guards or other product with a limited color range are not available in a compatible color.

Meeting the functional and budgetary requirements for walls may yield an excessive variety of materials. Visual chaos can result if colors are not carefully controlled. Sometimes, the technique used to try to alleviate this is to match colors in the various materials being used. This is seldom successful. A phenomenon called metamerism is apt to occur.

Metameric colors are colors that match in one type of light but do not match when the light source is changed. For example, a paint and a vinyl wall covering may match perfectly in incandescent light but not in flourescent light. Even when colors are carefully selected under the type of light proposed for the building, the actual site conditions will probably be different enough to adversely affect the match.

Another problem with trying to match colors exactly is that colors in different materials tend to fade and soil at different rates so that those that match initially will become different over time. It may be better to begin with a harmony that can withstand slight change rather than with a match that will look like a mistake with the inevitable distortions due to lighting and the inability to predict color change over time.

Lighting

Three considerations are pertinent in the relationship between lighting and the wall finishes: percentage of reflectance, specular reflections and grazing light.

PERCENTAGE OF REFLECTANCE. A light color wall will reflect more light than a dark color wall, an elementary but sometimes ignored fact. More luminaires are needed if walls are dark in color. If there is not coordination with the lighting designer regarding wall colors, insufficient light can be the result.

Lighting designers and electrical engineers will assume a 50–70 percent light reflectance from the walls unless informed otherwise. This is the recommended reflectance range for walls. It is the optimum range for visual comfort and energy efficiency. In most cases, the designer should select colors for large wall areas within this range. If darker colors are selected, be sure that the lighting plan and schedule are coordinated.

SPECULAR REFLECTION: While gloss finishes such as gloss epoxy paints and glazed tile are very easily cleaned, the specular reflection from these can cause visual discomfort, headaches and disorientation for some patients. These effects should be considered and the location of finishes carefully evaluated before gloss finishes are specified.

GRAZING LIGHT: Lighting very close to the wall rather than in the center of the space has several advantages. The light directly washes the wall; the wall is clearly defined and its use as a reflective light source is enhanced. In corridors, the discomfort of central sources beaming directly into the eyes of a patient on a gurney is avoided.

When the light source is located very close to the wall, the light grazes across the finish. This grazing effect can enhance textural qualities with increased shadow and highlight. It can also, unfortunately, emphasize construction joints and any imperfections in the work. If the light source is to be adjacent to the wall, joints should be oriented parallel to the direction of incident light and particular care taken regarding the quality of the finish. Slight imperfections can become eyesores under grazing lighting conditions. Textured surfaces can be used to conceal drywall joints and irregularities of wall surfaces.

Wear-Life Factors

As with floor coverings, the primary factors affecting wear life are **durability, appearance retention, maintenance** and **cost effectiveness.**

Durability

Impact from all types of equipment, especially from carts, is the type of damage most often sustained. Impact resistance is the most important durability characteristic to be evaluated. The degree will vary with the location, but high resistance to impact is an especially important determinant in corridors.

On the other hand, vandalism is probably a bigger problem with wall coverings than with floor coverings. Walls seem to attract graffiti and other types of deliberate defacing in toilet stalls, telephone booths, elevators and other places where people can pause unobserved for a few moments. Anxious persons seem particularly prone to defacing walls. Finishes resistant to various types of abuse can minimize this but, a person who is really persistant can vandalize almost anything. Resistant finishes need to be used in conjunction with space planning that provides as few unobserved, out-of-the-way spots as possible and establishes well-traveled public routes.

Appearance Retention

Staining, while not the problem that it is with floor coverings, is also a factor, especially for public and patient bathrooms and for patient room headwalls. Stain-resistant finishes such as Zolatone® or vinyl with Tedlar® or Prefixx™ are effective solutions. Ceramic tile is another good solution for bathrooms, provided a stain-resistant grout is specified.

Texture and color are effective in camouflaging slight damage. Concealing colors should be selected where stains can be anticipated.

Colorfastness should be investigated. In general, the darker and brighter colors will be most susceptible to fading.

Maintenance

Most wall finishes made for institutional duty can be cleaned with soap or detergent solutions or with standard commercial cleaners. Where stains are anticipated, the manufacturer's literature should be carefully read to see if there is a recommended antidote. To be certain, obtain a sample of the material and try it.

Flat paints will not wash well. They should be avoided where washing will be needed.

Some materials such as Zolatone, ceramic tile and some paint can be patched with good success. Others such as vinyl or rigid PVC wall coverings must have a whole section replaced for proper repair. This can be an important difference when comparing maintenance costs.

Cost Effectiveness

An inverse relationship frequently exists between initial cost and maintenance cost. Low initial cost is associated with higher maintenance costs and earlier replacement. For example, paint may last three years, good quality vinyl wall covering ten years and ceramic tile twenty years. To determine the best value, life cycle costing should be used; calculate annual cost based on initial cost, predicted life and maintenance requirements.

Balanced against this must be anticipated change and reconfiguration. If early replacement will be needed due to reconstruction of an area, this may mean replacement whether the finish material is worn out or not. In such a case, low initial cost would be very important and durability of little significance.

It is also important to have current costs and not to rely on remembered relationships of material costs. As technology changes, these relationships change. For example, the cost of ceramic tile becomes a factor of greater relevance as technological developments results in the production of many moisture-resistant, durable and easily maintained synthetic materials. Many of these are less expensive than ceramic tile and will do the job in locations where the use of ceramic is traditional. Each has advantages and limitations which must be weighed.

Organization of Chapters on Wall Finishes

For each functional area of the health care facility, advantages and limitations of the various wall finishes must be weighed. The following four chapters on wall coatings, vinyl wall coverings, heavy-duty wall surfaces and wall protection systems are intended to help the reader make knowledgeable decisions. The information in each is organized under six major headings. Several finishes are included in Chapter Eight, "Heavy-Duty Wall Coverings," and these are organized in the same manner: structure and properties, health and safety, types or classification, maintenance, installation or application, and specification notes.

Structure and Properties

Each finish has certain properties as a result of the ingredients used and the way they are put together. Understanding this structure will aid in understanding to what extent desirable properties are possible, help to judge the validity of glowing statements in the manufacturer's literature, and note omissions of vital facts in this literature. It should help define the critical questions to be asked for proper evaluation.

Health and Safety

With each finish, there are associated questions of health and safety. This section seeks to respond to those most frequently asked.

Types or Classification

Some wall finish materials are referenced by type. Others are referenced by classification. In either case, naming the category defines critical functional qualities. Paint and ceramic tile are classified by physical and chemical properties. Vinyl wall coverings are divided into types by performance. Other materials in the section are categorized by form or style.

Maintenance

In this section maintenance requirements are discussed. In evaluating any finish, it is essential to understand the equipment and labor that will be needed to maintain it. These will profoundly affect the total cost of the product. They must be added to the initial cost to make a valid assessment of the lifetime cost.

Installation or Application

First, it should be stated that this section is not a complete guide to installation or, in the case of paints, application. Most manufacturers give excellent installation instructions for their own products and these are typically found in the manufacturer's literature. Instead, the information presented here is intended to help in evaluating what type of installation will be most appropriate for the function of the space, problems that may arise with certain types of installations and other key points that may assist in material selection.

Specification Notes

This is not a complete guide to specification. Rather, it identifies sources for complete specification guides and notes some special points that are often not given the attention they deserve. It also identifies some details and refinements that are often overlooked.

Chapter Six

WALL COATINGS

WALL COATINGS have a recorded history of 20,000 years, extending back to the yellow, red and black wall coatings of the cave dwellers. Today, coatings cover a majority of the surfaces in the built environment. They provide protection for the underlying surface, sanitation and ease of maintenance as well as their original decorative function.

Coatings must be considered as part of a total coating system. A good coating is important, but equally important for satisfactory appearance and durability are the primers and the preparation of the surface to which they are applied. The major portion of this chapter focuses on paint systems. The last part discusses other coatings found to be especially good for health care facility use.

PAINT

Paints are the most commonly used opaque coatings. A good paint coating requires a high-quality paint film, a sound surface to receive the film, and a strong bond between the film and the surface.

Structure and Properties

There are many different kinds of paints; this can be confusing. To lessen this confusion and to comprehend the derivation of properties, it is helpful to understand the composition of paint. After the composition is clarified, a detailed discussion of various properties will be continued in the section "Classification."

As with any product, the properties of paint are determined by the components and the way these are put together. All paints are composed of three parts: (1) pigment, (2) resin and (3) volatile thinner. The resin and the thinner, together, make up the vehicle that carries the pigment. The proportion and chemical makeup of each part are what determine the properties of the paint.

Pigment

The primary purpose of pigments is to give color and opacity to paint. They are the most expensive ingredient in paint, with the deep-color pigments being the costliest of all. Pigments are fine, solid particles that remain insoluble in the vehicle. They remain suspended and do not dissolve. In this way, they are different from dyes which do dissolve.

Pigments provide opacity in accord with their degree of covering or hiding power. Hiding power varies greatly with the color of the pigment and its particle size. **Generally, the darker the pigment and the more finely ground, the more effective is the coverage.** Lighter-color pigments such as yellow and pink provide poor hiding power and require at least three coats for coverage.

Some pigments do not provide opacity. Translucent pigments are called extender or inert pigments and are used to control adhesion and sheen. The relationship of pigments to sheen is further discussed in the following section "Classification." An overabundance of extenders is often used in low-cost paints, reducing durability and hiding power.

Pigments are classified by color and opacity as white pigments, color pigments, metallic pigments and extender or inert pigments. They can be pure chemical elements or complex organic or inorganic compounds. One pigment is seldom used alone in a paint mixture. To obtain a certain color, several pigments may be used. The combination and proper proportioning of pigments is an exact science which has benefitted from the development of computers.

In the past, paint manufacturers provided only a limited number of packaged paint colors. Now, paint manufacturers supply a tint base, a medium base and a deep base to which exact quantities of pigments may be added. These bases and pigments provide color systems with as many as 1500 different colors.

Resin

Resins act as binders that hold the pigment together and form the dry film. The proportion of resin to pigment is critical; there must be just the right amount to bind together the pigment particles. Too high a ratio of pigment to resin will weaken the paint film, resulting in a fragile finish. This is why great care is needed in using additional pigment to modify a paint color.

Resins are also responsible for such properties as the paint's abrasion resistance, durability and stain resistance. Various resins are used to impart specific properties. These are further discussed under "Classification."

Volatile Thinner

The purposes of the volatile thinner are to act as a transfer agent to transfer the resin and pigment mixture to the surface being painted and to enhance penetration during application. Without the thinner, paint would be too sticky and thick to apply. Thinners may also be part of the curing process as will be discussed later. Thinners are either solvent based or water based.

Nearly all paints contain thinners. Cheaper paints contain excessive thinner which, when it evaporates, leaves a paint film that is too thin. When specifying paint, the ratio of thinner to resin and pigment must be checked. Better paints contain at least fifty percent resin and pigment. Cheaper paints contain more of the thinner that evaporates away and less of the components that form the finish coat.

Paints that have a high percentage of volume solids will cover better and provide a thicker dry film thickness (DFT). DFT refers to the thickness of the paint that remains after drying. Its measurement is expressed in mils (.001 in). Federal and most institutional specifications require a DFT of 5 mils for the combined thickness of the primer and all paint coats. The DFT should be measured during contract administration to confirm that requirements are met.

Health and Safety

Solvent-based paints are being increasingly regulated by the government, because they produce noxious vapors that are health hazards. When they are used, proper ventilation is essential. They should never be used in occupied spaces.

Water-based paints are non-toxic and produce few fumes and little odor.

Classification

Classification has taken place in accordance with certain properties deemed important for the specification of paint for functional purposes. Of primary importance in the selection of paints are: durability and other properties determined by the resins, degree of sheen determined by the particle size of the pigment, and the curing time determined by the method of cure.

In line with these selection criteria, the industry has established ways to organize or classify different types of paint. They are classified by: (1) resin, (2) sheen and (3) method of cure. These classifications bear a relationship to the components.

Resin = resin
Pigment size is a determinant of **sheen.**
A **solvent** is sometimes involved in the **method of cure.**

Resin

There are two basic classifications of paint: those in which the vehicle has a petroleum solvent base and those in which the vehicle has a water base. These are known as solvent-based and water-based paints. In solvent-based paints, the resins are dissolved in the solvent solution. In water-based paints, they are dispersed in a water emulsion. These types are further classified by the resins used with each.

The resins determine the most significant differences in the performance of paint. In addition to their binding function, the resins may impart extra hardness and strength, increase abrasion and chemical resistance, decrease drying time, and improve gloss, gloss retention and adhesion to the substrate.

RESINS IN SOLVENT-BASED PAINTS: Linseed oil from the flax plant and tung oil were the primary resins used for generations. Today, soybean oil has replaced linseed oil as the most common oil; it is less expensive and works well.

Alkyd resin paints have replaced oil paints as the most commonly used. These alkyd modified oils dry faster, are harder and have better color retention than ordinary oils. The more oil there is in the formula; the longer it takes to dry, the lower the gloss and the better the elasticity. Alkyd resin paints can be used on just about any wall surface except masonry. An alkali-resistant primer must first be used if they are to be applied to masonry.

Two-part epoxy resin paints are extremely durable and offer extra resistance to abrasion, moisture, chemicals and solvents. Epoxy resin paints can be used as a less expensive alternative to ceramic tile when these properties are essential.

Urethane resin paints are similar to epoxies and may be used when extra abrasion or chemical resistance is required. They are often used for floors.

RESINS IN WATER-BASED PAINTS: Today, all water-based paints are commonly called latex, whether or not they contain latex. Latex paints were first made with a synthetic rubber resin (styrene butadiene). They entered the market in 1948. These paints are hard, flexible, have good gloss retention and are rapid drying.

Latex can be used on most interior walls, including masonry walls. It should not be used over oil paint, as the more flexible latex paint can pull off the more brittle oil paint. This is a common problem which can be avoided by first covering the old oil paint with an oil or alkyd primer.

Largely replacing the original synthetic rubber resins in water-based paints are acrylic and vinyls such as polyvinyl acetate and polyvinyl chloride.

The most common resin is acrylic. It imparts excellent adhesion for all interior surfaces, has excellent hiding and self-sealing properties and flexibility, and very good resistance to water and alkali. The vinyl resins cost less and produce a somewhat softer film than the acrylic.

Latex paints have many advantages. They are easier and less expensive to make than oil paints, easier to clean up after painting, safe to use

Table 6.1

EVALUATION GUIDE: PAINTS

Property	Resin					
	oil	alkyd	epoxy	urethane	vinyl	acrylic
Abrasion Resistance	2	3	4	5	3	4
Hardness	2	3	4	5	3	4
Flexibility	3	3	5	4	5	5
Adhesion	4	4	5	3	3	5
Resistance to:						
Acid	1	2	5	5	3	3
Alkali	1	2	5	4	3	4
Detergent	2	2	5	4	3	3
Fading	3	4	3	2	5	5
Heat	2	3	3	3	3	4
Moisture	3	3	4	4	2	2
Strong Solvents	1	2	5	5	3	3

Legend:
  5 = excellent
  4 = very good
  3 = good
  2 = fair
  1 = poor

and store, non-toxic and produce little odor. Initially, their quality was not equal to that of oil paints, but the technology improves steadily and latex is being used in increasing quantities.

SPECIAL VEHICLES: Varnish-based and lacquer-based paints are pigmented versions of transparent coatings. Enamels, used frequently in health care facilities because of their hardness and durability, are varnish-based paints. A varnish is a combination of drying oils and natural or synthetic resins in a volatile thinner. An enamel is, thus, a category of solvent-based paints containing oils, resins and pigments. It is designed to flow and level well and give a smooth finish.

The term, enamel, is often loosely used. To some lay people, it connotes any type of durable, impenetrable surface with a high sheen. The finish is usually gloss but may be semi-gloss or, occasionally, flat. A flat enamel is produced by adding a flattening agent. This addition can affect some performance properties.

Lacquer-based paints dry quickly and are used when this special feature is needed. They are not as durable as some other paints.

Sheen

The sheen of a coating describes the degree of gloss reflecting from the surface when viewed at various angles. Paint sheen is classified as flat, semi-gloss or gloss.

1. Flat is almost free from reflection when viewed from angles less than 10° on a 60° glossometer.
2. Semi-gloss has some reflectivity when viewed at 30–40°on a 60° glossometer.
3. Gloss has smooth, almost mirror-like reflections when viewed at 70° on a 60° glossometer.

The term eggshell is commonly (and loosely) used to describe the sheen of a paint. Eggshell is used by manufacturers and the public to describe various flat and semi-gloss paints. Because the definition of eggshell is not standard, its use can be misleading.

Eggshell, satin, and velvet are just some of the terms used in the descriptive literature. Their definitions are not standard; satin in one manufacturer's paint may have a far different sheen from satin by another manufacturer. The degree of light reflectance determines the sheen. Standard categories define the range; non-standard classifications do not.

FLAT SHEEN: The quantity and size of pigment particles are major determinants of the sheen. Flat paint has a high pigment volume concentration and these pigments are coarsely grounded. The particles protrude from the paint surface and incident light is scattered in all directions. This diffusion results in low reflectance and a matte or dull surface appearance.

The protruding particles will pick up surface soil and, when scrubbed, will wear off to a shiny surface. Therefore, coarsely ground or flat finishes are inappropriate for areas of high traffic and hard use. A possible exception would be an area with concentrated use of computers. Part of the cause of eyestrain when working with computers appears to be due to reflection. A flat non-reflective wall surface could give some relief. The maintenance may be a worthwhile trade-off for extra staff comfort.

SEMI-GLOSS SHEEN: More finely ground pigment particles protrude less from the paint surface. Diffusion of incident light is less and reflectance is greater. This produces a semi-gloss finish. **Semi-gloss finishes are more soil resistant than flat finishes and can be washed with little damage. Semi-gloss is the paint of choice for most areas.**

GLOSS SHEEN: Gloss paints have the lowest pigment volume concentration. The particles are very finely ground and completely encapsulated within the binder, producing a smooth surface. Light reflects evenly from this surface, creating a gloss finish. Because the smooth surface does not pick up soil and the paint is protected from abrasion, gloss paints are more durable than flat or semi-flat. However, it should be noted that the high reflectivity of gloss finishes will emphasize any irregularity in a wall surface.

COLOR AND SHEEN: **A color in a flat finish is very different from the same color in a gloss finish.** Gloss finishes appear more pure and bril-

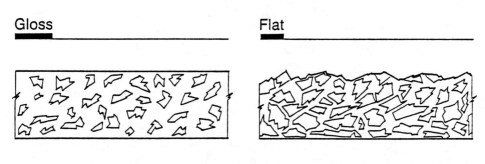

Figure 6.1 PARTICLE SIZE AND COATING SHEEN. Flat sheen paints have a high pigment volume concentration; pigments are coarsely ground and protrude from the paint surface. Gloss sheen paints have a lower pigment volume concentration; pigments are more finely ground and completely encapsulated within the binder.

liant in color, because they reflect light like a mirror. Flat finishes diffuse light and thus their colors appear less saturated than those of gloss colors.

One should always request a large finish sample in the sheen to be used before making the final selection. For example, a warm, rich gold in flat paint may look like day-old mustard in gloss. This could be especially distracting if used in a cafeteria.

Method of Cure

Curing refers to the hardening of the paint to achieve its full strength. It does not refer to drying. A few hours after application, a paint may feel dry, but until it is fully cured, it will be soft and vulnerable. Care must be taken during this curing time not to subject the paint to hard use or to cleaning. Until it has cured, it is not ready to be subjected to its full, intended use. The three main types of curing for solvent-based paints are oxidation, chemical and solvent evaporation. Water-based paints cure by coalescence.

OXIDATION: When paints cure by oxidation, they take in oxygen or oxidize to harden. Full hardness occurs after thirty to ninety days. Prior to the new technologies, this was just about the only way that paint cured. Oil and alkyd paints are oxidation-cured paints.

CHEMICAL: Chemical curing is achieved when two components, a catalyst and a resin, are mixed and then allowed to bond in the paint can for thirty to forty minutes. After application, full cure is achieved in five to fourteen days. Chemical curing tends to produce a hard, resistant surface. Epoxy and urethane paints are examples of chemically cured coatings. Chemical cures are not activated below 45° F.

SOLVENT EVAPORATION: In both chemical and oxidation cure paints, the solvent evaporates. It is used as a transfer agent and then evaporates away after drying. These paints differ from a solvent evaporation cure paint in which curing is achieved through evaporation of the solvent. Full curing requires only twelve to twenty-four hours. Solvent evaporation paints are expensive and not generally as durable as some others but have obvious advantages when time is of the essence. Lacquer-based paints are an example. They have highly volatile solvents which act as transfer agents and then as curing agents.

COALESCENCE: During curing of water-based or latex paints, the resins coalesce into a chewing gum like film as the water solvent evaporates. Curing of most latex paints requires forty to sixty days—about the same amount of curing time required in oxidation.

Water-based paints are undergoing extensive development. A new type of latex paint technology, called rheology, will produce durable latex paints that cure in only four days. Such research is proceeding because petroleum-based solvents are highly volatile and produce noxious vapors.

Maintenance

The cleaning of painted walls is highly dependent on the sheen. Walls coated with a flat sheen paint are seldom washed successfully. Washing breaks off the protruding pigment particles that diffuse the light, resulting in a change in the degree of sheen. The washed paint surface becomes more glossy. This is why a wall painted with a flat sheen may have glossy spots scattered over it. The effect is most noticeable when a dark-color paint is used. Generally, when a flat sheen wall is dirty enough to wash, it should be washed and repainted.

Semi-gloss and gloss paints can be washed, and soil should not be allowed to accumulate. It is recommended that they be washed once or twice a year to remove the routine accumulation of soil. Warm water plus a mild soap or commercially available cleaning products can be used. Abrasive cleaners should not be used, as they will scratch the gloss surface.

Application

Paint coatings are only as good as the care taken in application. **The best quality paint will fail if the surface is poorly prepared or inappropriate primers are used.**

Primers

Each coat of paint, from the first to the last, must adhere to the coat before it and must offer a "tooth" or surface to which each succeeding coat can bond. Primers are especially formulated paints which treat the substrate to which they are applied and provide adhesion for the finish coats. They are the first coat applied to the raw surface.

A primer must have enough resin to soak into the surface and still leave enough on the surface for bonding of the next coat. The resin in the primer acts as a sealer so that future coats can be applied without unevenly absorbing into the surface material.

The match of primer to surface and to topcoats must be made carefully. The paint manufacturer generally gives instructions regarding compatible primers for the particular paint and typical surfaces. The manufacturer should be consulted for all special circumstances.

Paints with alkyd resins should not be used on masonry or other alkali surfaces without an alkali-resistant primer. Latex primers offer alkali resistance. Block fillers composed either of latex or a solvent-thinned epoxy ester also provide resistance to alkali.

Surface Preparation and Site Conditions

Most paint failure starts at the surface of the substrate. Even the highest quality paint will fail if surface preparation is not properly done. The surface must be free of dirt, rust, scale, grease, moisture, scuffs, and loose, old paint. Surfaces can be cleaned with detergent solutions and solvents. Scraping of rust and old, loose paint can be done with sandpaper, handtools, power scrapers and sandblasting. When it is too expensive to remove all of the old paint, it must be sanded until it is smooth. A number of fillers are available to fill dents and cracks prior to coating.

When painting over old paint, the new paint must be compatible with the old. For example, a latex will not adhere to an oil-based gloss surface and will peel away in large pieces upon drying. A test patch of new paint over old paint should be done.

Any surface that is too smooth will repel paint. Therefore, glossy surfaces must be sanded prior to coating.

The surface must be thoroughly dry before application of coatings. Concrete should cure for at least four weeks prior to coating with latex paint. Because of their high water content and physical reactions, plaster and plasterboard must be coated with the proper paint. Some oil-based paints can be destroyed by plaster and must have a latex primer.

The holes in concrete block can be filled with a block filler for aesthetic reasons, or they can be left open to provide some acoustical qualities. Concrete block requires that paint be applied with a roller so that paint can be pushed into the holes. (A spray application can be followed by rolling.) Rough textures and porous surfaces increase the amount of coating material required.

Water-based paints should only be applied in temperatures of 50°–90° F. Oxidation and chemical-cure paints should only be applied in temperatures of 45°–90° F. Coatings should not be applied when humidity exceeds 85 percent or to damp or wet surfaces.

Method of Application

Application of paint to wall surfaces is done in three ways: by brush, by roller, and by spray gun. The size of the job and site conditions determines the type of tool.

BRUSH: Brushing is slow and is now used only for cutting in around trim and at ceilings and corners. Visible brush marks can be caused by too coarse a brush, an improperly thinned coating, too much brushing or too much ventilation.

ROLLER: Rolling is quicker than brushing and is commonly done in areas where people are still working or in renovation areas where the considerable masking needed for spraying will be time consuming and expensive.

SPRAY GUN: In areas of new construction where overspray is not a problem, spraying is the fastest method and provides the most even surface. Generally, all types of paint can be sprayed. When latex is used, it must be ground finely enough (must be gloss or semi-gloss) to flow smoothly through the nozzle for standard spraying. Flat latex can be sprayed using airless spraying and a large nozzle. Standard spray applicators break up the spray and spread it out. Airless spray applicators propel coatings through one hole at a very high pressure. Airless spraying is cleaner and faster than standard spraying. Less paint is needed and there is less overspray.

Specification Notes

In order to get accurate and directly comparable bids from contractors, it is necessary to clearly delineate on the drawings all surfaces to be coated and the material to be used for each. While marked floor plans are adequate for much of the project, elevations are necessary where there are changes in wall height and wherever there is a junction of two or more colors or materials on a plane. The layout and any details of this junction must be shown. These may seem obvious, but misunderstandings are common when there is not a drawing.

Changes in wall height are not always clear on the floor plan. Extra materials needed for higher walls may not get calculated. Furthermore, additional labor and the need to erect scaffolding can greatly increase the contractor's cost. If these are not calculated in the bid, the successful bidder may need to make a decision on whether to skimp somewhere or lose money.

Another critical area is to define the quantity of accent paints intended. Stronger and deeper paints are more expensive than pale or light colors. Locations may be shown on the drawings, noted in the schedule, or if specific colors have not been selected at the time of the bid, the percentage of accent colors should be stated in the specifications.

Sample submittals should always be required in order to confirm color selections. This is particularly important when color selections were made using one manufacturer and another manufacturer's paint is actually used on the job.

SPECIAL OPAQUE COATINGS

New opaque coatings are being developed which combine the best characteristics of paint and vinyl wall covering.

Like paint, they are:

1. Relatively inexpensive
2. Easy to repair when damaged
3. Mixable for exact color matches

Like vinyl they are:

1. Highly scrubbable
2. Highly stain resistant
3. Textured and matte in finish

There are several of these on the market and they are not all equal. Formulations vary. Consequently, physical properties vary and must be carefully compared. For most, spray application is required and the particular spray gun used will cause considerable difference in appearance. Appearance of an actual application should be carefully evaluated before accepting an "equal" to the product specified.

One special opaque coating that can be highly recommended is Zolatone. As with paints, Zolatone is composed of a vehicle, thinner and pigments. The vehicle is a chemically treated aqueous solution containing synthetic resins which Zolatone Process, Inc. defines only as a terpolymer. The thinner portion is aliphatic mineral spirits.

Zolatone is a polychromatic (multicolored) and textured coating. As in paints, the vehicle has pigment particles suspended in the solution. Unlike paints, the particles are of varying sizes and colors which, when applied, provide a finely textured surface. Highly contrasting colors can be used in the coating, but the richest and most successful surfaces are usually achieved when the particles are close in hue, value and chroma.

Also, unlike paint which must have a gloss finish to be highly durable, the composition of the terpolymer provides a durable coating with low light reflectance. Specular gloss measures less than $10°$ on a $60°$ glossometer.

Primers are required on all new surfaces. They are not usually required for previously coated surfaces that are properly prepared. The color coat can be applied to almost any interior surface using a primer formulated for the particular surface. Primers are available for drywall, plaster and masonry surfaces, wood, and non-porous surfaces such as ceramic, glass and metal.

For exceptionally demanding areas such as an aggressive chemical environment, a topcoat is available. This is a clear epoxy coating with excellent impact abrasion and stain resistance.

Application is by spray gun, usually by a specially trained contractor. The finish is dry in four to eight hours and fully cured in fifteen to twenty-one days.

The final sprayed coating provides a continuous film coverage with a DFT that is approximately three times that of standard paints. It has a class A flame spread rating when tested under ASTM E-84. Resistance to moisture, mildew, alkali and stains is superior and bacterial inhibition is good. The following is from test results published in the manufacturer's literature.

1. *Fire Safety:* ASTM Method E-84, Surface Burning Characteristics. Class A; flame spread 10, fuel contributed 5 and smoke developed 0. Equal performance under equivalent standards UL 723, NFPA 255 and UBC 42.1.
2. *Bacterial Inhibition:* U.S. Government Specification UU-P-510, Paragraph 4.4.2.1. Shows clear zone 5 mm from edge of test specimen using Staphylococcus aureus.
3. *Mildew and Fungus Resistance:* FED-STD-141B, Method 6271, evaluation of growth. Visually, no growth (organism Aspergillus oryzae).
4. *Stain Resistance:* ASTM Method D-1308. No staining from mild acids, chemicals, oils or foods.
5. *Alkali Resistance:* FED-STD-141B, Method 6141, drying and aging, and ASTM Method D-1308, resistance test. Aged film withstands 10 percent sodium hydroxide for three hours.
6. *Washability:* FED-STD-141B, Method 6141. Not more than 5 percent change in specular gloss and not more than 15 percent change in daylight reflectance.
7. *Specular Gloss:* ASTM Method D-523. Maximum 10 at 60°.
8. *Scrubability:* FED-STD-141B, Method 6142. Only slight signs of wear after 7500 cycles.

After full cure, the coating can be cleaned with regular liquid spray cleaners as recommended by the manufacturer. On any stubbon marks, chlorine-free, mild abrasives may be used. These should be tested in an inconspicuous area before use to determine effectiveness. Damage to the surface can be repaired by building maintenance personnel with touch-up guns.

Chapter Seven

VINYL WALL COVERINGS

VINYL wall coverings are extremely durable and serviceable. They are resistant to abrasion and fading and can be cleaned easily, giving them a long life and good appearance retention. When they are correctly specified, installed and maintained, they will outlive most paints. There is just one catch. While they may not be disfigured as easily as paint, once a tear or gouge does appear, it cannot simply be patched if appearance is to be retained. The entire strip must be replaced; this is often not done.

Structure and Properties

Vinyl wall coverings are chemical-coated fabrics. They are made of one or more layers of vinyl plastic adhered to a fabric backing. Both the vinyl face and the backing are manufactured in different weights. Weight is considered one criteria of durability. More important is the formulation of the vinyl face and the strength of the backing.

Two methods are used to make the wall coverings: (1) Calendering: hot vinyl compound is pressed with rollers. The resulting layer is then laminated to a fabric backing. (2) Plastisol: hot vinyl compound is spread over a moving sheet of fabric and fused to it. Both methods require very high temperatures.

As with all products, the components predict performance. An understanding of the components of the vinyl face and of the backing will help in appropriate product selection.

Face Components

The vinyl face is made up of polyvinyl chloride resin, plasticizers, pigments, stabilizers, fillers and perhaps some other additives. A protective finish or film may also be added.

119

POLYVINYL CHLORIDE RESIN: Vinyl resins were discussed at length in the chapter about resilient flooring. They impart the same durable qualities to wall coverings: resistance to abrasion, chemicals and bacteria. The vinyl formulation for wall covering is somewhat more susceptible to oil-based stains than that used for resilient flooring.

PLASTICIZERS: Pliability and processibility are imparted by plasticizers. Plasticizers may also augment other properties of the vinyl giving greater resistance to staining or abrasion or improving flame resistance. It is not possible to get the best of all properties. For example, achieving the ultimate in stain resistance might mean increasing flammability. The mixture of different plasticizers must be carefully balanced to achieve those properties desired for a specific vinyl.

PIGMENTS: Color is provided by the pigments. Because only certain pigments can withstand the high heat involved in processing vinyls, color selection is far more limited than with paint. Quality pigments are also expensive, especially the reds and golds. For these reasons, many lines are limited in their color range.

STABILIZERS: Stabilizers prevent resins from turning yellow under the processing heats and under prolonged light exposure.

FILLERS: Fillers may impart desirable characteristics such as toughness and heat resistance and act as a processing aid. They are also used to add weight and to lower costs. Excessive amounts of filler can seriously lessen abrasion resistance.

OTHER ADDITIVES: Flame retardants and fungicides are two examples of other ingredients that may be added. Antimicrobial additives to the vinyl coating are effective against growth of most mold, mildew, fungal and bacterial organisms.

FINISHES: Clear liquid finishes are applied to shield the vinyl from staining. Many of these have a matte sheen and do not change the sheen of the vinyl.

PROTECTIVE FILM: Where stains are a substantial problem, a vinyl wall covering can be further protected by specifying it with a laminated protective film. The most commonly used is Tedlar, manufactured by Dupont. Tedlar is a tough, transparent, fluoride plastic film. It is extremely resistant to stains, corrosive chemicals, solvents, light and oxygen. It does add a gloss sheen.

A more recent introduction in protective films is a product developed by Diversitech for use on its Boltawall wall coverings. This is Prefixx which prevents migration of most staining elements into the vinyl. The formulation is a proprietary secret, but test results show it to have a stain resistance similar to that of Tedlar. Both are slightly stained by only two of the critical staining agents: shoe polish paste and anthralin 8% burn cream. Both can be cleaned with strong industrial acids, alkaline cleaners and solvent-type cleaners. Neither will tolerate harsh abrasives.

Two advantages of Prefixx are that it does not alter the original sheen of the vinyl and there is less flattening of texture and grain than with Tedlar. It also has a very minimal affect on the color and pattern.

Vinyl wall covering with a protective film is often used in operating, emergency and treatment rooms, toilet rooms, laboratories and sometimes for headwalls in patient rooms. These protective films do add a significant cost.

Properties of Face Components

The vinyl formulation bears a direct relationship to abrasion resistance, cleanability, resistance to alkalinity, resistance to aging and colorfastness.

A summary of minimum requirements for properties of Types I, II, and III vinyl wall coverings can be found in Table 7.1. Vinyl types are discussed later in the chapter under "Types and Categories of Vinyl Wall Covering."

ABRASION RESISTANCE: This is a far less significant factor for a wall covering than for a floor covering. Tears in vinyl occur more often from a single blow than from constant wearing away. It can, however, be a factor in such places as outside corners. Formulation as well as thickness contributes to abrasion resistance. Resistance is measured by the Wyzenbeek abrasion test. Specification of a vinyl sustaining the minimum number of "double rubs" as shown in Table 7.1 helps insure sufficient abrasion resistance.

CLEANABILITY: Oil-based stains can be a problem; vinyl wall coverings with a stain-resistant finish should be specified for almost all locations in a health care facility. A simple test for cleanability is to mark a wall covering sample with ink and lipstick. After 24 hours, clean with anhydrous isopropyl alcohol. If no appreciable stain is left, the product should be sufficiently cleanable for use in public areas.

For areas subject to severe and constant staining, use of a film-coated vinyl wall covering is recommended.

RESISTANCE TO ALKALINITY: Many general-purpose cleaning agents are alkaline, a threat to vinyl. To test for resistance to alkalinity, a sample can be immersed in a solution of 1 percent sodium hydroxide for twenty-four hours. If no color change is evident, the vinyl should hold up to most general-purpose cleaners.

RESISTANCE TO AGING: Certain plasticizers can cause vinyl wall covering to become tacky as it ages. Compliance with the requirements of the heat aging test in Table 7.1 should prevent use of a vinyl that ages poorly.

COLORFASTNESS: Color fading caused by the affects of light can be avoided by specifying compliance with the requirements shown in Table 7.1.

Backing

The fabric backing of vinyl wall covering adds tensile strength and tear resistance. Four types of woven cloth fabrics are commonly used to back vinyl. These are scrim, Osnaburg, drill and broken twill. A fifth type of backing is a synthetic, a spunbonded polyester.

SCRIM: Scrim is the lightest quality woven fabric backing. It is used where minimum wall covering strength is required.

OSNABURG AND SHEETING: These are medium-weight woven backings of average strength. They provide adequate protection against normal traffic.

DRILL: For a somewhat higher traffic area, drill is a medium-weight, tear-resistant backing.

BROKEN TWILL: Broken twill is a heavy-weight woven backing for use in such places as elevators and service corridors where maximum strength and tear resistance are required.

SPUNBONDED POLYESTER: This synthetic backing comes in various weights. It is generally stronger than woven backings of comparable weight and can be used for most installations.

Properties of the Backing

Weight is often used as a determinant of impact resistance for vinyl wall coverings. More important indicators are tensile strength and tear resistance of the fabric backing. Also playing an integral part is the adhesion between the fabric and the vinyl face.

TENSILE STRENGTH AND TEAR RESISTANCE: Most tears are the result of a glancing blow. Tensile strength is the ability to resist the tensile forces of this blow. The strength of the backing is the prime determinant.

The backings used for the various types of vinyl were at one time all cotton. Many are now polyester/cotton blends. Blends are lighter in weight and less bulky and at the same time provide more tensile strength than pure cotton. For example, even though two vinyl wall coverings may have an Osnaburg backing, the tensile strengths can be quite different, depending on the ratio of cotton to polyester.

Because the same name does not necessarily denote equal performance and because many manufacturers do not list the composition of fabrics, test performance results become crucial. Tensile strength and tear resistance tests are included in Table 7.1. However, note that requirements are listed as minimum. Many products produce test results greater than these minimums and the added impact resistance is well worthwhile. Impact is the worst enemy of the wall finish in most health care facilities.

A good way to determine desirable minimums is to look up tensile and tear strength results of materials that have performed well on previous projects. With impact resistance being so important, it seems foolish to meet only the minimum requirements when many materials exist that far exceed these requirements. For example some Type II vinyls have a tensile strength in the range of 150×125 or 108×100 and a tear strength in the range of 75×75 or 55×50. Compare these with the minimum requirements shown in Table 7.1.

Reference Standards

The federal government set forth in CCC-W-408A, standards for minimums of breaking strength, tear strength, abrasion resistance, colorfastness to light, blocking, heat aging and crocking. Except for coating weight, coating adhesion and stain resistance (standards not addressed in 408A), requirements are the same as those shown in Table 7.1. Each method of testing is listed in Federal Specification CCC-T-191 which gives a detailed explanation of the test.

CCC-W-408A has recently been rewritten as CCC-W-408B. The major changes are that under 408B, physical requirements regarding tear and tensile strength minimums have been lowered and the finished weight requirement eliminated. At present, many manufacturers continue to reference CCC-W-408A in their literature. Others cite both 408A and 408B.

In a reaction to this lowering of standards, major manufacturers, who belong to the CFFA (Chemical Fabrics and Film Association, Inc.) developed their own standards: CFFA-W-101-A. This standard does not conflict with 408B; it reestablishes the higher minimum of 408A for tear and tensile strength.

Table 7.1

CFFA MINIMUM REQUIREMENTS FOR WALL COVERINGS

Property	Test Method	Type I	Type II	Type III
Total wt., minimum oz/sq yd	FS 191, 5041	7	13	22
Coating wt., minimum oz/sq yd	Para. 7.1.1	5	7	12
Coating adhesion lbs for 2" width	ASTM D751	4	6	6
Shrinkage, maximum W × F	Para. 7.1.3	2.1 × 1.0	2.0 × 1.0	2.0 × 1.5
Cold crack resistance ½ 20°C	Para. 7.1.2	None	None	None
Tensile breaking strength lbs, minimum W × F	ASTM D751	40 × 30	50 × 55	100 × 95
Tear strength, (a) scale reading, minimum W × F	ASTM D751	14 × 12	25 × 25	50 × 50
Abrasion resistance (b) double rubs, minimum	FS 191, 5304	200	300	1000
Color fastness to light after 200 hours	FS 191, 5660	No change	No change	No change
Blocking, scale rating, maximum	FS 191, 5872	Scale #2	Scale #2	Scale #2
Heat aging, (c) 7 days at 158°F	FS 191, 5850	2	2	2
Crocking, scale rating, minimum	FS 191, 5651	Good	Good	Good
Stain Resistance (d)	ASTM D1308b	No effect	No effect	No effect

Legend:

W × F = warp × filler

Test Method Applicable Documents:

FS 191	= Federal Specification CCC-T-191, Textile Test Methods. Number following 191 is test method number.
ASTM D751	= Standard Methods of Testing Coated Fabrics by American Society for Testing and Materials.
ASTM D1308	= Standard Method for Test for Effect of Household Chemicals on Clear and Pigmented Organic Finishes.
Para.	= Paragraph from CFFA-W-101-A.

Notes:

a.   Tear Strength — Type I is tested without the augmenting weight. Types II and III are tested with the augmenting weight.

b.   Abrasion Resistance — tested using #220 grit, pressure at 3 pounds and tension at 6 pounds.

c.   Heat aging — exposure condition is 158°F ± 3° (70°C ± 2°C) for seven days.

d.   Stain Resistance — test period is twenty four hours. Reagents used are 50% ethyl alcohol, 5% acetic acid, 1% sodium hydroxide, soap and detergent solutions, orange juice, butter and catsup.

Types and Categories of Vinyl Wall Covering

Types (old classification)

The federal government identified types of vinyl wall covering by weight with performance standards for each weight (Federal Specification CCC-W-408A). Three types were defined by weight and recommended uses given. Although 408A has been superseded, these types continue to be common terminology.

The federal specification was given in ounces per square yard. It should be noted that vinyl wall covering for institutional use is manufactured in 54" widths and is actually sold, not by the square yard, but by the linear yard.

$$1.5 \times \text{oz/sq yd} = \text{oz/linear yd.}$$
$$\text{e.g. } 1.5 \times 7 \text{ oz/sq yd} = 10.5 \text{ oz/linear yd.}$$

Table 7.2 shows the government standards and translates these to ounces per linear yard. It also shows the commonly used backings and recommended uses.

Table 7.2

VINYL WALL COVERING TYPES

Type	oz/sq yd	oz/lin yd	Backing	Use
I	7.0-13.0	10.5-19.5	scrim	areas of low abrasion; offices, patient rooms
II	13.0-22.0	19.5-33.0	sheeting, osnaburg & drill	areas of average use; public corridors, dining rooms, lounges
III	over 22.0	over 33.0	broken twill	areas of hard use; service corridors, food service

Type III vinyls wear well in areas exposed to extraordinarily hard use and are often used as a wainscot in locations exposed to damage by moving equipment. Choices, however, are very limited and the vinyl is expensive. Alternatives, such as the durable wall coverings discussed in the next chapter, should be evaluated.

Categories (new classification)

Although reference to Types I, II and III is still being made, new standards have been officially adopted. The American Society for Testing and Materials (ASTM) had adopted new standards for classifying wall covering by durability characteristics rather than composition and weight, ASTM F-793. This is in line with CCC-W-408B where, as previously noted, references to composition and weight were deleted.

Under ASTM F-793 a category code related to durability has been assigned. Categories I, II, and III in this standard apply to decorative products for light use. Categories IV, V and VI are comparable, respectively, to Types I, II and III.

The new standard does not place new restrictions on wall-covering manufacturers; in some ways it is more lenient. There may be considerable confusion regarding categories and types while the new standard is becoming established.

Health and Safety

Flame Resistance

Wall coverings are also classified according to their flame resistance. The standard used in most regulatory districts is ASTM E-84, the Steiner Tunnel Test for Surface Burning Characteristics. Public corridors are generally required to have a class A rating. This is not difficult to achieve, as there is a great variety of vinyl wall coverings with a class A, ASTM E-84 rating. Classes and equivalent flame ratings are:

Class	Flame Rating
A	0–25
B	26–75
C	over 75

Typically, smoke development is required to be below 50. The smoke development ratings of many vinyl wall coverings are in the range of 5 or 10.

A vinyl wall covering which exudes a non-toxic vapor at a temperature lower than that at which it contributes to flame has been developed by B. F. Goodrich. When the wall is heated to about 300° F by such things as a fire in the next room, a short circuit in a through-the-wall heating unit or a neglected curling iron, the vinyl wall covering gives off an odorless and colorless vapor that will set off the alarm on an ionization-type smoke detector.

Mildew Resistance

There is another classification to which the word class is applied. Wall coverings are called:

1. Class 1 if the backing **is not** mildew resistant
2. Class 2 if the backing **is** mildew resistant

Vinyl wall coverings can also contain bactericidal additives to inhibit microbiological growth.

Maintenance

Soil, grease and oils should not be allowed to accumulate. It is recommended that vinyl-covered walls be washed once or twice a year to remove the routine accumulation of soil. Warm water plus a mild soap or commercially available vinyl cleaning products can be used. Do not use abrasive cleaners, steel wool or solvent-type cleaners.

For stain removal, the manufacturer's recommendations should be followed. Isopropyl alcohol or naptha can usually be used. Many vinyls are scrubbable. These are an appropriate choice for most areas. A soft bristle brush should be used.

Tedlar and Prefixx are non-porous and prevent migration of staining agents into the vinyl. Most stains will clean off with water, even months later. For tough problems, strong solvents like acetone, or methylene chloride, can be used without damage to the protective film or to the vinyl substrate.

Acrylic films are sometimes used as a protective coating on vinyl wall coverings. These must be cleaned within twenty-four hours or stains will migrate through the finish and permanently stain the vinyl. They cannot be cleaned with solvent-based products, as the solvent will damage the finish and the vinyl wall covering.

When vinyl is gouged or torn, the entire strip containing the defect must usually be replaced, as the edges of the patch are typically difficult to conceal. If the vinyl has faded badly, even the new strip may be difficult to blend with the rest of the wall.

Installation

Master specifications suitable for editing are available from both AIA (The American Institute of Architects) and CSI (Construction Specifications Institute).

As with all architectural finishes, site conditions and condition of the substrate are very important for proper installation. A minimum temperature of 60° F and humidity of 20%–40% should be maintained for three days before, during and continuously after installation.

It is best if the permanent building lights are installed and operational so that the lighting conditions for the installation are the same as those under which the vinyl will be viewed.

The substrate should be smooth and free of defects, with moisture not exceeding 4 percent. Primers should be used as recommended by the manufacturer. A release coat should be used if a primer is not used. Previously finished surfaces should have a sealer applied so that there is no bleed through of the former finish.

The manufacturer's instructions should always be read and followed. Important points, some of which may be included in the manufacturer's instructions, are:

1. Use panels in exact order as they are cut from the roll.
2. Install panels on the hanging surface, reversing (top to bottom) every other panel of non-match patterns unless otherwise instructed by the manufacturer.
3. Fill in over doors and windows in sequence with full height strips, using panels in consecutive order from the roll.
4. Seams must be butted and not lapped, as vinyl will not adhere to itself.
5. Vertical joints shall not occur less than six inches from outside or inside corners.
6. Remove excess adhesive from each seam before making the next seam. Immediately clean adhesive residue from all adjacent surfaces.
7. Any variations in color or pattern match should immediately be communicated to the manufacturer's representative for inspection before proceeding further with the installation.
8. The cement used with rubber or vinyl base moldings will not adhere permanently to vinyl. Vinyl-wall-covering strips should be trimmed so there is only one-half-inch overlap of molding. This one-half-inch tolerance is needed to compensate for any unevenness in the floor.

Specification Notes

A wall covering heavy enough for the job should be specified but do not overspecify. There is a tendency to specify a Type II product throughout the building, not only in corridors, but in offices as well. This makes the job more expensive than it needs to be.

Do not specify solely by weight, as fillers are sometimes used to meet required weights, while other requirements may not be met. Other physical requirements should also be stated in the specification.

Always obtain a large sample before making the final selection. It is difficult for most people to visualize the effect of a large area using only a small sample. The larger sample will avoid many unpleasant surprises for both client and specifier.

The designer must be sure that the client understands that in horizontal patterns such as a grass cloth, the vertical seam will be visible.

Extra wall covering should be purchased for repair and for potential renovation work in adjacent areas. This is especially important if a custom color is specified. There are minimum-quantity stipulations for custom colors. Often, they cannot be bought in the small quantities needed for renovation or additions to the initial work.

Chapter Eight

HEAVY-DUTY WALL COVERINGS

WHILE PROPERLY selected coatings and vinyl wall coverings may suffice for an entire facility, other wall surfaces should be considered for their special properties. Both the initial cost and installation for the materials discussed in this chapter are higher than the cost of most coatings or vinyl wall coverings. However, the replacement period is much longer, as they are less subject to scratching, gouging and other kinds of wear and tear. Maintenance time is generally less, resulting in savings in operating costs.

The relative permanence of these materials can be a limitation, in that reconfiguration of spaces can be a problem. With some, patching after removal of a wall can be difficult. If the material is no longer suitable for the changed function of a space but is still in good shape, it may be difficult to justify the cost of replacement.

There are locations where the durability, strength and ease of maintenance of these materials outweighs any limitations that may exist. The value gained may be well worth the expense. Of particular relevance to health care facilities are ceramic tile, carpet and various synthetic wall coverings.

CERAMIC TILE

The same properties that make ceramic tile an appropriate floor finish also make it worthy of consideration as a wall finish. Ceramic tiles are durable, non-fading and easy to maintain. They are hard, strong, fireproof and resistant to chemical attack. Because glazed tiles are appropriate for walls, there is an even greater color and texture range than for floors where only unglazed tiles are recommended.

Both vitreous and glazed, non-vitreous tiles can be used for walls. The non-vitreous tiles are not resistant to moisture attack from the back. Care must be taken in installation so that water cannot seep behind the glazed tile face. Another limitation is that tile is a poor sound-cushioning material. This makes it inappropriate for locations such as patient corridors.

Structure and Properties

As previously discussed, the properties of the various kinds of ceramic tile are determined principally by the following variables: body composition, method of forming, degree of vitrification, and glazed or unglazed. (To review these, refer to Chapter Four.)

Health and Safety

Health and safety factors of a fire-resistant and hygienic surface are well met by ceramic tiles. They are fireproof and, therefore, meet the strictest fire codes. The tile face is moisture resistant and will not support organic growth. Any moisture problems are with the grouting. In locations where water is present, the grouting must be specified, as moisture-resistant or mildew and bacterial growths will likely occur. It is also important that the grouting completely cover and protect the sides of non-vitreous (therefore, porous) glazed tiles that are often used for walls. If water penetrates behind the glaze of these tiles, not only is hygiene a problem, but the bond to the substrate can be weakened or broken.

Types of Tile

Several of the vitreous tiles used for floors are also used for walls. Because structural strength is seldom a consideration on vertical surfaces, the thinner and less heavy porcelains and ceramic mosaic tiles are appropriate choices. Another important consideration for walls is the glazed, non-vitreous tile, commonly known as wall tile.

Vitreous tiles

Porcelain tiles and ceramic mosaics of porcelain or natural clays are impervious to moisture and are stain resistant. They are very durable and appropriate in areas of hard use, such as public rest-rooms, central showers, and janitor's closets. They can be glazed if a sheen or special color is desired for appearance.

Paver or quarry tiles could be used on walls where extraordinary strength or impact resistance is needed. These might be considered for the kitchen.

(Refer to Chapter Four for a more complete description of these vitreous tiles.)

Glazed Tile or Wall Tile

Glazed tile greater than six square inches is often called wall tile, a somewhat confusing term, as many other ceramic tiles can be used on walls. Glazed tile, itself, is also a confusing term, as it does not refer to any tile with a glaze. Instead, it refers to a soft-bodied, porous tile to which a glaze has been added to make the surface impermeable to water. In other words, it refers not to tiles where glaze is purely decorative but to those for which the glaze has a necessary protective function. If the glaze were omitted in these soft-bodied, glazed tiles, the tile would be highly vulnerable to water and non-functional.

At the same time, the decorative aspect of the glaze has been most highly developed in these tiles. Because they are used primarily as wall tiles and not subjected to the impact and abrasion born by floor finishes, the decorative possibilities are expanded. Materials that would not withstand floor abuse are used to give a broad array of color, color intensity, texture and sheen. Most give a durable wall finish, but it is important to note any limitations stated by the manufacturer.

This white-bodied tile has a high proportion of kaolin. Flint is added to reduce shrinkage, hold the tile together in the firing process and help marry the tile to the glaze. Feldspar, the glass-forming agent, is not used. It is replaced by talc. Talc lessens expansion of the tile when the unglazed surface comes in contact with and absorbs water. Shale may be introduced for harder, denser tile. The tile body is non-vitreous; it is porous and has a high absorption rate.

Glazed tile is made by dust pressing. The tile may be double fired or single fired. In double firing the clay is pressed into shape and the tile is fired. A surface glaze is then applied and the tile fired a second time. In single firing, the tile is formed and the glaze applied to the unfired tile. It goes through the kiln only once and at a higher temperature than in the double-firing process. Single-fired, glazed tiles are called monocottura by the Italians, who developed the process.

Some argue that the glaze is more firmly bonded to the clay body in the single-firing process. Others argue that the older double-firing method produces a more impervious tile. Economics are in favor of the single-firing process; it is less costly.

There is great variety in glazes, and technology promises more. Glazes can be clear or colored. The surface imparted may be plain, speckled, textured or patterned. Multiple colors may be more expensive, as each color is laid on and fired separately in the conventional process. Glazes may form a matte, gloss, or crystalline finish. A crystalline glaze is usually somewhat stronger than the others.

Glazed wall tiles have been the material traditionally used in areas where moisture and water are present. They continue to serve well in patient bathrooms, operating rooms and hydrotherapy rooms. One precaution should be observed. A gloss sheen, single color, glazed tile with no surface texture or mottling will show water spots when hard water is used. While this is not harmful to the tiles, their use in showers is not recommended, as they will have a spotted appearance unless wiped down after each use.

In evaluating whether to use a glazed tile or a non-glazed vitreous tile for a wall finish, considerations can be summarized as follows:

Advantages of glazed tile

A broad range of colors and finishes are available.

Dirt seldom adheres to a glazed tile. Any soil that does cling such as oily vapor deposits can be easily wiped off.

A non-vitreous glazed tile is less costly than a vitreous tile.

Advantages of vitreous tile

A vitreous tile is stronger and more rugged than a non-vitreous tile.

Moisture is not absorbed through the back.

Maintenance

Ceramic tile is a durable, easily maintained material with excellent appearance-retention characteristics. All types can be easily cleaned with water or, if especially dirty, with a mild detergent solution. Glazed tiles accumulate less dirt and are even easier to clean than non-glazed tiles.

While ceramic tile is very durable, broken tiles do occur. Tiles broken years after the initial installation may be difficult or impossible to match. Extra tiles should always be purchased in the beginning for later replacement.

No grout has been developed which is as good as the tile, itself. The grout lines are the location where moisture penetration problems occur.

When water gets behind the glaze to the body of porous-bodied tiles, problems do occur including expansion and contraction and subsequent cracking, especially cracking and chipping of grout. Adhesion to the wall can also be affected. It is a simple procedure to replace tile, but it may not be so simple to cure the underlying moisture problem.

Grout is also more vulnerable to staining than is the tile, itself. Latex additives to a Portland cement grout will make the grout less absorptive. Sealers that reduce porosity are also available. As for floors, epoxy grouts should be considered. Silicone and urethane grouts are also stain-resistant options for walls. Darker-colored grouts will show staining less than lighter-colored ones.

Installation

The same mortars and grouts are used for walls as for floors. When using the full-bed mortar method, the bed is thinner at 3/4" or 1" thick. In addition to those methods discussed in Chapter Four, two other materials can be used for walls.

Organic Adhesive (Mastic) Systems

Solvent-based adhesive systems, also known as mastics, cure very quickly and are easy to use. They are low cost, lightweight and flexible. The grouts resist staining. They are water repellant and suitable for locations with intermittent wetting such as shower enclosures. However, bond strength varies greatly among the many brands available. Solvents in some of the adhesives are irritating to some people, and air circulation at the work site may be a critical factor. Some of the systems remain flammable after evaporation of the solvent and could not be recommended for health care use.

Elastomeric Grout Systems

Silicone, urethane and modified polyvinyl chloride are elastomeric grout systems used in pre-grouted tile sheets. These are flexible grouts that allow the sheets to be installed without cracking the grouting. When pre-grouting is used, field grouting between the sheets should be done with the same material.

Silicone is used both for pre-grouted sheets and for other installation work where its attributes are desired. It cures rapidly and is resistant to staining, moisture, heat, mildew, cracking, crazing and shrinking. (It must not be used for kitchen countertops or other food-preparation surfaces.) It has excellent adhesion and is flexible enough to stretch and bend with normal building movement.

These elastromeric grouts will involve costs beyond that of a Portland cement grout.

Specification Notes

The most complete specification information for installation of ceramic tile is published by the Tile Council of America in their annual publication, *Handbook for Ceramic Tile Installation.* All methods in the handbook have been researched and tested. A detailed description of each and appropriate specification information are given. Charts showing recommended applications are included. It is a must for the person who is actually writing the specification.

Tile selection and proposed setting and grouting methods should be confirmed with the manufacturer's representative as to appropriateness for function and substrate. Condition of the wall is important and provisions for proper preparation by the tile setter or under his or her supervision should be made in the specification.

Beyond selection of the tile and installation information, the specifier should keep in mind the following points:

Ceramic tile walls are usually finished with various types of moldings or trim tiles. Inside and outside corners may be needed. If tile is used as a wainscot, a bullnose finish is typically used. If moldings are desired, be sure they are available. Many ceramic tiles, especially European products, do not have matching trim tiles.

Wall tiles are usually not the same dimension as tiles used for floors. When it is desired that the module of the wall tile match that of the flooring tile, the tile used on the floor can be continued up the wall. However, glazed wall tile should never be used on the floor to achieve a match.

Specify the layout of the tile. Detail it on the drawings. Written instructions such as "herringbone" are open to misinterpretation. Drawings are the only sure way to communicate the desired layout.

Quantities should be specified with 2 percent extra of each color and size. This will facilitate quick replacement of any damaged tiles and assure color match. Unlike color in many materials, ceramic colors remain true. Tiles stored for many years will match previously installed tiles, provided they were originally from the same lot. It is important to standardize and so limit materials that must be stored.

Remember to specify the color of the grout. Darker grouts show less soiling.

CARPET

Carpet is a heavy-duty wall covering especially suited for corridors in areas with patient rooms. It is rugged, showing little effect from the bumps and knocks of cart traffic. However, a hard-loop pile will show greater effect than a cut pile or a soft-loop pile. Carpet cushions the sound of impact and also absorbs airborne sounds. Psychologically, carpet provides a warm, hospitable atmosphere.

If carpet is to be used, it is particularly important that selection and installation be done with care. While slight imperfections seldom show on the floor, they are apt to be emphasized on the wall, where they are at eye level and where the effects of lighting are quite different.

As with all wall coverings, down lighting along the wall can be a grazing light that emphasizes any change in the level of the surface. This can have a positive effect in emphasizing a handsome texture or a negative one in highlighting even minor flaws.

Structure and Properties

The two main ways that a wall carpet may differ from the carpet used on floors are in weight and fiber type. As with floor carpet, texture and pattern are important in concealing seams.

WEIGHT: The carpet can be lighter in weight, as it is not subjected to traffic wear. A lighter-weight carpet is also much easier to handle in the installation process. Standard floor carpets with a face weight as high as thirty ounces per square yard have been successfully used, but twenty-two ounces per square yard provides easier installation and approximately the same protection. These "low end" floor carpets give very good service as wall carpets.

Not only can low end floor carpets be beneficially adapted for wall use, there are also several lines of carpet made specifically for wall use. Manufacturers of these have adopted vinyl wall covering sizes and terminology. Width is usually 54" and weight is quoted as total weight per linear yard. A typical product is thirty ounces per linear yard. This would be twenty ounces per square yard. (See "Vinyl Wall Covering," Chapter Seven, for conversion figures.)

Note that this is total weight rather than face wight. Whatever the weight, pile height, tightness of construction and resilience will make a difference in the amount of protection and acoustical absorbency achieved. Typically, wall covering manufacturers are giving only total weight in their literature, while traditional carpet manufacturers give both face weight and total weight.

FIBER TYPE: There is a broader range of suitable fibers for wall carpet than for floor carpet where nylon is the fiber of choice for heavy-duty institutional wear. In fact, nylon is seldom used for the wall, as other fibers are less expensive and will perform well in this less demanding location. Various synthetics are commonly used, including polyester FR, olefin and modacrylic.

TEXTURE: Many of the carpets made especially for walls are constructed with a multi-level pile forming vertical ribs. Vertical seams are well concealed in this ribbing which also enhances the textural qualities and gives a subtle variation to the color.

There is one precaution regarding a level, cut pile: finger writing is possible. In locations where there is the potential for graffiti, this texture should not be used. Four-letter words can be avoided by using a short loop pile.

COLOR: As with floor carpet, a medium value works best. Too light and the dark soil shows; too dark and the lint becomes evident. The backing color is also important, as white can show through, especially at eye level.

Health and Safety

In most regulatory districts, the requirements for fire resistance for wall finish materials in exit corridors is very strict. A class A flame spread under ASTM E-84 or the Life Safety Code is required. Other applicable codes are NFPA 701 and UBC 4202A. Manufacturers are producing wall carpet material in polyester FR, olefin and modacrylic that comply with these requirements. It is much harder to achieve this with a nylon (another good reason why nylon is seldom the fiber used in carpets selected for walls).

Types of Carpet

In selecting a carpet for a wall covering, there are two categories from which to choose: a lightweight floor carpet or a carpet made especially for a wall covering. Either can perform well. The principle limitation of the floor carpet is its twelve-foot width which makes installation difficult. It is heavy to lift and can pull away from the wall before the adhesive is dry. This difficulty is sometimes lessened by cutting the carpet into two six-foot widths. An advantage of the floor carpet is that it is usually less expensive.

Carpets made specifically for wall coverings are typically made in narrower widths. Coral and Knoll both carry an excellent wall carpet with similar specifications. Both of these carpets are 54" wide, 1/4" thick and weigh 30 ounces per linear yard. They are polyester FR and have a flame resistant backing. The backing is important for dimensional stability. It also helps retard fraying at the cut edges.

Several other carpets specifically designed for walls are in a line of carpets carried by Design Tex. These are 100 percent olefin, 39" wide and have a class A flame spread rating.

Maintenance

In general, soil is not a major problem with wall carpet; routine vacuum cleaning is all that is needed. One problem location, however, is the area around hot-air ducts. This area will become soiled over time and could be a consideration in the location of carpeted walls.

Use of a powerful tank-type vacuum cleaner is the best method of routine maintenance. Clean with a ceiling-to-floor motion. If the carpet has any spots or stains, they can be treated with a mild detergent solution. Let the solution do the work. Wipe gently and then blot; do not rub. If a mild detergent solution is not effective, other cleaning solutions, such as concentrated rug shampoos or spot cleaners that dry to a powder, should be tried in accordance with the carpet manufacturer's literature.

Of all the fibers used, olefin is probably the most resistant to harsh cleaning solutions. Olefin is always solution dyed, and even undiluted bleaches will not remove the color.

As with floor carpets, the most important factor in complete removal of spots and stains is immediate action. With prompt attention, most can be removed. Good communication between nursing and environmental services and good response from environmental services are essential to the use of carpet.

Installation

The surface receiving the carpet should be clean, dry, smooth, structurally sound, thoroughly sealed and primed. An oil primer is recommended. On previously painted walls, the surface should be sanded and any glossy finish removed. Any previous wall covering must be removed.

Adhesive should be in accordance with the carpet manufacturer's recommendations, usually a multipurpose latex, and is typically applied to the wall surface. "Open" time or setting time after spreading the adhesive and prior to carpet application is more critical than in floor installation. If the adhesive is not properly tacky, the carpet tends to fall from the wall.

Carpet is installed from top to bottom between two plumb lines for perfect vertical alignment and minimal trim. Carpet strips should be hung in consecutive order as taken from the roll.

Any excess material should be trimmed using a broad knife to hold the wall covering in place so that no movement occurs. After installation, the wall carpet should be smoothed with a short hair brush.

In locations dominated by union labor, there may be jurisdictional disputes over whether the floor carpet layers or wall covering installers will install the wall carpet. This is especially true for carpet normally intended for floors. This should be resolved prior to preparing the Contract Documents.

Specification Notes

Carpet may be applied as a full height covering or as a wainscot. There is certainly more sound control in a full height application and it is often more effective, visually. A wainscot is sufficient for wall protection, as most abuse occurs on the lower portion.

When carpet is used as a wainscot, the top edge must be finished. Vinyl edge mold with a rounded profile is functional, and the material and form are consistent with the softness of carpet. Metal edge molds are not recommended, as they dent when bumped and have a stark visual contrast with the carpet.

Textured, vertical ribbing conceals seams well.

OTHER WALL CARPETS

It is worth mentioning one more fiber used for wall carpet. This is sisal. While sisal carpets may not be the answer to many health care facility concerns, they are an excellent answer in elevators and telephone bays where graffiti is a problem. They are soil and stain resistant and writing on them is very difficult. Their scratchy texture is good reason to stay away from the wall.

These sturdy carpets are made with a class A flame spread rating. They have a low smoke rating and are impervious to cigarette burns. Good noise reduction can be achieved with an NRC of 60 to 65. They are static free.

WALL FABRICS

While most wall fabrics would be used in low maintenance areas, there are some that sustain heavy usage. Two of these are of a woven polyolefin marketed as Tek-Wall™ by Maharam and Amoweve® by Amoco. The woven olefin is acrylic backed for stability and fray resistance. Being of olefin, they can be cleaned, if necessary, with undiluted chlorine bleach with no deleterious effects. This is an attribute that is greatly favored by maintenance and nursing staffs.

The cost and performance of these woven polyolefins are impressive. Cost is comparable to a Type I vinyl. However, they sustain cart traffic like a Type III or better. They are very difficult to rip or tear. Hospitals are using them successfully in high traffic corridors and in patient rooms. The test results are impressive:

Wyzenbeek abrasion resistance; exceeds 75,000 double rubs (Tek-Wall) or 50,000 double rubs (Amoweve).

Fade resistance; minimum 200 hour fadeometer rating (Tek-Wall) or 100 hour (Amoweve).

Tensile strength; warp, 284 pounds; filling 410 pounds.

Flame spread rating; class A as tested under ASTM E-84, NFPA 255, UBC 42.1, ANS 2.5 and UL 723

Maintenance

Polyolefin is non-absorbent, resulting in easy cleaning. Routine cleaning as recommended by the manufacturer includes such methods as wiping, washing and vacuuming. Some users say that dry brushing works very well for most all soil. Soil such as crayon marks and shoe scuffs can be removed by brushing with a soft bristle brush. Washing should be tried after dry brushing or vacuuming. Solvent cleaners should not be used, as they can mar the surface with a dissolving action.

Water-based staining materials have little or no effect on the face of the material. However, water coming through sheetrock to the backside (such as with leaking pipes) does cause stains that are extremely difficult to remove.

Installation

Tek-Wall is hung with a heavy-duty vinyl adhesive using much the same procedure as that used for vinyl wall coverings. Double-cut seams as recommended by the manufacturer are generally used, although butt seams have been successfully used in some installations.

With this material, it is necessary to have a high-quality installer. The material is stiffer than vinyl. When wrapping around outside corners, it is necessary to have six to eight inches of wrap around so that the fabric lays flat and does not pop up. Where a narrow wrap is necessary, such as at a window recess, contact cement can be used at the seam.

This is a tough material and a sharp blade is required for cutting. It is even more difficult to cut after installation such as when outlet boxes must be installed after the fabric has been installed.

Specification Notes

If a monolithic look is desired, the weave must be carefully selected. Fabrics that have a medium to heavy texture, such as a basket weave, do not seam well; seams have an appearance similar to grasscloth seams. These are very visible and many people find them obtrusive.

There is yet another heavy-duty woven textile suitable for hard use. This is Xorel™ from Carnegie Fabrics. This is a proprietary fiber, and the manufacturer does not wish to reveal the generic fiber from which it is derived. Its performance attributes rival those of Tek-Wall and Amoweve. Its appearance is more lustrous or iridescent. Test results include:

Wyzenbeek abrasion resistance: no wear after 100,000 double rubs.

Colorfastness (AATCC 16A): class 5 or 4.5 after 80 hours.

Tensile strength (ASTM D-1682): warp, 335 pounds; filling 262 pounds.

Tear strength (ASTM D-2261): warp, 60 pounds; filling 60 pounds.

Flame spread rating: class A as tested under ASTM E-84; class 1 as tested under ASTM E-648.

Resistant to growth of fungi, bacteria and staphylococcus.

Maintenance

This is a non-absorbent wall covering and very stain resistant. Complete testing information on many different stains is available from the manufacturer. As with all materials, quick removal is the best way to assure complete removal.

Cleaning instructions from the manufacturer recommend wiping with a damp cloth, washing or cleaning with a solvent-based cleaner.

Installation

Vinyl adhesive is used for installation. Care must be taken in the installation and having a well-qualified installer is important. The fabric is tough to cut and stiff to wrap around corners. The following instructions from the manufacturer's literature give some indication of the critical nature of the installation: (Capital letters are instructions from the manufacturer.)

1. Double cutting is recommended. Use a DOUBLE CUTTER to avoid blade contact with the wall.
2. Cut the drops consecutively including pieces over doors and windows. USE NEW BLADE FOR EACH SHEET.
3. Hang the drops consecutively.
4. Reversing sheets may be necessary at times.
5. Do not paste more than two drops at a time.
6. Do not let glue set up longer than five minutes or the fabric may peel off the sheetrock paper when the overlapped edge is peeled.
7. Drop should be rolled after pasting, NOT FOLDED.
8. Xorel is a woven fabric. Do not tape the face of the fabric or yarns may be pulled out when tape is removed.
9. DO NOT USE SEAM ROLLER OF ANY KIND AT THE SEAMS OR EDGES. Smooth the seams with a plastic scraper.
10. To clean any excess adhesive at seams, wipe with a slightly damp sponge and dry immediately with a terry towel.
11. If Xorel tends to curl away from the top or bottom of the wall, prime the top or bottom edges of the wall with adhesive. Allow to become tacky before hanging fabric. For very difficult corners, determine where the fabric will reach the corner and then, with rough sandpaper, lightly sand the paper backing. This will make the fabric less rigid at these points so it can be more easily turned.

SEMIRIGID PLASTIC WALL COVERINGS

A PVC/acrylic alloy is made into a wall covering that is semirigid, resilient, tough and durable. It is resistant to marks, scratches and abrasions. It is also resistant to fractures and dents and to chemicals and stains. Use is recommended for areas where damage and graffiti would necessitate frequent painting of walls or replacement of wall covering. It has been successfully used in such difficult locations as surgery, psychiatric patient rooms, wainscots in service corridors, service elevators and materials handling areas.

Structure and Properties

The PVC/acrylic alloy has outstanding impact resistance. Impact resistance is tested using the notched Izod method, ASTM D-256. For PVC/acrylic sheet, 10 to 15 foot-pounds per inch of notch, depending on the thickness used, is typical. This test is explained in the next chapter.

PVC/acrylic is dent, gouge and abrasion resistant. These properties are enhanced with integral color throughout the material and a textured surface that helps disguise any blemishes that do occur. The textured surface also softens glare and light reflectance.

PVC/acrylic sheets are thermoplastic and can be vacuum formed for corners and other applications. Corners can also be constructed using preformed moldings available from some of the manufacturers of the sheet goods. Joints on the planar surface of the wall can be butt joints, or vertical joint strips can be used. It is important to read the manufacturer's instructions regarding tolerances recommended for expansion and contraction of the material. Some of the manufacturers also make a wainscot molding for a finished edge in a wainscot application.

PVC/acrylic sheet is made by a limited number of manufacturers: Acrovyn® by Construction Specialties, Kydex® by Rohm and Haas, and Pro-Tek® by Pawling.

Table 8.1 is a listing of products made by each and includes information on thicknesses, colors and moldings available.

Health and Safety

In accordance with ASTM E-84, "Standard Method of Test for Surface Burning Characteristics of Building Materials, 0.028" and 0.040" thick materials meet requirements for class 1 construction when applied with the recommended adhesive. The thicker materials which have even greater impact resistance typically meet class 2 or class 3 requirements.

Table 8.1

COMPARISON OF PVC/ACRYLIC SHEET PRODUCTS

Product	Thickness	Colors			Moldings				
		St	Cus	Tex	IC	OC	VJ	W	O
Acrovyn®	.028 & .078	13	13	10	X	X	X	X	X
Kydex®	.028 to .250	19	0	1					
Pro-Tek®	.028, .040 & .060	7	9	1			X	X	X

Legend:

St standard colors
Cus custom colors
Tex textures
IC inside corners
OC outside corners
VJ vertical joint molding
W   wainscot moldings
O   other products, e.g. corner guards, bumper rails

These materials are sold in four foot by eight foot sheets. Kydex also comes in three and five foot wide sheets. The thinner grades, .028 and .040, also come in 120 foot long rolls.

Custom colors are available with minimum order requirements.

Other material protection includes corner guards, base molds, bumper and hand rails, and door and frame protectors. These are discussed in the next chapter.

Smoke development is low in the thinner materials but in the thicker ones may reach 350–450. When heated to 400° F or above and when burning, HCl fumes are released.

PVC/acrylic is moisture resistant and will not support organic growth.

Maintenance

PVC/acrylic semirigid wall coverings can be cleaned with standard commercial wall cleaners. It is stain resistant and most stains are readily removed. Because the color is integral and permeates the entire thickness, it withstands repeated scrubbing.

While heavy damage is rare, the panel cannot be patched. Instead, the entire panel must be replaced.

Installation

All wall surfaces must be clean, dry, level, smooth and free of all irregularities to provide a good adhesive grip and smooth application. Adhesives should be as recommended by the manufacturer.

It is important that removal of excessive adhesive be performed concurrently with the installation. At this time, warm, soapy water will do a satisfactory cleanup job. If the adhesive is allowed to dry, it is very difficult to remove.

Specification Notes

Design criteria must be communicated. This would include inside and outside corner conditions (use of molding or formed corners) type of vertical joint (butt or vertical joint strip) and use of wainscot molding if applicable. Specific directions must be given as to whether moldings will match or contrast with the panels.

If vertical joints are required at specific locations, this must be shown on the drawings. If more than one color is used, color locations must appear on the drawings or in the color schedule.

PLASTIC LAMINATE

Plastic laminate is another material sometimes used on walls. Specifically, elevator walls are often finished with plastic laminate. Plastic laminate is discussed in Chapter Seventeen.

Chapter Nine

WALL PROTECTION SYSTEMS

OFTEN, an entire wall does not need heavy-duty protection; only portions are particularly vulnerable. Sometimes, full protection is desirable but not affordable. At other times, even a tough durable wall finish needs additional protection from bumping and ramming by the ubiquitous cart. In each of these cases, there are protective devices available. By using these in combination with the wall covering, an effective protection system can be designed.

This is a particularly tricky area in the design of an interior finish plan for a hospital. If protective devices are poorly selected or located, the result is battered walls. On the other hand, an overabundance may minimize wall damage but at the same time create visual chaos and cost far more than necessary.

In hospitals, especially, repair and refurbishing costs are high. Damage from everyday abuse can be a major expense; carts of all kinds and their drivers are the major offenders. Discussed in this chapter are corner guards, bumper and handrails, and door and door frame protection. These all function to provide protection beyond that of the wall finish, itself.

Structure and Properties

The degree of protection afforded by these devices is highly dependent upon the material from which they are made and upon their form and type of attachment to the wall.

Materials

The materials most frequently being used for protective additions today are PVC (polyvinyl chloride), both rigid and flexible, rubber and stainless steel. A polycarbonate, Lexan™, has limited use.

Before discussing these materials and their attributes as wall guards, it may be helpful to clarify some terminology. PVC, a hard and rigid thermoplastic, is often simply called vinyl. This is imprecise and can lead to confusion. There are many vinyls, of which PVC is only one. Each has its own properties. Some important vinyls used in buildings and an example of their use are PS (polystyrene) for insulating foam, PMMA (polymethyl methacrylate), also called acrylic, for skylights, PVAc (polyvinyl acetate) for adhesives, PVB (polyvinyl butyral) for tough upholstery fabrics, PC (polycarbonate) as a substitute for glass and many others.

Although these are all derived from the same basic vinyl group, common terminology is not uniform. Some include the name vinyl and some do not. **Furthermore, the term vinyl, as commonly used, means polyvinyl chloride only, leading to considerable confusion.**

To avoid confusion as much as possible and still recognize prevailing terminology in the product literature, terms used in this chapter will be:

PVC: rigid polyvinyl chloride.

Vinyl: resilient polyvinyl chloride; a plasticizer is added to the compound resulting in a tough, flexible PVC. Plasticizers are liquid or solid materials that are blended with plastics to make them softer and more flexible than would otherwise be the case.

Acrylic: the term commonly used for PMMA.

Lexan: A trade name that has begun to function as a generic term for polycarbonate.

PVC: Both PVC and a PVC/acrylic alloy are used for rigid guards of all types. PVC is a tough, impact-resistant material. The commonly used toughness test, ASTM D-256, is known as the Izod Impact Strength Test. It measures the impact of a weighted pendulum striking a small notched bar.

The energy needed to break the specimen, expressed in foot-pounds per inch of notch, is called its impact strength. The impact strength varies according to formulation. As a class, PVCs vary upward from 0.4 foot-pounds per inch. Manufacturers of wall protective systems cite impact strength ratings from 18 to 28.8 foot-pounds per inch of notch.

PVC resists abrasion and gouges. Because the color is integral (molded clear through the material) and not just a surface coating, scrapes that do occur are less noticeable than they would be if a different color substrate were revealed. To further conceal marks, the surface is generally textured.

Pendulum Impact

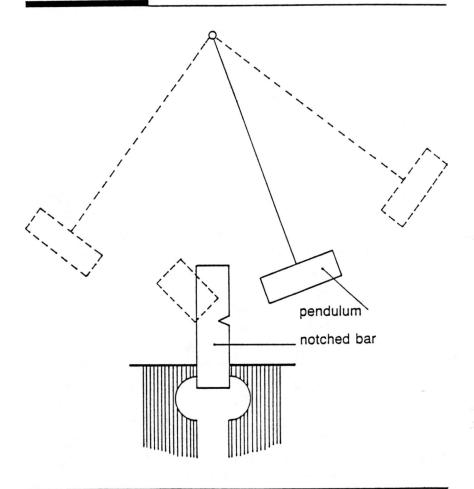

pendulum

notched bar

Figure 9.1. IZOD IMPACT TEST METHOD. The impact of a weighted pendulum striking a small notched bar of the test material is measured in the Izod impact test. The energy needed to break the specimen, expressed in foot-pounds per inch of notch, is designated the material's impact strength.

VINYL AND RUBBER: Vinyl, as noted above, is the term that will be used for flexible PVC. This material and rubber have properties that are very similar. They are tough, flexible and resilient. Their formulation is similar to that of resilient floorings and base molds. Typically made by manufacturers of resilient flooring who also make base and other moldings, their colors are usually limited to about six which match those of the manufacturer's base molds. This can be advantageous when it is desirable to match colors of base molds and guards.

For flexible vinyl and rubber, impact resistance is tested in accordance with ASTM D-1822, a method used for plastic materials too flexible or too thin to be tested in accordance with ASTM D-256.

STAINLESS STEEL: The traditional corner guard was of stainless steel. It has important health and safety features, being non-flammable, non-toxic and non-absorbent. It is the most rigid of the materials used for corner guards. However, it is also susceptible to dents from severe impact and to scratches. These dents and scratches are not repairable. Stainless steel is institutional and cold in appearance, making it psychologically inappropriate for some patient areas.

LEXAN: This is a polycarbonate plastic. The Lexan used for protective guards typically has an impact strength of 16 foot-pounds per inch of notch when tested under ASTM D-256. It is available in solid colors and clear. Clear Lexan has the advantage of letting the wall color show through. It is attached with countersunk screws. (Adhesives are not an option, as they would show through the clear material.) While the clear Lexan may be a visually unobtrusive solution, the screws do show and may be considered objectionable. With the clear Lexan, there is no camouflage for the scratches that may occur.

WOOD: In handrails, one other material deserves attention. This is wood. The beauty and warmth of wood make it a desirable aesthetic choice. Wood being a cellular material is somewhat resistant to impact. This same cellular nature means that its surface will absorb moisture and soil unless this is counteracted with a non-porous finish. Other limitations of wood are that it can splinter, will become scratched and gouged and it is flammable. It will also warp if not properly kiln dried.

Care taken in sanding will minimize splintering. Flame retardents impregnating the wood can be used (with the small area involved, this may not be necessary). Last but not least, while wood is more easily disfigured than PVC, it can also be more easily repaired. Damaged PVC must usually be replaced. Wood is relatively easy to refinish. The problem is that maintenance staffs often do not get around to doing it. Use wood only when a high level of maintenance is exhibited in existing buildings.

Structure

There are two types of structure used for the guard, itself. One is simply a single piece of material formed to the desired shape. This single component is fastened directly to the wall.

The second type of structure is a two-component guard. This consists of a extruded aluminum retainer that is firmly attached to the wall and a rigid plastic cover that snaps into the edge channels of the retainer. The components and the connection between them are designed so there is an air cushion between the two materials that dissipates the shock of impact. The rigid plastic cover protects against abrasive damage.

Health and Safety

Fire Safety

These wall protection systems are intended for institutional use where fire codes are strict. They are made to meet class 1 and class A requirements.

RIGID PVC: The applicable tests for flame spread are ASTM E-84, UL 723, NFPA 255 and UBC 42-1.

FLEXIBLE VINYL AND RUBBER: Flame resistance is tested in accordance with ASTM 635-74. These components typically meet a self-extinguishing standard.

LEXAN: This is tested in accordance with ASTM D-1929 and a self-ignition temperature of 650° F or greater is typically required. Lexan has been tested with a self-ignition temperature of 1000° F. The NBS smoke chamber test, NFPA 258, may be required. It is usually required that the optical smoke density be under 450.

STAINLESS STEEL: Stainless steel is a non-flammable material.

Biogenic Factors

PVC is not an absorbent material, nor is it chemically reactive. Therefore, it is stain and chemical resistant. Being non-absorbent, it is also resistant to the growth of bacteria and fungi. Nevertheless, some manufacturers have added antimicrobial agents to the vinyl resin to further minimize organic growth.

Stainless steel is non-absorbent and will not support growth of bacteria or fungi.

For handrails, cleanliness is extremely important, as they are used successively by many people.

Handrail Safety

A safety concern of importance and one which is much more apt to be overlooked than that of fire safety has to do with the design of the handrail. A handrail should be able to be easily grasped. Security and comfort are especially important to weak or older people who depend on the rail. In some regulatory districts, the design is restricted by codes for the handicapped. Proper handrail design includes:

1. A round cross section or rounded corners; at the top so that sharp corners do not cut into the hand and at the bottom so that fingers can obtain a grip
2. A horizontal dimension between 1 1/4" and 2", formed so that the hand can envelope the rail
3. A distance of at least 2" from the wall for knuckle clearance
4. Protected ends; ideally, a return to the wall so that nothing will catch under the rail end
5. A non-flexing top portion for a secure feeling when leaning on the rail

Types of Protection

Heavy-Duty Corner Guards

As everyone who has ever tried to maintain a facility knows, corners are particularly vulnerable to scrapes, nicks and gouges. The guards developed to protect corners are of two main kinds: (1) a heavy-duty, two-part guard with an air cushion between the parts to absorb the shock of severe impact; and (2) a medium-duty, single-component guard adhered directly to the wall for medium-traffic locations. For the heavy-duty applications, there are two types of mounting for these corner guards: flush mounted and surface mounted.

HEAVY DUTY, FLUSH MOUNTED: Built into the wall construction these are typically used in new construction and extensive remodeling. They are best installed for the full height of the corner. It is recommended that both retainer and guard be installed to project two inches into the ceiling. This provides a simple means of handling ceiling height variations.

The retainer is designed to accept dry wall or plaster plus the finish used, including thick finishes such as ceramic tile or carpet. When coatings or vinyl wall coverings are used, they can be carried across the face of the retainer flange and returned 90° into the void between the retainer and the guard. A smooth, trim look can be achieved with the flush-mounted corner guard.

Most manufacturers make provisions for installation of a cove base by furnishing an aluminum base as part of the retainer system. Over this, the standard building base mold can be applied.

HEAVY DUTY, SURFACE MOUNTED: These are appropriate for corner protection in existing buildings where the walls have already been built, especially if existing walls are plaster. They are also used in new construction for concrete block and for poured-concrete columns.

Surface-mounted corner guards can be full height or any desired partial height. Unlike the flush-mounted guards which extend above the ceiling, surface-mounted guards terminate at the ceiling. Closure caps are used at the ceiling and at the bottom where the guard ends above the vinyl base mold. For partial-height guards, caps are used to close the top gap. In some brands, these closure caps are available only in black or in a limited color line. In others, it is possible to match any of the corner guard colors.

The surface-mounted corner guard protrudes from the corner and does not have the trim look of the flush mounted. However, it is more adaptable to a number of situations and is less expensive.

FLUSH MOUNTED AND SURFACE MOUNTED: Most brands of both types of guards have 90° corners with a bullnose, 1 1/4" radius and a sharp nose, 1/4" radius, 135° corners and recommended configurations for endwalls. Some can provide angles other than 90° or 135°.

Most of the high-impact-resistant corner guards are of the air cushion type with extruded aluminum channel and PVC cover guard. For more industrial-type applications such as loading docks, thick (3/4"–7/8" or more) rubber guards are available. These are surface mounted directly to the wall and are resilient enough to bounce off heavy equipment and withstand the hard knocks and jolts.

Medium-Duty Corner Guards

Mounted directly to the wall using adhesives or countersunk screws, these are not as resistant to impact as the "floating" systems which absorb shock; these rigidly mounted systems will transmit shock to the adjoining wall area. However, they do provide protection against lighter-weight equipment, and the initial cost of materials and installation is lower.

A number of materials are available, including PVC, vinyl, rubber, stainless steel and Lexan.

Resilient vinyl and rubber corner molds are produced with 85° corners to pressure fit a 90° corner where they are generally attached with adhesives. Standard lengths are 48" and 54". Some have a tapered top. Custom, full-height guards are available in some lines. Of all the materials in this category of medium-impact resistance, these are the most

Flush Mounted

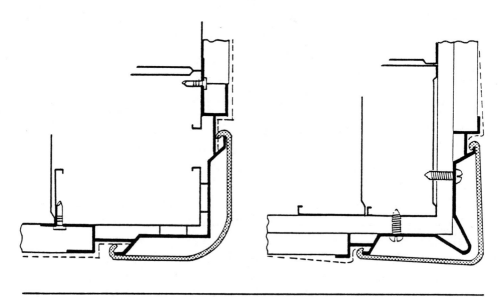

Surface Mounted

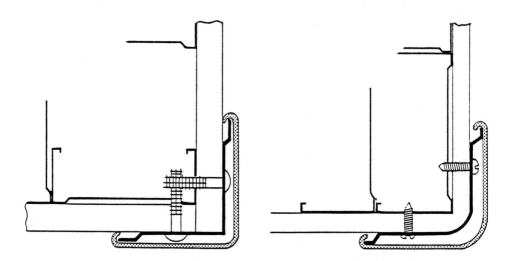

Figure 9.2. FLUSH- AND SURFACE-MOUNTED CORNER GUARDS. Illustrated are typical, heavy-duty two-part corner guards. The concept is to position the guard, using an aluminum retainer with an air cushion between guard and retainer, to absorb the shock of severe impact. Flush-mounted guards are typically used in new construction. Surface-mounted guards can be added to existing walls and used for concrete block, poured concrete and other types of construction that do not accept the flush-mounting details.

used and for good reason. Their resilience does help in absorbing the shock of impact, although they are not as resistant as the heavy-duty guards. They are easy to install and comparatively inexpensive.

Stainless steel, as was noted earlier, is the most rigid of the materials used for corner guards. The resultant non-resilience combined with the method of direct attachment to the wall means that shock will be transferred to the walls. Hairline cracks in adjacent walls sometimes result. A more resilient material with greater ability to conceal scratches is a better corner guard solution.

Lexan acts much the same as stainless steel when used as a corner guard.

Horizontal Wall Guards

Horizontal wall guards from wheel hub and ankle height to waist height offer protection from vehicles and consequent relief from repair costs. Used in conjunction with handrails, these combine maximum protection with essential pedestrian safety. They are made in three main types:

1. The bumper rail is mounted against the wall and used purely as a wall guard. Both the one-component and two-component structures are used.
2. The combination bumper/handrail is mounted out from the wall where it can be grasped. This is typically the two-component structure.
3. The handrail is used where impact resistance is secondary. The construction is that of a typical handrail.

These guards must be firmly affixed to the wall to function properly. Blocking behind the wall is usually required.

BUMPER RAILS: Many bumper rails are constructed in a manner similar to the heavy-duty corner guards. An extruded aluminum retainer strip is fastened to the wall. A rigid plastic cover of embossed PVC is snapped onto the retainer with an air cushion remaining between the two components. This performs in essentially the same way as the corner guard of the same construction.

With the horizontal protectors, there are some variations on this theme. Portions of the aluminum retainer not exposed to impact may be left uncovered; the vinyl becomes an insert rather than a cover. These inserts can be made of a rigid PVC but more often are of a soft, resilient vinyl that is thicker than the PVC. A thick resilient vinyl may also be

**Rigid Cover with
Bumper Cushion**   **Rigid Cover**   **Flexible Insert**

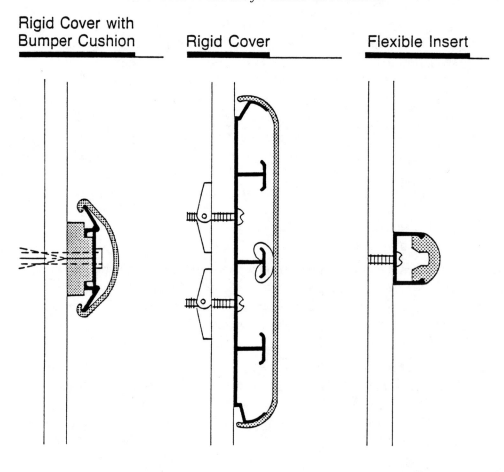

Figure 9.3. BUMPER RAIL STYLES. Bumper rails come in a wide variety of styles and sizes. Style, size and location on the wall must be specified in accordance with the dimensions of equipment and type of impact anticipated. The two-part bumper rail, using an aluminum retainer and rigid plastic guard with air cushion between, works on the same principle as the heavy-duty corner guard. This assembly can be backed by a cushion for even greater impact resistance. Flexible plastic inserts can be used in the aluminum retainer for slightly less demanding situations.

embedded in the retainer rail with only a small air space behind. In evaluation of these rails, two important points emerge. First, there should be a cushioning effect that lessens the transfer of the shock of impact to the wall. Second, the simpler the mechanism holding the two components together, the better; lots of little clips and springs become an installation and maintenance irritation.

    There are also wall strips that attach directly to the wall for light-duty protection. These are often used at chair rail height in offices and might well be used in lobbies and waiting areas. PVC and Lexan are used. With the clear Lexan, the countersunk screws can be obtrusive. When directly attached to the wall with no buffering air cushion, a soft, resilient vinyl strip would be more useful in absorbing impact. These are available for both institutional and industrial applications.

BUMPER/HANDRAILS: Bumper/handrails are a variation of the two-component bumper rail construction but mounted at handrail height and some distance from the wall so that people can grasp the rail for support. It is seldom acceptable to simply move a bumper rail to the appropriate height, as bumper rails are not designed to be easily grasped by the hand.

HANDRAILS: Any handrail will also serve as a bumper rail but may not sustain severe impact as well as those specifically designed with the bumper function as a primary design criteria. A simple round or oval

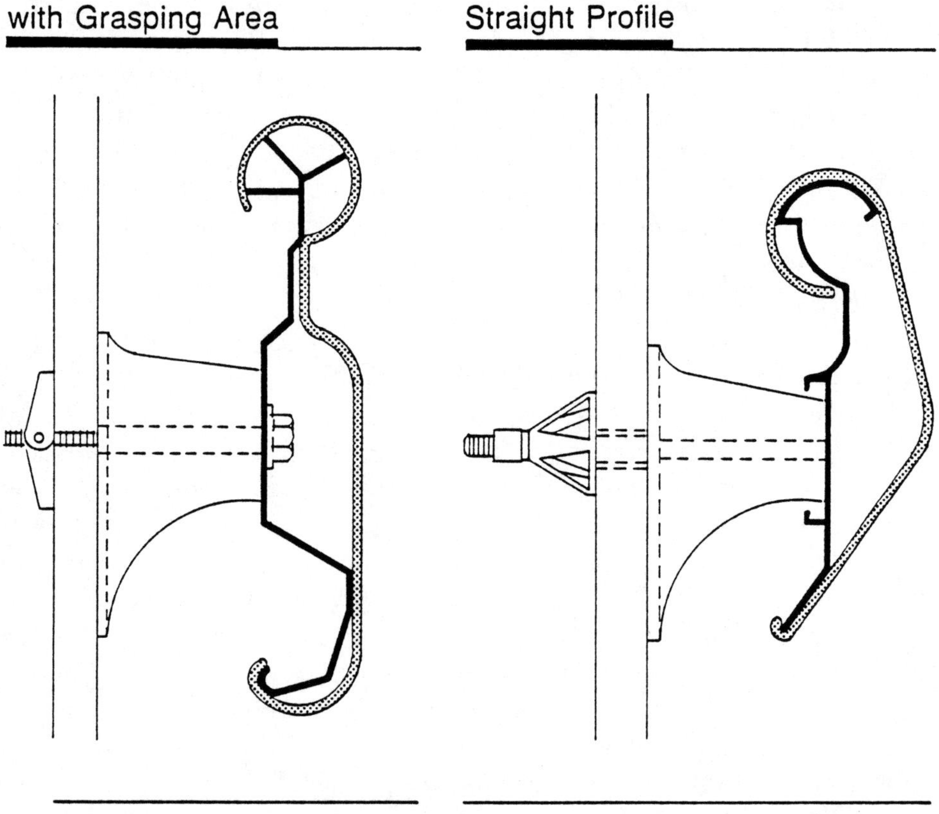

with Grasping Area   Straight Profile

Figure 9.4. BUMPER/HANDRAIL CONTOUR. It is important that a bumper rail intended for use as a handrail be of a configuration that is easily grasped. In general, the more rounded the top of the rail, the easier it will be to grasp. Handrail design is addressed in the subsection on "Health and Safety" under the section "Handrail Safety."

rail can serve as a handrail. It may be of steel or aluminum, brushed or polished, or finished with brass or chrome. Wood, as noted earlier, can also be used. In locations where carts are expected, scratch and mar resistance may be best obtained with a cover of rigid PVC.

Door and Door Frame Protectors

There is less traffic through any one door than down the corridor, but the door is where the turn is made and the space narrows. These are conditions for collision; doors and door frames are particularly subject to crashing and banging.

Two materials are the most commonly used door materials: wood and plastic laminate. A solid-core wood door is very durable, but the surface will be scratched, gouged, and marred over time. The natural pattern of the wood will disguise some of these marks. The door will maintain its appearance longer if the color of the finish is similar to that of the natural wood. This will enhance the camouflaging power of the pattern, as a break in the surface will show little color difference. In addition to its warmth and beauty, a big advantage of wood is that it can be refinished at a relatively low expenditure of time and money.

Plastic laminates will be discussed in much greater detail in Chapter 17 on "Casework." They have a durable finish and are more resistant to abrasion and impact than wood. However, impact damage is also more visible than it is with wood. Chips of plastic laminate are broken from the door and the substrate is clearly visible. The only way to repair this is to remove the entire laminate finish and replace it with a new layer of plastic laminate.

The same materials that are used as protective devices on walls and corners are used as protective shields on doors. PVC, stainless steel and Lexan are all used.

STAINLESS STEEL: The same limitations apply for door protectors as for corner guards; it dents and is subject to scratching. In fact, it is delivered to the job site with a protective covering. Perhaps, this is the first clue that scratching will be a problem.

LEXAN: Clear Lexan is sometimes used over wood doors so that the beauty of the wood will show through. This effect is better initially than later when, with scratches, it becomes less clear.

PVC: PVC or a PVC/acrylic alloy work well in this application. A number of sizes and types of application are available:

1. Full door cladding
2. Kick plates from 12"–24" high

3. Molded door-edge protectors
4. Push plates

Door frame protection is available in thermoformed profiles to fit many wood or metal door frame configurations. There is also a two-component system for door frames similar to corner guard and bumper rail systems. This will give maximum impact protection for door frames in highly vulnerable locations.

Maintenance

PVC, vinyl and rubber are easily cleaned with detergent solutions and with standard commercial cleaners. In the two-component systems, if the vinyl is ever damaged beyond use it can be popped out and replaced without replacing the entire product. Although a new piece of PVC is needed, little labor is involved.

Installation

Of primary concern to the designer is the installation height of horizontal wall guards. A handrail or combination bumper/handrail is typically required to be mounted at about 34 inches above the floor so that it functions properly to support people. Whether this height protects the wall is dependent on the particular equipment used in the building.

About the only way to determine the mounting height for a bumper rail is to inventory existing equipment and planned new equipment, paying special attention to the height of protrusions that will hit the wall. Once this inventory is done, the particular best combination of wall finish and wall guards can be determined, along with the best size and the extension from the wall.

Needs may differ throughout the facility according to equipment, function of area and the people using the area. By analyzing these three aspects, initial installation, maintenance and replacement costs can be balanced. For some corridors, a system incorporating a heavy-duty wall covering, corner guards and two horizontal wall guards may be the only answer to constant replacement. In other locations, an appropriate coating or vinyl wall covering and medium-duty corner guards are all that is needed.

Specification Notes

In the selection of a system, the following are items to note.

Corner Guards

1. Are all the necessary angles available?
2. On flush mounted, is provision made to extend the base mold over the retainer if this is desired?
3. On surface mounted, do end cap colors match guard colors if this is desired?
4. Is the endwall configuration suitable; two corner guards can be used or some manufacturers provide flush-mounted continuous wrap-around corners for some wall thickness dimensions.

Horizontal Rails

1. Are end pieces and caps available in the desired color?
2. Is the form of the end configuration designed for safety?
3. Is the form of the handrail well contoured for grasping?
4. Is the mounting distance of the handrail from the wall sufficient?

Overall

1. Will the available colors be suitable? Most manufacturers provide a half dozen or so neutrals, including black. These may or may not blend with the building color scheme. A few manufacturers provide a number of pastel and bright hues.

Part III

WINDOW TREATMENT

Chapter Ten

INTRODUCTION TO WINDOW TREATMENT

WINDOWS integrate the interior of a building with the outside world. For people inside, they provide a pleasing visual escape. Daylight can enter buildings through windows. The warmth of the sun can also enter, as can fresh spring breezes when windows are operable. In addition to these salubrious effects, windows may allow glare, excessive summer heat and cold winter air to disrupt a carefully controlled environment. The hard glass may annoyingly reflect sound and privacy may be lost. Window treatment allows a degree of control on the effect of the window on the interior environment.

The interior environment of any space is generally affected by the external environment. In the case of window treatment, this influence is particularly strong. Window coverings are part of a larger window system. External conditions which influence the design of the window system are the orientation of the windows to the sun, the direction and strength of the prevailing winds and the existence of shade trees, buildings and windbreaks. Differences in conditions on various sides of the building may dictate different window treatments.

Differences in function of the space may also dictate different window treatments. For example, while treatment of all windows is important, special care should be given to the patient room window. The patient may be confined to the room as much as twenty-four hours a day. The window may be the major contact with the outside world. Even when confinement is less severe, it is important that the relationship between the bed and the window is such that the patient can see out, and glare and privacy can be easily controlled.

Components of Window Systems

The window, along with all adjacent controls, is a window system. The window system consists of:

1. Exterior appendages such as sunscreens, shutters and architectural projections.
2. Window framing components such as weather stripping, caulking, framing materials and operating controls.
3. Window glazing such as multiple, tinted and reflective sheets.
4. Interior window treatment such as drapery, blinds and shades and the associated hardware.

While the focus of this book is on interior finishes, a very brief discussion of the other elements of the system is relevant. Each has an influence on the choice of interior window treatment. It should be noted that the interior window treatment will also affect the exterior appearance of the building. **Close communication between the architect and the interior designer is essential in coordination of the total system.**

Exterior Appendages

Awnings and building or roof overhangs limit direct solar radiation into the interior. These can be designed to shade the windows only at certain times of year, keeping out the hot summer rays and allowing their penetration in winter. Shades of fiberglass or PVC designed for the outside of the building are efficient solar filters. These can be automatically controlled or manually controlled from the interior. When exterior shading devices are used, interior control of solar radiation is less critical.

Window Framing Components

An essential function of the framing components is to provide a tight seal against air leakage. A snug seal allows greater flexibility in the design of the window treatment.

With operable windows, the direction that the window opens and the way the hardware protrudes will affect the type of window treatment. Tracks for the window covering must not interfere with window operation. Draperies and blinds must clear the window in their open position. The window covering location must be compatible with cranks and other opening devices.

Window Glazing

Double- and triple-glazed windows are much more effective insulators than single-glazed windows. They are almost always worth the extra cost.

Tinted glass, reflective glass and various films are often used to lessen entry of solar radiation into the interior. However, they do not provide the flexibility that allows this same solar radiation to enter when it is beneficial for heating and daylighting. Well-designed window coverings do provide this flexibility.

Double-glazed windows with blinds sandwiched between are manufactured. These provide control of solar radiation and the blinds remain clean as claimed. However, many institutions using them report undue maintenance problems.

Interior Window Treatment

Commonly used window treatments are draperies, horizontal blinds, vertical blinds and shades. These will be discussed in Chapters Eleven and Twelve. Prior to discussing specific window treatment, it is appropriate to consider the health and safety, environmental and wear-life factors of window treatment.

Health and Safety Factors

The primary health and safety concern with window treatment is flammability. Another concern is the ability of the user, who may be infirm or handicapped, to control the positioning of the window covering.

Flammability

Flammability codes in use vary considerably from one jurisdiction to another, as do the testing methods and the required degree of flame resistance. It is imperative that the specifier know the codes specific to the building location. Most regulatory bodies will require approval of any flame retardant to be used, a certificate of flame resistance and a sample of drapery fabric to be used. While most flammability codes address all types of window treatment, the greatest concern is with drapery. (See Chapter Eleven "Drapery" for more detailed code information.)

The following terminology must be understood in order to understand the fire codes. Definitions are based on ASTM D 123-85, Standard Terminology Relating to Textiles.

Flame Resistance: The property of a material whereby flaming combustion is prevented, terminated or inhibited following application of a source of ignition. Flame resistance can be an inherent property of the basic material or product, or it can be imparted by specific treatment.

Flame Resistant: The government-mandated description for certain products that meet established governmental conformance standards on specifications when the product is tested by a specific method.

Flame-Resistant Fabric: (1) A fabric whose fiber content or topical finish makes it difficult to ignite and slow to burn. (2) A fabric treated with a flame-retardant finish to meet code standards for flame resistance.

Flame Retardant: A chemical applied to fiber, yarn or fabric to impart flame resistance. This term should not be used as an adjective except in the terms "flame-retardant treated" or "flame-retardant treatment."

Flame-Retardant Treatment: A process for incorporating or adding flame retardant(s) to a material or product. The term flame-retardant treatment does not apply to fabrics that are inherently flame resistant.

Control of Positioning

For effective control of the environment, the user must be able to control the position of any window covering. Window coverings are designed with control mechanisms in the proper place for typical window locations and the average user. Health care facility users are often not average, and care must be taken to insure that the controls can be easily reached and operated with minimal effort.

Automated control systems for opening and closing draperies for patient rooms if the budget permits, can be located in the bedside table, overbed table or a control paddle on the bedrail or pillow.

Environmental Factors

Window treatment is often erroneously viewed as only an aesthetic element in an interior environment. Used in conjunction with other components of the system, the primary purpose is control; that is, to control light, temperature, acoustics and privacy.

Light Control

The degree of light control required in a space is dependent upon any exterior shading devices, orientation of the space to the sun and the function of the space.

In a northern exposure, little light control may be needed. Southern, western or eastern exposures will have much more variability in the amount of light entering, both throughout the day and during different seasons. For these exposures, over-bright light and glare must be controlled. Glare coming from light sources can be direct, or it can be indirect, bouncing off interior reflective surfaces.

The function and surface finishes of the space determine the degree of control needed for quantity of light and for glare.

A space used for audiovisual presentations should be able to be completely darkened. In fact, a space primarily devoted to this use might best be located in the central portion of the building. A space equipped with video display terminals (VDTs) requires the utmost in glare control. As computers become more and more abundant in health care work, the problems of screen reflections and poor contrast will affect more and more people. A combination of filtered daylight along with proper selection and careful location of electric lighting fixtures must be carefully coordinated.

A space with dark surface finishes may require an abundance of light, while a space with light surface finishes may be adequately lit with much less light. Shiny finishes will contribute to glare, while matte finishes will help mitigate glare problems.

Temperature Control

Temperature control is directly related to energy conservation. The more effectively passive controls such as interior window coverings can be used, the less energy will be needed to maintain optimal temperatures for human comfort.

John I. Yellot, professor at Arizona State University, explored combinations of glass and shading materials to find which would be most effective in controlling undesirable solar radiation in buildings, yet provide the best illumination. "Yellot and his colleagues found that double clear glazing in combination with a tighly woven white shade on tracks offer the best all around, all season performance. Venetian blinds, and some tightly woven, white or light colored draperies offer good alternatives to shades."*

In accordance with the laws of physics, heat energy flows by: (1) conduction, (2) convection and (3) radiation. Significant amounts are transmitted through the window system in each of these ways. Techniques to control interior temperatures must address all three methods of heat flow. **In general, the higher the insulating properties, the tighter the fit; and the lighter the color of the window treatment, the more energy conserved.**

---

*Zoehrer, Richard. "Energy Efficiency Can Be Improved With Good Window Management." *Contract Magazine*, December, 1980, p. 68.

CONDUCTION. In considering conduction, or the transmission of heat by a conductive material, the main principle is to insulate the interior from the adverse exterior temperatures. The transfer of heat by conduction will be diminished by using materials that resist conduction. The measure of thermal resistance is the R-value. The higher the R-value, the more resistant the material.

The opposite of R is C, thermal conductance. Metals conduct heat readily. They have a high C-value and a low R-value. Glass conducts heat less readily and plastics still less readily. Foam-like synthetics such as polystyrene foam as well as fibrous minerals such as fiberglass conduct it very poorly; these materials have a high R-value and are effectively used as insulators.

However, heat savings do not increase in direct proportion to the R-value. Rather, the relationship can be described by a curve as illustraed in Figure 10.1. The most significant savings would be gained by using a window covering with a R-value of 2 or 3. Anything beyond 4 or 5 would probably not be worth the additional cost of the material, as the incremental heat savings are small.

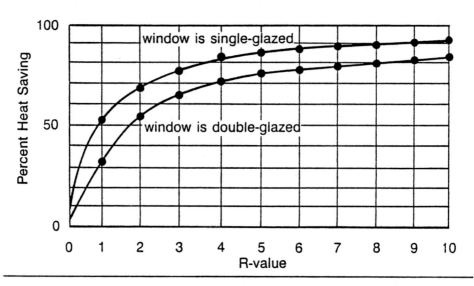

Figure 10.1. PERCENT OF SAVINGS VERSUS R-VALUE. The figure illustrates the percent of heat saving achieved on a cold night in winter by application of a thermal shutter, of a given R-value, to a double-glazed or single-glazed window that is airtight. An outdoor wind speed of twelve miles per hour is assumed. (Adapted from William Shurcliff, *Thermal Shutters and Shades*, p. 28. Printed with permission of Brick House Publishing Company, Andover, MA.)

R-values are good indicators but should not be taken overly seriously. The manufacturer's listed R-value is meaningful and probably reliable. However, it is that of the material only, assuming an infinite sheet of material. The effective R-value of the material should be evaluated within the context of the entire window system, not for the material alone.

When not moving, air is a good insulator. Many good insulating materials are based on the principle of containment of numerous small pockets of air, for example, building insulation materials based on polystyrene foam or fiberglass batts. The use of several layers of material with layers of still air between can also effectively increase the accumulated R-value of the materials. Quilted shades and lined draperies take advantage of this principle as does double glazing.

There is also a layer of air between the glazing and the window covering which can act as an insulator if the air is still. Moving or circulating air will have the opposite effect and effectively decrease the R-value. This moving air is discussed under "Convection."

CONVECTION. In considering convection, or the transmission of heat by moving air, the key points are: first, protect against air leakage through the system during periods of heating and cooling; and second,

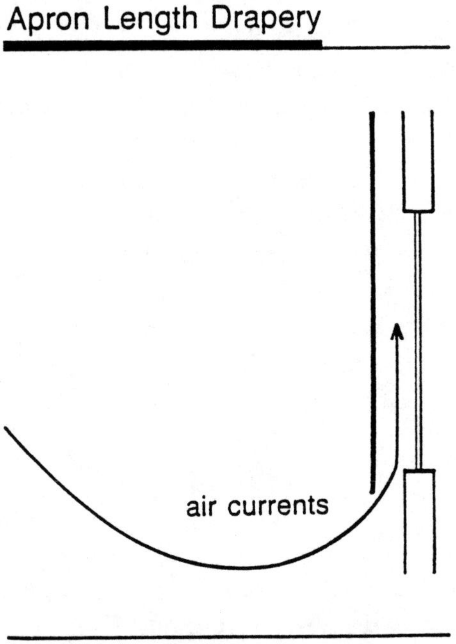

Apron Length Drapery

air currents

Figure 10.2. CONVECTION AT THE WINDOW. Air circulation occurs readily when there is a gap greater than one-half inch between the glazing and the window covering. This condition always exists with apron-length drapery and may also exist with other drapery lengths.

protect against air circulation between the glazing and the window covering, especially during heating periods.

Any gaps or cracks in the window system such as at the mullions, sash or frame joints will allow air flow from outside to inside, or vice versa. To prevent this, the window must be tightly sealed. This is best accomplished within the framing and glazing portion of the window system but can also be affected by a good seal between wall or frame and window covering. Unless the window system is fairly well sealed, heat loss by air leakage can exceed that lost by conduction.

In addition to air flow through the system, air circulation can occur within the system. As mentioned previously, there is a layer between the glazing and the window covering that may act as an insulator if the air is still. Distance is also a factor. When the distance between the glass and the covering is less than one-half-inch thick, little air circulation will occur. When the distance between the glass and the covering is greater than one-half-inch thick, convection or movement of air occurs readily. Thus, a shade next to the window may be more effective than a drapery farther from the window.

When the distance is over one-half inch, edge seals can be used to lessen convection currents. In fact, with a well-constructed, tightly sealed window, the edge seal need not even be tight. A gap of one-quarter inch or less will not generate adverse air circulation.

RADIATION. In considering radiation, the main principle is to keep out solar radiation in the summer and to let in solar radiation in the winter. In the winter, it is also important to keep within the room the radiant heat energy emitted from objects and people.

Radiant heat energy is transferred in three ways: (1) transmittance, (2) absorption and (3) reflection. Any material put between the rays of the sun and the interior environment will transmit some of the energy, absorb some and reflect some. It will also transmit, absorb and reflect energy radiated from objects and people in the interior.

Clear glazing will transmit a very large proportion of radiant energy. This effect is beneficial in bringing the heat of the winter sun into the interior. It also means easy entry of summer heat and dissipation of interior heat on winter nights.

An opaque black fabric will absorb a very large proportion of radiant energy. This in turn will both radiate and conduct heat; the process be-

Solar Radiation

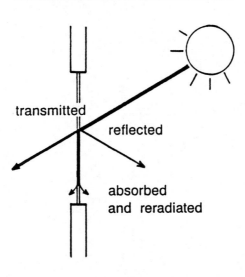

transmitted

reflected

absorbed
and reradiated

Figure 10.3. TRANSMITTANCE, ABSORPTION AND REFLECTION. Radiant heat energy is transferred in three ways. The characteristics of the surface receiving the radiant energy determine the percentage that is transmitted, absorbed or reflected. Clear glazing will transmit a very large proportion.

comes quite complex. On a sunny day, the combination of black fabric and glazed windows with little air circulation between can cause a heat buildup so great that the glass becomes excessively hot. If it lacks sufficient expansion space, it may crack.

A white material will reflect much of the radiation, preserving heat on the side of the barrier from which it originates. A shiny sheet of aluminum or metallized fabric will reflect even more. The metal also has a low emissivity which enhances the R-value of a layer of still air next to it.

Emissivity refers to the property of all materials to emit radiant energy. The hotter the object and the blacker the object, the more energy is emitted. Mirror-like objects emit very little. The lower the emissity of a material, the higher its R-value. A sheet of polished aluminum combined with a layer of still air has a thermal resistance comparable to a one-half-inch sheet of Styrofoam™ and the adjoining still air.

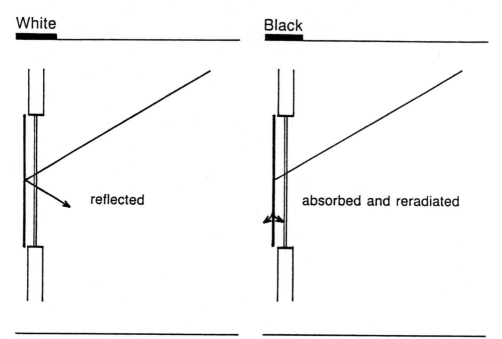

Figure 10.4. EFFECTS OF WHITE OR BLACK WINDOW TREATMENT. An opaque white fabric will reflect a large proportion of radiant energy, preserving the differential between hot and cold spaces. An opaque black fabric will absorb a large proportion of radiant energy. This is, in turn, re-radiated and can cause a heat buildup between window covering and glazing. With enough heat, window breakage can result.

Acoustical Control

As with radiant heat, sound is also transmitted, absorbed and reflected. Soft porous materials absorb sound; hard non-porous materials reflect it. Window glass is a hard reflective surface. Sounds reflect off the glass and back into the space. There is little problem when window areas are small. When glazed areas are large, a space can be unacceptably noisy due to this reflected sound.

Privacy Control

One of the most cherished advantages of windows is the visual access to environments beyond our immediate one. However, there are times when visual privacy is either necessary or desirable. The desire for a view may conflict with the need or desire to be unobserved. Obviously, window coverings can provide the occupant of a space with a choice for openness or privacy.

Conflicts of Control Properties

The reasons for window-covering selection may conflict. For example, north light produces little interior glare and is an ideal working light. But admitting the north light in winter may also admit a prevailing, cold, north wind. Or in another example, a large window may allow a beautiful view but cause a distracting sound level. The conflicts are almost limitless. The designer must find the window system that will resolve the conflicts in the optimal way.

HVAC System

Window treatment systems and HVAC (heating, ventilating and air conditioning) systems must work together to control the thermal climate of the building. They must also be located so as to be physically complementary. HVAC units are generally located on exterior walls next to glazed areas. Window treatment is, obviously, also located on exterior glazed walls. The potential for conflict has been realized on all too many buildings where coordination did not take place during an early phase of the design.

Wear-Life Factors

In addition to considering the various components of the window system and the control functions, the specifier must consider the wear-life requirements of the potential window covering. Primary among these are durability, ease of maintenance and cost effectiveness.

Durability

Window treatments are not walked upon like flooring, sat upon like chairs or spilled upon like tables. However, there are three main ways they can be damaged. **Solar radiation** is the primary destructive force; it weakens many fibers. **Moisture** is another enemy. Materials used in window coverings must be dimensionally stable to withstand the moisture condensation at the window. Condensation is particularly troublesome on older metal windows. The third enemy is abrasion. **Abrasion** of fibers can be a problem, because window coverings are constantly being opened and closed.

Appearance Retention

Two of the properties most important to durability are also important to appearance retention: resistance to solar radiation and resistance to moisture. Solar radiation fades many dyes. Staining elements are dissolved in moisture taken in by drapery fibers. When the moisture evaporates, stains remain.

Maintenance Factors

Any system that is not properly maintained will lose functional effectiveness and become shabby in appearance. Maintenance is closely associated with wear life. Without proper maintenance, durability and appearance-retention properties will not reach their full potential.

The window system must be designed so the owner can properly clean and repair it. Special requirements of the various window treatment alternatives must be considered. For some products special equipment must be used or special techniques employed. For example, fiberglass drapery requires a dedicated washing machine, because glass particles remaining in the machine can become embedded in fabrics washed in later loads. Textiles made of synthetic fibers must be washed in water with a temperature below 120° F. If cleaning is to be contracted out, this should be a decision and not a surprise. Vertical blinds are easier to maintain than horizontal blinds, as one blade can be replaced without disassembling the blind. They are also easier to keep clean as dust does not collect on them as it does on horizontal blinds.

Cost Effectiveness

Cost effectiveness does not necessarily mean a low initial cost. Total life cost of a material and its installation must be evaluated. This includes the cost to maintain it and replace it at the end of its useful wear life. It also includes the cost effect on other systems and on people. The following are important total life components:

1. Initial cost
2. Maintenance costs, including housekeeping and maintenance
3. Replacement period and costs
4. Energy costs; lighting and HVAC
5. Staff efficiency
6. Patient comfort

In a comparison of initial costs, mid-range vertical blinds and draperies are about equal. Standard horizontal blinds can be as much as 60 to 70 percent less costly.

Organization of Chapters on Window Treatment

Each building interior has a set of situations which need to be resolved in the best possible way. The next two chapters discuss specific window-covering choices and the information needed to evaluate them. The information is organized under the following headings: structure and properties, health and safety, types, fabrication (for drapery only), maintenance, installation, and specification notes.

Structure and Properties

The materials used in window treatment determine the performance of the end product, as does the type of treatment: draperies, blinds or shades. Understanding what can be expected of each type, fabricated in specific materials, will help to answer the critical questions.

Health and Safety

With each material used, there are associated questions of health and safety. While these are a part of structure and properties, in health care health and safety merit special attention.

Types

In window treatment, type is an indication of the manner in which the covering is drawn across the window. Of all the properties, type would most strongly affect the environmental-control properties and the ambience of the space.

For draperies, there are two sections on types: one for drapery and one for track.

Fabrication

The information required for drapery differs in one way from all the finishes previously discussed: Drapery is not fabricated at the manufacturing plant. Rather, material is ordered which is then fabricated by a drapery house in accordance with the designer's fabrication specifications. Therefore, an additional section on fabrication is included in Chapter Eleven, "Drapery."

Maintenance

In evaluating any finish, it is essential to understand the equipment and labor that will be needed to maintain it. The cost of these will profoundly affect the total cost of the product. It must be added to the initial cost to make a valid assessment of the lifetime cost.

Installation

First, it must be stated that this section is not a complete guide to installation. Most manufacturers of drapery track, blinds and shades give excellent instructions for the mounting of their own products. These instructions are typically found in the manufacturer's literature. Instead, the information given here is intended to help in evaluating what type of installation will be most appropriate for the space, problems that may arise with certain types of installations, and other key points that may assist in material product selection.

Specification Notes

This is not a complete guide to specification. Rather, it identifies sources for complete specification guides and notes some special points that are often not given the attention they deserve. It also identifies some details and refinements that are often overlooked.

Chapter Eleven

DRAPERY

D RAPERY is frequently selected as a window treatment because of its softening effect and because many people associate it with the comfort of home. These characteristics make it especially appropriate for patient rooms in hospitals and rooms in nursing homes. The textural qualities of drapery and the opportunity for pattern make it an element that can provide psychological warmth and comfort in a room that all too often appears cold and intimidating with its array of high-tech equipment. These qualities counteract the institutional atmosphere and provide a softening effect not only in the patient room but also in public areas such as lobbies and waiting rooms.

The properties of draperies are principally determined by the fiber from which they are made and the way these fibers are put together or woven. Thus, the major portion of information in the first section "Structure and Properties" is concerned with the fiber and the weave.

Structure and Properties

Properties of Fibers

One fiber or a blend of fibers can be used to construct the drapery fabric. Each fiber has its own characteristic properties which must be understood to specify the best fabric for the particular application. The fiber properties most important for the wear life of health care draperies are dimensional stability, resistance to light and heat, and abrasion resistance.

DIMENSIONAL STABILITY. This important factor in shape retention is a prime requirement for any fabric that hangs freely. The most noticeable changes in drapery length, both sagging and shrinking (sometimes called "hiking up"), are in response to changing humidity. The effects of changes in humidity are resisted by non-water-absorbing or hydrophobic fibers such as polyester and fiberglass. These moisture-resistant fibers tend to be dimensionally stable and the drapery maintains its shape. Moisture resistance of fibers also helps prevent staining, as water-soluble staining materials are not absorbed into the fibers to be deposited when water evaporates.

In addition to the fiber, the construction is important to dimensional stability. This will be discussed in the section about weaves. The longer the drapery, the more important dimensional stability becomes.

RESISTANCE TO LIGHT AND HEAT. Drapery fabrics are exposed to massive doses of solar radiation. Temperatures as high as 300° F can occur between fabric and window glass. This solar radiation is the cause of the disintegration of fabrics, sometimes known as sun rot. Both light and heat can cause sun rot. They also cause fading which, while it does not destroy the material, will certainly destroy the appearance. Fabrics in southern and western exposures are most vulnerable to this problem. The effects of solar radiation can be diminished by using sun-resistant fibers and dyes. They can also be lessened by using linings, blinds or shades in conjunction with draperies.

ABRASION RESISTANCE. In order to perform its control functions, a drapery is constantly being opened and closed. As it is drawn, it may rub against protrusions from the window and abrasion may occur. Fiberglass, a fiber sometimes specified for institutional draperies, is particularly vulnerable to abrasion. If fiberglass is to be used for draperies, it is imperative that nothing rub against the drapery as it is drawn. The wear life can be considerably shortened because of lack of abrasion resistance.

Classification of Fibers

Fibers can be broadly classified as natural or man-made. Natural fibers are produced from inherently fibrous materials found in nature. Plants furnish cellulosic fibers. Animals are the source of protein fibers.

To make man-made fibers, a chemical solution is forced through a spinneret to produce single or multiple filaments. These filaments are conditioned in various ways as described for nylon in Chapter Two, "Carpet." They may be crimped and twisted for resilience, bulked for loft, or texturized. Man-made fibers can be grouped as regenerated cellulosics, synthetic long-chain polymers and mineral fibers.

These categories are shown in Table 11-1 with some of the more familiar fibers in each.

Table 11.1

CLASSIFICATION OF FIBERS

Natural Fibers		Man-made Fibers		
Cellulosic	**Protein**	**Regenerated Cellulosic**	**Synthetic**	**Mineral**
Cotton	Wool	Rayon	Nylon	*Fiberglass
Linen	Silk	Acetate	Olefin	
		Triacetate	Saran	
			Acrylic	
			*Modacrylic	
			*Polyester	

*indicates the fibers used most often for draperies for health care use.

A drapery fabric made totally of natural fibers is not recommended for health care use. However, natural fibers are sometimes used in blends for fabrics that are suitable. Because of this, it may be useful to briefly discuss their properties.

Fibers for health care draperies are found in two of the man-made fiber classifications. Fiberglass, a mineral fiber, is often used. Modacrylic and polyester are the synthetics commonly used.

CELLULOSIC FIBERS: Cotton has relatively good tensile strength and abrasion resistance. It is absorbent and can be dyed easily in a wide variety of saturated and subdued colors. It is also receptive to many chemical and additive-type finishes, including flame retardants. Cotton is not inherently flame resistant and in order to be used must be treated with flame-retardant chemicals. Because of its high absorption ability, dimensional stability is poor. Cotton is degraded by sunlight.

Linen fibers are obtained from the flax plant. They may be identified on the label as either flax or linen. Linen fibers lack resilience and are subject to abrasion. They have a limited capacity to accept dyes. In common with other cellulosic fibers, they are not flame resistant. However, the fibers are resistant to sunlight, firm in body and interestingly slubbed in texture. They also give body to a fabric when used in combination with other fibers. They are often used in small proportions such as 10 percent of the fiber content to give a special texture and hand to drapery fabrics.

PROTEIN FIBERS: Wool is exceptionally resilient and has fine draping qualities. It is resistant to soil and has good soil-releasing properties during cleaning. It is highly absorbent and has an excellent affinity for dyes. Insulating qualities for both thermal and acoustic control are excellent. It is also inherently flame resistant. A severe limitation of wool fabrics is their tendency to shrink and sag. The high absorption rate that contributes to affinity for dyestuffs also contributes to dimensional instability. Compared to most fibers, wool is relatively expensive.

Silks can be readily dyed in brilliant shades. They are luxurious in appearance and feel. They are also very expensive. Fabrics of silk are luxury fabrics used for very special applications. When used, they must be protected from bright sunlight, as their solar resistance is poor. Both lining and interlining are advisable when using silk.

REGENERATED CELLULOSIC FIBERS: These fibers are extracted from woody vegetable material. Rayon, acetate and triacetate are examples. They are little used in contract design work, as they will not tolerate the wear and tear of commercial and institutional installations. Because of their low cost, they are sometimes used in combination with other fibers.

MINERAL FIBERS: These are extruded directly from natural mineral solutions. Only one of these, fiberglass, is commonly used in the manufacture of textiles. Fiberglass is important in health care drapery fabrics and will be discussed further in the following section on "Fibers for Health Care Draperies."

SYNTHETIC LONG-CHAIN POLYMER FIBERS: Synthesized primarily from petrochemicals, these are chains of like molecules linked end to end. In general, they are thermoplastic, non-absorbent, smooth, non-porous, non-allergenic and impervious to moths and mildew. Improvements are continuously being made in the synthetic fibers. Modifications constantly improve both appearance and performance.

Synthetic long-chain polymers commonly used in fabrics are nylon, olefin (polypropylene), saran, acrylic, modacrylic and polyester. Of these, only modacrylic and polyester are extensively used in drapery for health care facilities. Before discussing these, a brief statement about other synthetics may be helpful.

1. Nylon is highly susceptible to sun rot and to fading upon exposure to the sun.
2. Olefin is low cost but hard to dye, heat sensitive and tends to pill.
3. Saran is light resistant and colorfast, soil and flame resistant; it has good properties but is heat sensitive, very heavy and used mostly in blends.
4. Acrylic can be given loft and bulk to look like wool, but it is not inherently flame resistant and the use of flame-retardant chemicals on acrylics has not yet been successful.

Fibers for Health Care Draperies

In order to be considered as suitable for health care use, a fiber for drapery must have the wear-life factors of dimensional stability and light resistance. Abrasion resistance is also important. The health and safety factor, flame resistance, is mandatory. The properties deemed essential for health care draperies are found in modacrylic and polyester fibers and, except for abrasion resistance, in fiberglass fibers. Each has several other advantageous properties and, inevitably, some limitations. Once fibers are selected that meet the essential criteria, investigation of other properties can commence.

MODACRYLIC: Modacrylic is a modified acrylic with most of the positive properties of acrylic plus flame resistance and better light resistance. It can be given a high bulk, making it a good thermal and acoustic insulator. Modacrylics are usually about 70 percent of a fabric's content, permitting 30 percent to be blends of other yarns such as linen, rayon, acetate or saran. Even with 30 percent non-flame-resistant yarns, these fabrics can meet fire codes. Some trade names are Dynel®, Verel®, Leavil®, SEF®, Cojun® and Cordelan®.

Advantages
Light resistance
Dimensional stability
Flame resistance
Abrasion resistance sufficient for drapery
High tensile strength
Good resilience
Ability to have high bulk
Antistatic

Limitations
No significant limitations
Cannot be laundered in hot water

POLYESTER FR: Polyester FR (flame resistant) is the version of polyester used in institutional drapery. It is used extensively, especially when a smooth, tightly woven fabric is desired. It has good dye affinity, providing an opportunity for bright and intense colors. Its smoothness and good dye affinity make it an excellent print cloth.

Polyester is frequently used as a blend with cotton. Because of its poor dimensional stability, cotton is risky to use in buildings with in-wall air conditioners. With central air conditioning, humidity control is better. Polyester is a fiber often used for cubicle curtains as is a polyester and cotton blend. Some trade names are Dacron®, Fortrel®, Kodel® and Trevira®.

Advantages

Light resistance
Dimensional stability
Flame resistance
Abrasion resistance
Superior resistance to rot
Permanent body
Wrinkle resistance
Good dye affinity
Good draping quality

Limitations

Spun yarns tend to pill
Stains (oil-based) are hard to remove
Collects static electricity
Cannot be laundered in hot water

FIBERGLASS: Fiberglass is the mineral fiber important in drapery fabrics. It is the most stable yarn made. It will not swell or shrink even with great humidity changes. It is a good insulator and will not rot or fade even in the strongest sunlight. It will pass all fire codes; in fact, it is fireproof and will not burn at all. In addition, it is a low-cost fiber.

Except for a serious susceptibility to abrasion, the performance characteristics of fiberglass are excellent. It is in aesthetics that fiberglass falls short. Colors are limited and deep colors are impossible to obtain. Texture and sheen are also limited and draping qualities are poor. Advances in technology continue to lessen these visual limitations.

The enemy of fiberglass is abrasion. The yarn will eventually break if the drapery rubs against rough surfaces at a window or if the fabric is washed in an overloaded washing machine or one with vigorous agitation. Fibers also tend to abrade during drapery fabrication. Some trade names are Beta®, Fiberglas®, and PPG®.

Advantages

Light resistance
Dimensional stability
Flameproof
Low cost
Good insulator

Limitations

Low abrasion resistance
Special equipment needed for laundering
Poor draping qualities
Limited color selection

Properties of Weaves

Weaves are also important to the properties of the fabric. While there are other types of construction used for drapery fabrics, weaving is by far the most common. Most of the following comments would hold true, in concept, for fabrics constructed by other means. Principle contributors to the effect of the weave are the degree of openness and the amount of bulk. Weaves are classified as open, semi-open and closed. They can be thin or bulky; this property is also determined by the bulk of the yarn. Weaves affect light transmittance, privacy, heat conductance, acoustics, dimensional stability, slippage and appearance.

LIGHT TRANSMITTANCE: The more open the weave and the thinner the fabric, the more light is transmitted.

PRIVACY: The greatest privacy is achieved when the fabric is tightly woven of opaque yarns. Obtaining visual privacy may well conflict with other needs such as maximum light transmittance.

HEAT CONDUCTANCE: The least heat is conducted when a high bulk yarn is used in a weave that incorporates many small air spaces in a thick or bulky fabric.

ACOUSTICS: For absorbing sound, one of the best materials is a fabric with lofty yarns separated by noticeable air spaces. These are the same qualities as those for good heat insulation.

DIMENSIONAL STABILITY: Loosely constructed fabrics are likely to sag more than tightly constructed ones. A balanced cloth (weight of warp yarns equals weight of horizontal filling yarns) or one with a heavier warp than filling will tend to be stable. If filling yarns are heavier than warp yarns, sagging can be a problem. In some loosely constructed fabrics, a "net" of very thin translucent yarns is used to stabilize the fabric.

SLIPPAGE: This is a fabric fault caused by warp and weft or filling yarns sliding over each other. Slippage will cause unevenness in the color and texture of the fabric. It is prevalent in loosely woven fabrics. Slip resistance is essential for casements.

Open and loosely woven yarn benefits from some types of stabilization such as leno weave or malimo construction. Leno is a variation of plain weave (see Chapter Fourteen for weave types), where pairs of warp cross between insertions of filling yarns. A malimo construction is one in which stitching yarns knit the weft onto the warp. Solar Loc® is a popular malimo fabric. Slippage is also alleviated by the use of a fuzzy or rough yarn.

Leno

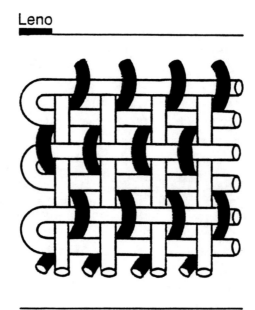

Figure 11.1. LENO CONSTRUCTION. Leno is a fabric construction in which warp ends are twisted between insertions of filling yarns. Slippage in loosely woven fabrics can be minimized by using leno construction.

APPEARANCE: Besides their functional importance, weaves have great visual impact. Drapery fabrics should always be held up to the window during evaluation. Appearance at the window is substantially different from that of the fabric lying on an opaque surface.

Health and Safety

Flammability

While most health care installations must meet a defined flame-resistance rating, the specifics of the codes vary considerably from one regulatory district to another. In some instances, where requirements are quite liberal, the conscientious designer may specify a fabric that exceeds the local flame-resistant requirements. This both benefits patient safety and insures against the day when regulations become more strict. There is a sufficient variety of flame-resistant fabrics available to make it a foolish risk not to specify one of these.

For drapery fabrics, NFPA-701 (National Fire Prevention Association), Vertical Flame Test is the required test standard under the Life Safety Code. This test has two basic parts: afterflame and char length. Afterflame is the amount of time, measured in seconds, that it takes a fabric to self-extinguish after being exposed to a flame. Char length, measured in inches, is the length of fabric charred by the flame.

Regulatory districts may or may not use the NFPA-701 Vertical Flame Test. In lieu of, or in addition to, this standard, they may use their own test or one devised by another regulatory district. The most frequently quoted standards are those of the cities of Boston and New York and the state of California. Discussion of these codes is found in Chapter Thirteen, "Introduction to Upholstery Fabrics."

Fibers can be inherently flame resistant or can be made flame resistant with a flame retardant. Inherently flame-resistant fibers are modacrylic, polyester FR, saran and wool. Fiberglass is flameproof.

If it is desired to treat fabric with flame retardant, samples should be tested first. Properties such as the color, texture, absorption and degree of stiffness may be affected by the chemical additives. Significant differences in the draping qualities of the fabric may result. However, many fabrics can be successfully treated. It is incumbent on the designer to be certain.

Control of Positioning

Bright light and glare can be disorienting to the elderly, especially to those with cataracts. If the control functions of drapery, especially that of light control, are to be fully realized, the individual must be able to adjust the drapery.

Unless attention is given to location and height, the control can be difficult for the elderly or handicapped to operate. It should be low enough for persons in wheelchairs and easily found and reached by all. Specification of the proper length of the baton for hand-traversed drapery is often overlooked.

Skin Irritation

As noted earlier, fiberglass is very susceptible to abrasion. The tiny glass particles that break off are irritating to the skin. Some people are more sensitive than others to this irritant. Especially sensitive persons experience severe itching and reddening of the skin. This can be a problem in the drapery workroom, and some workrooms charge extra to fabricate fiberglass draperies.

The abraded particles are seldom a problem in the building, itself, as long as dedicated laundry facilities are maintained. Patients and staff seldom handle draperies for more than a moment, but if draperies are laundered with other fabrics such as sheets, the glass particles become embedded in the other fabrics and can cause severe irritation.

Types of Drapery Systems

Two main types of fabrication systems are used for pleated draperies; these are the pinch pleat system and the snap tape system. Each must be coordinated with the appropriate track system. There is also a third system, Paneltrac®, manufactured by Kirsch, which utilizes flat, unpleated lengths of fabric. Each type of drapery can be made in three basic lengths: floor, sill and apron (below sill). Each can be lined or unlined.

Pinch Pleat System

Pinch pleating is the traditional fabrication method. Each pleat is attached to the drapery track with a hook that has been inserted in the drapery heading. The pleats can be stitched or a pleater tape can be applied to the heading and special hooks inserted in the tape to form the pleats. The stitching means more time in initial fabrication but less time for the first and subsequent hanging, as the special hooks are time consuming to insert. Stitched pleats are crisper than pleats formed with pleater tape.

A pinch-pleated system requires more stacking room at the sides of the windows than any of the snap tape systems.

Snap Tape Systems

Snap tape systems require less stacking room and may be easier to maintain, since pins do not need to be removed and reinserted when draperies are taken down for cleaning. The snap tape systems which do not have stitched pleats are more quickly fabricated. For those systems which lay flat when removed from the track, both mending and cleaning are easier. These advantages make snap tape the system of choice for most health care use.

In this method of construction, a tape with snaps evenly placed along it is applied to the heading. The snaps are joined to their counterparts (snap carriers) on the track so that pleats are formed. The snapping can be time consuming. Also, some care must be used in taking down the drapery for cleaning so as not to rip the tape from the fabric.

There are three prevailing styles. These are listed below, along with the name applied to each by two major manufacturers.

Style	Kirsch	Graber
Stitched	Accordia-fold®	Stack Pleat®
Folded	Archifold®	Neat Pleat®
Rolled	Ripplefold®	Roll Fold®

Stitched

Accordia-fold   Stack Pleat

Folded

Archifold   Neat Pleat

Rolled

Ripplefold   Roll Fold

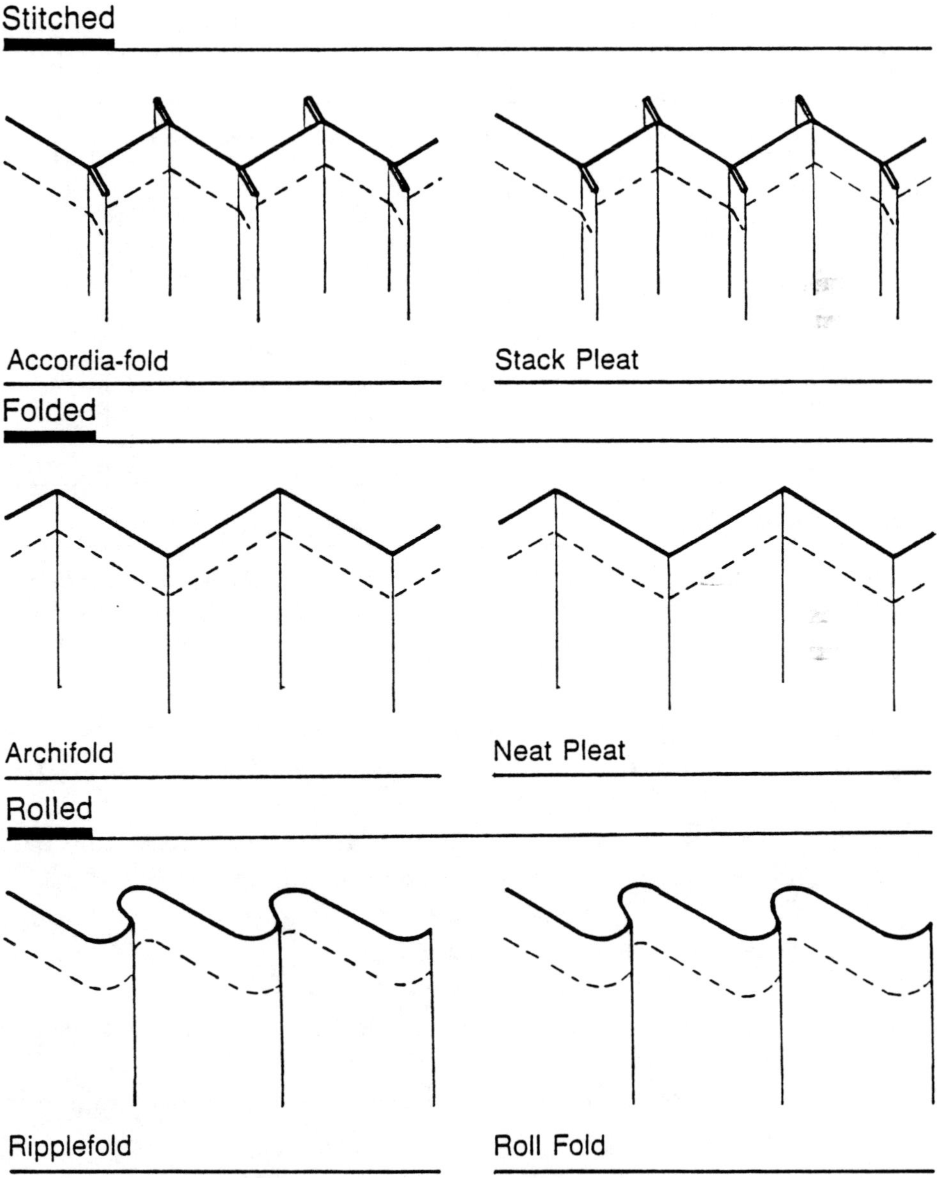

Figure 11.2. SNAP TAPE SYSTEMS. There are three prevailing styles of snap tape systems. An example of each as made by two major manufacturers is illustrated.

CHARACTERISTICS OF SNAP TAPE SYSTEMS: Certain constants are characteristic of all snap tape systems.

The drapery is suspended under the track; unless the track is recessed, it will be visible. This differs from the pinch pleat system where the track can be concealed or not when the drapey is drawn closed, depending on the way the system is specified.

Snap Tape Systems   Pinch Pleat Systems

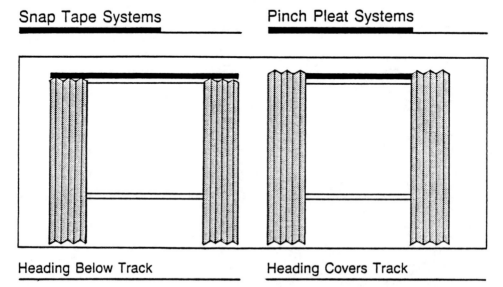

Heading Below Track   Heading Covers Track

Figure 11.3. RELATION OF DRAPERY HEADING TO TRACK. In each of the snap tape systems, the drapery is suspended below the track. In pinch pleat systems, the drapery is usually positioned in front of the track but may be suspended below the track if desired.

Different snap spacings are available so that pleat depth and width can vary. In general, closer spacing should be used for shorter drapery and lighter-weight fabrics.

The width needed for stacking to the side of the window will be dependent on the snap spacing selected and the number of pleats.

VARIATIONS IN SNAP TAPE SYSTEMS: Some variations that should be considered in the selection process are noted below.

Either a center overlap or a center butt closing is used. The overlap closing provides more control over air leaks, while the butt closing presents a more uniform overall appearance.

In two of the systems the drapery can be flat for cleaning, while in the third it cannot.

Overlap Closing

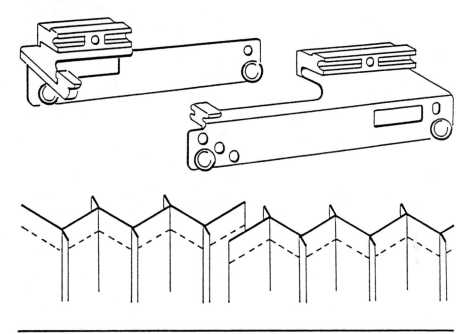

Butt Closing

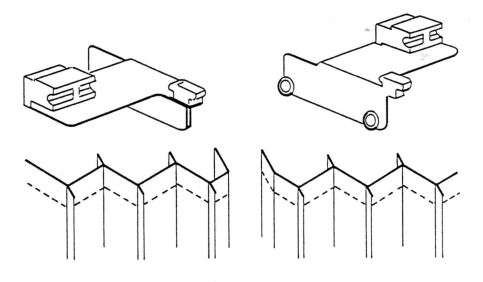

Figure 11.4. OVERLAP AND BUTT CLOSINGS. The overlap closing best controls air leaks, while the butt closing presents a more uniform overall appearance.

These variations occur as noted in the following brief descriptions

1. *Stitched style:* These have a stitching which emphasizes the pleats formed by the snap system. This can be advantageous with fabrics that have a soft body. Either an overlap or butt center closing can be used. In this style, the drapery does not lie flat when removed from the track.

2. *Folded style:* This pleating system presents a sharply tailored effect with a uniform exterior and interior appearance. The center closing is butt type. When removed from the track, the drapery will be flat for cleaning.

3. *Rolled style:* Rolled or rippled styles present a soft appearance which is the same on both exterior and interior. A butt-type center closing is used. The drapery will lie flat when removed from the track.

Paneltrac®

Paneltrac is a window treatment system manufactured by Kirsch. It consists of a multi-slotted track to which flat panels of fabric can be attached with Velcro®. The panel is fabricated just as any snap tape drapery panel, except Velcro is stitched to the top instead of some type of tape for pleating. A weight is inserted through the bottom hem for smooth hanging. There can be a substantial savings in the cost of fabric, as about half as much fabric is needed for this system as is needed for systems where pleating is used.

The panels can all be drawn to one side where they stack within the dimension of one panel, or they can be bi-parting and drawn to both sides of the window. The Paneltrac system provides a way to have a simple, clean-cut drapery solution. It is especially effective in contemporary rooms where it may be used as a very subtle window treatment.

It can also be used effectively when the window treatment is used as artwork, and it is not desirable to have it gathered in pleats at the side of the window. With Paneltrac, one panel will remain visible and flat at the side of the window when the drapery is drawn open. If the drapery is to be drawn fully off the window, the wall to the side of the window must be wide enough to accommodate the width of a panel.

Drapery Fullness

In general, drapery fullness should be greater for lightweight fabrics than for heavy fabrics and greater for shorter drapery than for long.

Fullness is expressed in percentage of fabric panel width to pleated drapery width. For 100 percent fullness, the width of the unpleated fab-

Track and Sliders

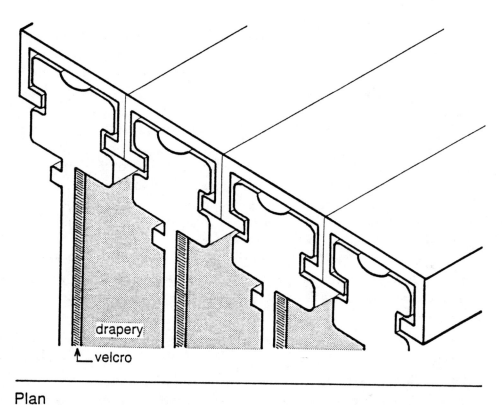

drapery

velcro

Plan

stacking space

stationary panel

One Way Draw

Figure 11.5. PANELS ON TRACK. The perspective section shows drapery attached to sliders with Velcro tape. The plan illustrates a one-way draw installation, with the track positioned so that drapery will cover the window. Track with drapery can be stacked to the right when window covering is not desired.

ric panel is two times the width of the pleated drapery. This is a suitable fullness for the mid range of fabric weight and length. Seventy percent fullness may be sufficient for heavy fabrics, and sheers may require 200 percent fullness (a fabric panel width three times the pleated drapery width).

Length of Drapery

Drapery can be specified as floor length, sill length, or as a specific distance below the sill (apron length).

FLOOR LENGTH: This is generally specified as one-half inch AFF (above finished floor). Any higher than this will encourage convection currents between glazing and fabric. However, a non-stable casement should be specified one inch AFF to prevent its dragging on the floor at times.

SILL LENGTH: The standard is one-half inch above the sill. Drapery just grazing the top of the sill is probably the best length for thermal control. However, it is an almost impossible length to obtain and maintain. Any shrinking or sagging will substantially change the gap, and most likely it will change it unevenly across the width of the drapery. The thermal advantages are lost and the visual appearance can be disastrous.

APRON LENGTH: This is the safest length in terms of visual appearance. A slight change in drapery length will not be apparent, but thermally it leaves a lot to be desired, as there is no way to control the air gap at the bottom.

Drapery Linings

Drapery linings have two main functions: (1) to protect the drapery fabric from the sun and (2) to contribute thermal control. Linings are also used where the appearance of the drapery fabric is not what is desired on the exterior of the building, such as with prints, or to give a consistent exterior appearance where a variety of drapery fabric is being used. A lining will change the opacity and light transmittance which may or may not be advantageous.

Lining fabrics used to protect drapery must have exceptional sun resistance. It is not cost effective to reline draperies, and rotted linings will be unsightly even if the drapery fabric is still good.

Any lining material will provide extra thermal control, as an insulating layer of still air is added between the lining and the drapery fabrics. Careful selection of the lining will mean still greater control. A white lining will reflect solar rays. Some linings are constructed of insulating materials. There are also linings of metallic fibers which give additional thermal control due to their low emissivity and high reflection value.

Drapery Fabrication

For proper drapery fabrication, instructions must be included in the specifications. Otherwise, bidders will each bid their own method, making it difficult to compare bids. In order to keep their prices low, bidders may plan to use fabrication shortcuts when methods are not specified. This can result in inferior quality.

Fabrication of the drapery is a sequential process as follows:

1. Goods are placed on a light table to check for defects in the fabric.
2. The fabric is cut, avoiding the occurrence of any defects in the drapery lengths. The proper hang of the finished drapery depends on square cuts, i.e. cutting along a weft or filling yarn of the fabric. The fabric must also be cut so that any pattern will match.
3. The selvedge is removed. Lengths of fabric are joined on the serger which also overcasts the edges.
4. A double four-inch hem is formed. This dimension may be less for sill length draperies, but good draping quality depends on a hem deep enough to weight the bottom. A blind stitch machine is used to fasten hems. On the highest quality draperies, hems are hand stitched. For lined draperies, the lining goes through this same process (steps 1 through 4).
5. For lined draperies, the lining is attached to the drapery fabric allowing for a 1" drapery fabric foldback on the lining side of the drapery. For unlined draperies, a blind stitch machine is used to fasten double 1 1/4" side hems.
6. The drapery is tabled to insure squareness and the length is adjusted from the top.
7. The heading is fabricated. For pinch pleats, a stiffening material is encased in the top heading after which the pleats are stitched. If tapes are used, the manufacturer's instructions should be followed. For Paneltrac systems, Velcro is stitched to the top.

Thread should match the color of the drapery fabric and must be compatible with the properties of the fabric. Monofilament nylon must not be used in areas exposed to sun; nylon disintegrates in the sun. It may be used for stitching pinch pleats.

There are at least two manufacturers, Ado and Gardisette, whose drapery textiles are made to be fabricated quite differently. The fabric is woven with a durable and flexible, covered lead weight along one edge. This edge becomes the bottom of the drapery, where it forms a very narrow weighted finish edge (no hem) that contributes to the even hanging of the drapery and is aesthetically crisp and clean.

Because the fabric is designed to be "railroaded," (hung with the warp direction parallel to the floor), the drapery can be very wide with no seams. This is especially advantageous with casement fabrics. Both manufacturers have available an extensive line ranging from airy casement to heavy drapery fabrics. Most of these are of fire-resistant polyester.

Draperies are fabricated by Ado and Gardisette with their own pleating systems or with a heading system designed for common snap-carrier track systems such as Graber Roll Fold or Kirsch Ripplefold.

Types of Track Systems

The selection of a track system must be coordinated with the drapery heading system, the method of operation, the visual appearance, the location and size of the window and the weight of the fabric. Each track system has limitations to the fabric weight it will support. These limitations are identified in the manufacturer's literature.

Shape and Function

Most track systems for contract drapery fall into three broad categories. All can be recessed or surface mounted in a ceiling installation or can be wall mounted.

DUAL-CHANNEL TRACK: Dual-channel aluminum track systems are generally used when a concealed raceway for traverse cords is required.

SINGLE-CHANNEL TRACK: Single-channel aluminum track systems are generally used when hand-traversed operation is required. Operation is via wand attached to the master carrier.

C-SHAPED TRACK: C-shaped steel drapery track systems can be used with either cord- or hand-traversed operation. They are generally restricted to drapery systems of pinch-pleated fabrication. The tracks tend to be less expensive than aluminum channel tracks.

Other Hardware

In addition to the track itself, master carriers for butt or overlap closing and direction of operation must be identified. Master carriers and snap carriers must be specified as slide or ball bearing. Ball-bearing carriers are used for large expanses and heavier fabrics. For cord-traversing systems, standard-duty or heavy-duty end pulleys must be selected. Heavy duty is recommended for all public and staff areas and for patient rooms. For hand-traversed systems, the baton length must be specified.

Draw Cord Systems

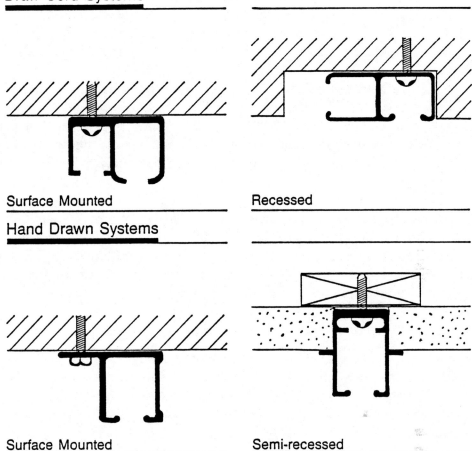

Surface Mounted   Recessed

Hand Drawn Systems

Surface Mounted   Semi-recessed

Figure 11.6. TYPICAL TRACK SECTIONS. Drapery track can be dual channel for concealed cord traverse or single channel for hand traverse. It can be surface mounted or recessed.

Maintenance

The specification of good quality track is important to the maintenance of drapery installations. Track maintenance consists mostly of replacement of small pieces of hardware that break and traverse cords that wear out. If these are properly specified, little track maintenance will be needed. Cords of braided polyester or nylon are abrasion resistant and wear well.

The major maintenance item is the cleaning of the drapery fabric. Each fabric has its own cleaning requirements. It is important that the building owner have cleaning instructions from the manufacturer of the fabric, especially when the fabric is a synthetic or fiberglass. Many laundry personnel are familiar with washing cotton fabrics and do not realize that the methods used to launder cotton can destroy fabrics of manmade fibers.

Synthetics can usually be washed or dry cleaned; the manufacturer's directions should be followed. When they are washed, low water temperatures, usually below 120° F, are mandatory. Hot water will permanently disfigure the fabric. Most synthetics will not require ironing; if light touching up is desired, pressing must be done at a low temperature setting.

Fiberglass is always washed. It requires special handling and equipment. It must not be spun or tumble dried; drip drying is mandatory. Machines must not be used to wash other items, as glass particles remaining in the machine can become embedded in fabrics in the next wash load. A night spent between bedsheets washed after fiberglass draperies would be conducive to much scratching but little sleep.

Installation

It is essential that the mounting of drapery hardware as well as the fabric and fabrication be coordinated with the HVAC (heating, ventilating and air conditioning). This should be accomplished during concept development for the building project. If building design decisions are completed before window treatment is considered, it may be not only impossible to design the optimal system but difficult to even find a compatible window treatment system.

The existence of a suitable surface, thermal considerations, aesthetic considerations, the method of window operation and the size and location of the operating hardware determine the mounting location.

The attachment of the window treatment hardware must be to a solid surface. If it is mounted to drywall or plaster beyond the window frame, there must be a stud or plate for attachment. Likewise, there must be a solid surface above the ceiling finish material; blocking is usually needed. Coordination with the architect is essential. All studs, plates and blocking for attachment should appear in the construction documents for the building. If they do not, extra time and expense will be involved in properly securing the track and other hardware.

In renovation, old plaster surfaces are often crumbly and brittle. They may need to be broken away and reinforcement added.

Ceiling mounts tend to control convection current between glazing and drapery, as there is little space for air to escape. Ceiling mounts can be on the surface, recessed in the ceiling plane or recessed in a cove.

Wall mounts can be on the window frame or on the wall beside the window. The track should be mounted high enough above the window so that any visible heading stiffener or tape does not show on the exterior. The standard minimum is four inches.

Consideration should be given to mounting track far enough to the side of the window to accommodate the stacked width of the drapery beside the window. This way the total glass area can be exposed and full advantage can be taken of the view or the warming winter sun. Most track system manufacturers have available information on stacking widths.

The method of window operation (casement, awning, sliding, double-hung) can affect track location, especially if the window opens inward. Protruding operating hardware can rub against the drapery fabric if the track is incorrectly located. Conflict between the open window or operating hardware and the window treatment is a fairly frequent problem which can easily be avoided.

Specification Notes

For specification of track systems, standard CSI and AIA formats are available. As far as this author is aware, no such standard exists for specification of the drapery. A sample specification which includes track and drapery is included in Appendix B at the end of the book.

It is essential to consider drapery, track and associated hardware as one system. One contractor should be responsible for the total system. All too often, track and hardware are in the architectural contract and drapery in a separate interiors contract. When separate contractors are responsible, coordination can be a major problem. If difficulties arise (as they are apt to when two contractors are in charge of one system), responsibility is passed back and forth. Resolution can be time consuming and expensive.

In the case of window treatment, the need for coordination between the interior designer and the architect cannot be stressed too strongly. Whether they are from the same or different firms, they must cooperate in specifying the window treatment system if it is to fit the building, be properly installed, and meet the client's needs.

There are four important submittals that must be included:

1. Certification that the drapery meets the regulatory requirements.
2. Samples of each fabric from the dye lot to be used for the work for verification purposes.
3. A sample of one complete operating unit, including track and drapery for each type required. This can be a small-scale or full-size unit. It will be used as a standard of workmanship for all work on the project.
4. Shop drawings for special components and any conditions which are not fully detailed or dimensioned in the manufacturer's data.

Be sure that the length of the baton for hand-traversed drapery is appropriate for the window height and the potential users.

To assure intent of the design, clear and complete drawings and schedules are necessary. Information should include:

1. Elevations showing every condition for types of windows, tracks and drapery.
2. Plans showing location of each length of drapery track. Ends of track should occur only at mullions or other defined vertical separation. Direction of traverse and location of operating controls must be indicated.
3. Details showing position of window treatment with respect to glass, window frame, wall surfaces, blocking, and HVAC units. Mounting details, including surface and recessed mounting, pockets and valences, should also be shown. Special conditions such as at inside and outside corners and curved walls should appear on the drawings.
4. Schedules will probably be required where more than one type of track or drapery is used, although, depending on the complexity, it may be possible to include the information in the drawings. Schedules can include information regarding size and type of track, type of operation (hand, cord or motorized), track color, drapery color and pattern, and length of drapery. These must be carefully coordinated with the specification.

It should be noted in the specification that size information in the drawings is for bidding purposes only. Site measurements should be required prior to ordering and fabrication. Accurate site measurements taken when construction work is complete are critical for the proper fit of drapery.

Elevation

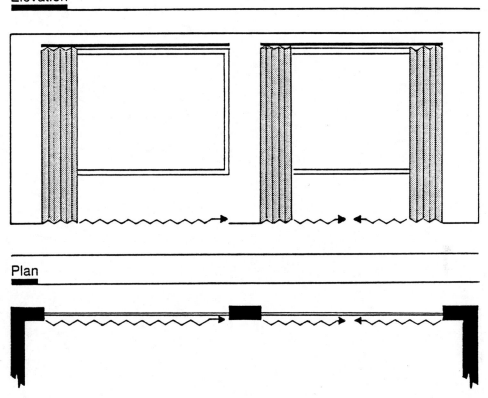

Plan

Figure 11.7. DRAWINGS OF DRAPERY CLOSING. The plan drawing illustrates how a typical elevation drawing can be translated into clearly illustrated traverse directions for the construction drawings.

Chapter Twelve

BLINDS AND SHADES

BLINDS

BLINDS CONSIST of a set of vanes or louver blades which can be rotated about their axes to form either a closed, planar set that restricts passage of light and air, or an open set that freely permits such passage. Blinds are called horizontal or vertical, so named because of the direction of the vanes or louver blades.

Structure and Properties

The properties of blinds are primarily a function of the materials used for the vanes and the rotation movement of the vanes when the blind is drawn over the window. The rotational ability contributes to excellent control of light and privacy.

Originally, blinds were made of wood. Today, most blinds are made of metal, usually aluminum, or PVC (polyvinyl chloride). Aluminum vanes have a factory-applied finish consisting of a chemical conversion coating topped with a baked-on synthetic resin finish coat. Finish coats come in a wide array of colors. Polished and satin finish aluminum, chrome, and other metallic finishes are available too. PVC vanes are integrally colored. They are tough, low maintenance, inexpensive, and a good insulation material. The hard, non-porous character of these materials favorably affects both their environmental and wear-life qualities.

Some vertical blinds are made of fabric. The properties of fabrics are identified in Chapter Eleven, "Drapery." However, for blinds, many of the fabrics are treated with vinyl or other plastics. While the fabric retains its textural appearance, environmental and wear-life qualities can be substantially changed by the addition of these plastics.

Light Control and Privacy Control

Blinds are very versatile. They can be rotated to block the sun while permitting a view, to provide privacy while allowing light to enter, or to be completely closed. In addition to rotational capability, the vanes can be drawn completely off the window to expose the total window surface.

Perforated metal and PVC louver blades are manufactured. Perforated louvers, while only about 13 percent openness, provide a view of the outside while protecting the interior space from glare and heat. White, opaque perforated louvers will reflect as much as 65 percent of the solar radiation striking the window. Perforated vinyl louvers provide a high degree of energy-loss protection, flexibility in light diffusion, and a clear view through the louver.

At least one manufacturer makes horizontal blinds of transparent polymeric resins. These act like sunglasses for windows, filtering out excessive glare and ultraviolet rays while allowing a full view of the outside environment.

Temperature Control

A number of properties affect temperature control: the color, the material, the fabrication and the way the blind fits the window. Blinds of light color or metallic materials reflect heat. Some horizontal blinds are available with different colors on each side of the slat, allowing the inside to be color coordinated with the room and the outside to be white. This can be useful in hot climates where the main objective is keeping out solar rays. It will not be useful in cold northern climates where keeping heat in the room is the major concern.

Blinds of PVC or a textile fabric are better insulators than metal blinds. However, the fit of the blind to the window and containment of still air between the blind and the window probably have a greater effect on the insulation value than the differences in materials. The specification of blinds that can be tightly shut and fitted to the window with minimal air gaps greatly influences the degree of temperature control.

Acoustic Control

Little acoustical control is provided by most blinds, as they are of hard or non-porous materials. A PVC blind would provide slightly better sound cushioning than a metal blind. A perforated blind would be slightly more effective than a non-perforated. Some vertical blind blades are of fabric, but they would provide little better sound control, as the fabrics are tightly woven and treated with plastics for dimensional stability. These plastics fill in the pores and diminish sound-control properties of the fabric used.

Ambience

In general, blinds will give a crisp, clean-cut appearance somewhat dependent on color and texture. A textile fabric as used in some vertical blinds gives these blinds a softer look similar to that of drapery.

Durability and Appearance Retention

Most of the blinds used in health care work have vanes or blades of metal or PVC. With these materials there is little problem with durability. They are light and heat resistant so they will not deteriorate or fade in the sun, moisture resistant so they are dimensionally stable and not easily stained, and abrasion resistant.

With horizontal blinds, it is the ladders that may be of materials vulnerable to the ravages of sun, moisture and abrasion. Since vertical blinds do not have ladders that hold the blades in place, they are less vulnerable.

With vertical blind blades made of fabrics, it is difficult to generalize about the durability and appearance retention. While they may be similar to that of fabrics discussed in Chapter Eleven, "Drapery," all have been treated to give them stiffness and dimensional stability. These treatments could substantially affect and probably improve other properties such as solar and abrasion resistance.

Health and Safety

Flammability

With blinds, there is little concern about flammability. While there must be adherence to the required codes for window treatment, the metal and PVC from which the majority of blinds are made are inherently flame resistant. Most fabric blinds available for institutional use are of inherently flame-resistant materials. It is essential to provide certification that the code requirements are met, but there is little likelihood that the desired blinds will fail to meet the requirements. With PVC, toxicity of smoke is a question that has not yet been answered.

Control of Positioning

Considerations regarding location of operating hardware so it can be found and reached by the elderly and the handicapped are the same as those for drapery. Operating controls for rotating the vanes may be cords, bead chains or wands. The wands can be difficult to operate for people with arthritic hands.

Types of Blinds

Horizontal Blinds

Horizontal blinds consist of a head rail, bottom rail, vanes, ladders, a tilting mechanism, a lifting mechanism, and installation brackets. Ladders support and maintain vanes at the proper spacing and alignment in open and closed positions. When standard fabrication techniques are used, the vanes cannot be tightly closed.

To achieve tight closure for light and heat exclusion, the rear of the vane must be notched at the ladder, and rout holes offset at the lift cords, to enable vanes to touch one another when closed. This is done by a limited number of manufacturers. One manufacturer who does have this option available in what is labeled an audiovisual blind, is Hunter Douglas.

Side channels are sometimes used to reduce light leakage or air circulation at the edges of the blinds. These channels can also be used on windows located in doors to keep the blind from flapping when the door is opened or closed.

Vane widths most often come in one-inch (narrow) or two-inch (standard) sizes, although other widths are offered by some manufacturers. "Micro" or very narrow vanes are useful for some installations such as windows in doors with shallow frames. Generally, blind units with 1-inch wide vanes are limited to widths of 12 feet and a maximum area of 100 square feet, and blinds with 2-inch wide vanes are limited to widths of 16 feet and a maximum area of 135 square feet.

Most one-inch-wide vanes are manufactured in aluminum. They are less obtrusive in appearance than blinds with two-inch vanes because of their slimmer profile and the use of nearly invisible ladders made of cords rather than tapes. Another advantage of the one-inch vane is the smaller-size head rail required. Wider vanes can be of aluminum, steel, or polyvinyl chloride.

Ladders should be of abrasion-resistant materials. Cord ladders can be of braided polyester and tape ladders of reinforced vinyl tape.

Two functions are involved in the operation of horizontal blinds: rotating the vanes and drawing the blind up and down. Rotation can be controlled by a cord or a wand. The wand can be a problem for persons with lack of coordination or arthritic hands. Up and down movement is usually controlled with a cord.

Controls can be placed on both operational functions if this is desired for appearance or maintenance reasons. Rotation can be limited to a specified angle with a tilt control. Up and down movement can be limited to housekeeping and maintenance staffs by tucking the control cord above the head rail. This is a good option for lobbies and long corridors where blinds are apt to be carelessly jerked up and down.

Vertical Blinds

Vertical blinds consist of a track system (traversing or non-traversing), louver blades, a pivot mechanism, an operating device (bead chain or a wand) and installation brackets and fittings.

The louvers are manufactured in a variety of widths from 1" to 7", with 3 1/2" and 4" sizes being the most common. The blinds can have a head and sill track or a head track only.

Initially, it was necessary for vertical blinds to have tracks at both bottom and top of the window. New developments in hardware in the 1970s made possible the single track vertical (track at top only). New technology in materials made possible louvers which could hang straight and even without the bottom track.

Manufacturers have developed techniques to use a great variety of materials in louvers that will not twist, warp, unravel, stretch, sag, or curl. There are very few problems. However, it is always beneficial to inspect an installation of the material being considered. Materials include: aluminum, polyvinyl chloride (PVC), perforated PVC, fiberglass—woven and knitted, vinyl-coated fiberglass, synthetic fabrics, vinyl-impregnated fabrics, laminated fabrics, laminated mylar, laminated wood veneers, and macrame.

Wood and macrame must be treated with fire retardants. Laminations are usually made upon aluminum louvers. PVC louvers are also manufactured with grooves at the side to accept fabric or wall-covering inserts. Any inserts must meet flammability requirements.

Vertical blinds can be fabricated to close tightly without gaps between the louvers and can, therefore, be more energy efficient than horizontal blinds.

Two functions are involved in the operation of vertical blinds: rotation or pivoting of the louver blades and traversing or drawing the louvers across the window. Pivot mechanisms should be geared and can be controlled with either a bead chain or a wand. The bead chain is easier for arthritic fingers to operate. For traversing, the louver blades are attached to carriers of metal or acetal resin-molded plastic. The plastic is quieter in operation. For long wear, the cord can be braided polyester or nylon.

Sometimes, chains are used at the bottom of the louvers to connect each one to the next. The purpose is to keep the louvers moving together when they are being operated. These are generally not necessary for most installations of PVC or aluminum louvers. When unnecessary, the chains should be avoided, as they tend to break and are difficult to repair. For proper repair, the entire chain must be replaced.

The chains are helpful when there is a convector unit opening directly below the blind. They restrain movement in the air current. They are also useful to control fabric blinds that will be operated frequently. Most fabrics are less abrasion resistant than PVC or aluminum, and the louvers rubbing against one another will eventually show wear. The chains would be unnecessary on short fabric louvers, as they do not sway enough for abrasion to be a problem.

Maintenance

A disadvantage of horizontal blinds is that dust accumulates on the horizontal surface of the slats, necessitating frequent cleaning. Dusting is accomplished with a special instrument which has multiple narrow brushes that fit between the slats, making it possible to dust several slats at a time. Occasionally, they will need to be wiped with a damp cloth using water or a cleaning solution. It is seldom that a slat will need to be replaced, but if the need occurs, disassembly of the blind is necessary.

Vertical blinds are much easier to maintain than horizontal blinds. They collect no more dust than a wall and require little housekeeping attention. Maintenance is also simple, as louver blades can be replaced individually if the need arises.

Installation

Blinds can be recessed within the window frame or attached to the outside on the frame or the wall. For inside mounting especially, accurate measurements are essential. Check to make sure that the brackets fit the intended location. Make sure that blinds and window-operating hardware do not interfere with one another.

Blinds are an excellent option for clerestory or other high windows. Extended controls can be provided for their operation. Blinds are also a good solution for other difficult conditions such as sloped and "greenhouse" type windows, arches and other shapes where they can be custom cut to fit, and for windows with interior-mounted air conditioners.

Other installation information is similar to that for drapery.

Specification Notes

For specification of blinds, standard CSI and AIA formats are available. These are very helpful in making sure that important details are not omitted.

Shop drawings should always be requested for special components and any conditions which are not fully detailed or dimensioned in the manufacturer's data.

Information on the drawings and the schedules is very similar to that needed for drapery.

SHADES

A shade is a device that consists of a flexible sheet or sheets that can be drawn up or down over the glazing. The traditional standard shade is unrolled to cover a window or rolled up when a covering is not desired. Some shades are operated in a manner similar to a horizontal blind.

Structure and Properties

Most of the properties of shades derive from the materials used. A great variety of materials have been used to achieve some very specific purposes such as special quilts for the utmost in temperature control or transparent films allowing full vision while reducing heat and glare.

Light and Privacy Control

Shades can be transparent, translucent or opaque. Most of the transparent shades are engineered to reduce heat and glare, and protect interior furnishings from sun fade while allowing full vision to the exterior. These can serve beneficially when privacy is not an issue. Translucent shades perform similar protective functions and allow a soft, diffused light to enter when they are drawn closed. They provide daytime privacy but, depending on the specific shade, may provide little privacy at night when interior lights are turned on.

Opaque shades allow no exterior light when drawn for privacy control. However, many of the standard shades can be attached at the bottom of the window rather than the top. The opaque shade may provide more desirable options when mounted at the window bottom. Attachment at the bottom provides the option of rolling the shade partway up the window for privacy while still admitting light at the top. This is not an appropriate solution for public areas, as it is too easy to tamper with this type of mounting.

Temperature Control

Shades are a very cost-effective means of temperature control. They are relatively inexpensive and if properly selected provide excellent temperature control. They can be tightly fitted for good control of convection. Some roller shades are available with extruded side channels and with valence and bottom sill sealing devices to provide a very tight fit. Magnets have also been used as sealing devices. Conduction is dependent on the R-value of the material used, and many of the shade materials have been designed with high R-values. Solar radiation control is best with a white or metallic shade cloth.

Acoustic Control

Many of the shade cloth materials are hard and non-porous and provide little sound control. On the other hand, shades of quilting would provide good sound control. The specific material must be evaluated as to its porosity and bulk.

Ambience

Shades can effect a clean and simple ambience. They can be opaque or translucent and are made in a variety of handsome textures. A simple valence or headboard also provides some decorative possibilities.

Durability and Appearance Retention

Durability, in shades as in other types of window treatment, is most affected by light and heat resistance, moisture resistance and abrasion resistance of the materials used. Because many materials are used, it is difficult to generalize. However, most materials used in shades specifically made for contract use either have these properties inherently or are treated to have them to a sufficient degree.

For roller shades, the traditional and most common type of shade, there is another consideration. The material used should have a high tensile strength, as operation involves pulling directly on the shade material.

The durability of a shade is also dependent on the mechanism for lifting and lowering the shade. Good hardware must be specified. Roller shades using a spring-return roller system can be a problem if poor-quality springs are used. For cord-operated shades, the cord should be of braided polyester. A minimum of one foot of extra fabric length (longer than the window) should be specified to allow for people overextending the shades and pulling them off the roller.

Health and Safety

Flammability

Shades can be made in a variety of materials greater than that of drapery and blinds combined. Almost any material can be used. If the material is too rigid, it can be cut into strips and woven; if it is too flimsy, it can be laminated to a suitable base material or impregnated or coated with vinyl. With the great variety of materials possible, it is essential that flammability codes are examined, understood and met. A discussion of flammability is in Chapter Eleven, "Drapery."

Cleanliness

Shades are the easiest of all the window treatments to keep clean. They are especially good for sunny nursery areas where cleanability and dust control are critical.

Control of Positioning

Dangling cords are easy to see and easy to pull but unsightly. More subtle pulls such as a small ring or plastic sleeve on the lower edge of the shade present a better appearance but may be difficult to see and hard to grasp.

Types of Shades

Roller shades are the traditional shades and the one that most people think of when shades are mentioned. A recent version of the shade is the pleated shade, which pleats up rather than rolling up. This is a crisper rendition of the Roman shade, which has long been popular in residences but has limited application in institutional work.

Roller Shades

The rolling process is usually accomplished by a spring return. Also used are springless roller systems which utilize beaded chain and continuous cord loop. These can be controlled somewhat more accurately than a spring roller shade. Another operating mechanism is a gravity-activated take-up spool and ribbon drawtape. Shades can also be motor operated.

Shades can be attached at the top or bottom of the window. They can be installed inside the jambs or on the room surface of the jambs. Some roller shades are available with extruded side channels and with valence and bottom sill sealing devices to provide a very tight fit.

Shades are especially suited for automated, computerized control. Solar controls can adjust the shades as the sun exposure changes.

Shades are manufactured in a wide variety of materials, from transparent films to thick quilts. Materials include: transparent mylar, polyester film, metalized polyester film, fiberglass, vinyl, woven aluminum, woven wood, macrame, and laminations and coatings of many kinds.

Transparent mylar and polyester films provide full vision to the exterior, reduce heat and glare, and protect interior furnishings from sun fade. Metalized finishes can be controlled for transparency or opacity. Woven aluminum and wood, macrame and textile fabrics can be woven in varying degrees of looseness and tightness and in high or low bulk. Laminated and coated shades range from translucent to room-darkening finishes.

Another kind of material used for shades is quilting. Quilted fabrications consist of several flexible sheets attached to one another in series to form a thick, soft, flexible assembly. The multi-layer construction usually contains an insulating layer with a high R-value such as a fibrous continuous-filament polyester. Often, one layer is a fabric with a highly reflective metal finish.

Pleated Shades

A type of shade that is relatively new in the market is the pleated shade. This consists of a permanently pleated piece of fabric that draws upward and is operated in a manner similar to a horizontal blind. These can fold up to 1" per 4' drop, making them inconspicuous in the up position.

Pleated shades are often made of translucent polyester fabrics that filter the sunlight. A micro-thin layer of aluminum may be bonded to the base fabric. The translucent quality is maintained in the metalized fabric. Completely opaque fabrics are also available.

Roman Shades

Roman shades pull to the top in horizontal folds. They are operated with a control attached to a series of cords threaded through loops attached to the back of the fabric. A very soft look can be achieved. These shades are used infrequently in contract work.

One Roman shade that has been especially developed for thermal control is Roman Shade V by Zenith Insulator Products in Duluth, Minnesota. It consists of a four-layer quilt of:

1. Decorative interior fabric
2. Metalized polyethylene vapor barrier
3. Non-woven batting — Thinsulite® by 3M
4. Roclon® thermal suede-insulated drapery lining.

The shade pulls to the top in horizontal folds. When the shade is lowered, magnets form a draft-free seal against the window casing.

Maintenance

A properly selected shade cloth requires little housekeeping attention. It will collect little dust, and if moisture resistant, staining will not be a problem. Operating devices will need to be replaced from time to time; springs come loose, cords and pulls break. Probably, the biggest problem is that the fabric is pulled off the roller with careless handling.

Installation

Installation information is the same as that for blinds.

Specification Notes

Specification notes are the same as those for blinds.

Be sure to specify an adequate length to minimize problems with the fabric being pulled from the roller.

Part IV
UPHOLSTERY

Chapter Thirteen

INTRODUCTION TO UPHOLSTERY FABRICS

THE INITIAL discussion in making a decision on upholstery fabrics is often the evaluation of textile versus vinyl. Each has appropriate applications, but before exploring these some definitions might be helpful.

Literally, textile refers to a woven fabric or material for weaving. It comes from the Latin word textere, "to weave." This is also the derivation of the word, texture, and most textiles have a textural identity. This literal definition is commonly extended so that **the word, textile, includes all fabrics constructed from fibers and yarns.** Using this extended definition, knitted fabrics would be included as a textile.

Vinyl upholstery fabric is the most commonly used of a class of fabrics known as chemical-coated fabrics. **Chemical-coated fabrics are made by forming a resin sheet which is given additional strength by applying it to one face of a backing of natural or synthetic fibers.** This resin sheet forms a non-fibrous, durable protective surface. Chemical-coated fabrics are also formed using urethane, acrylic or polyester, although these are not typically used for heavy-duty upholstery fabrics. Sometimes, the chemical sheet is used without a backing; this does not have the strength to be used for a good-quality upholstery fabric.

Health and Safety

Health and safety issues such as biogenic factors and electrostatic propensity will be discussed in the following two chapters on textile and chemical-coated upholstery fabrics. The issue of flammability and applicable codes is a confusing one. It will be addressed here, as the same discussion is relevant to both types of upholstery fabrics.

215

Flammability

The possibility of fire and the fire resistance of materials is always of concern to those responsible for facilities where many occupants are incapacitated to some extent. In the case of most attached, architectural finish materials, concerns for safety have been addressed in national regulations and codes which are used in a fairly standardized manner across the United States. This is not so with codes regulating the use of upholstery fabrics.

Flammability of upholstery fabrics is policed by a multitude of regulations. According to Richard Zoehrer in a December 1983 article in *Facilities Design and Management*, there were at that time more than 300 different regulations for flammability control in simultaneous use by government agencies, states and municipalities in the U.S.A. Today, there still exists across the country a confusing array of local and regional codes.

However, there are some standards that are being used most frequently by local regulatory agencies and some tests to which manufacturers of upholstery fabrics most frequently submit their materials. Standards most frequently cited are Boston Fire Department (BFD), New York and New Jersey Port Authority (NYNJPA), and California Bulletin 117.

In order to understand the relationship of these standards and others to upholstered furniture and building fires, it is helpful to look at the development of a fire.

Stages of Fire Development

Fires progress through a series of stages. Three stages are commonly identified as: (1) incipient, (2) growth and (3) fully developed fire conditions.

Stage 1, incipient, is the introduction of the ignition source and the actual ignition of the item. A fire remaining in the area of the initial ignition is a stage 1 fire. Of concern, is the performance of an item, such as furniture, in exposure to a smoldering source, such as a cigarette, a small flame or a radiant ignition source.

Stage 2, growth, concerns the performance of the item from the time of apparent ignition up to the condition of full involvement such as when an entire room is involved in the fire. The heat generated may cause the fire to "flashover" to adjoining spaces. Of concern are the spread of flame and the production of heat, smoke and toxic combustion products.

Stage 3, fully developed, considers the contribution of the item to the fire once a fully developed fire situation has occurred. Of concern are the rate of burning and the heat and smoke released by the item.

Regulatory Approaches

The concept of fire stages suggests three regulatory approaches:

1. Control of ignition—measure **ignition resistance** of materials.
2. Control growth of fire—measure **flame spread** and heat- and smoke-release qualities.
3. Limitation of contribution to fire—measure fuel load and heat-release qualities.

Flammability testing methods and regulations presently in use for upholstered furniture address ignition resistance and flame spread qualities.

None of the currently used tests measure the heat-release qualities or the fuel load of upholstered furniture. Underwriters Laboratories cites research showing that "resistance to smoldering ignition bears little relation to the perfomance under growth or fully developed conditions."* Furniture that resists ignition may or may not perform well once the fire has started.

The following are summary descriptions of flame spread and ignition resistance tests which are being used with some frequency. This includes the most frequently quoted BFD, NYNJPA and California standards, each of which has an open flame test for the fabric component.

FLAME SPREAD: The tests used to measure flame spread for upholstery padding and fabric are the Tunnel Test and the Radiant Panel Test. The Tunnel Test is commonly used for many types of architectural finishes. Both the Tunnel and Radiant Panel Tests are used for carpet and are fully described in the chapter on carpet.

RESISTANCE TO IGNITION: In tests developed for ignition resistance of upholstered furniture, three testing methods are generally used:

1. a vertical flame test where the sample is held vertically and ignited by an open flame. Many of the vertical flame tests are based on the test procedure and apparatus as specified in Federal Specification CCC-T-191, Method 5903.
2. a 45° flame angle test where the sample is held at an angle and ignited by an open flame. Most of these are based on U.S. Department of Commerce Commercial Standard 191-53.

*Underwriter Laboratories, File R8044, p. 6.

3. a cigarette ignition test where a cigarette is the source of ignition.

The open flame test methods are all currently used with components such as fabric and padding tested separately. For each of these methods, a specific flame source is applied for a designated amount of time. Length and time of afterflame, afterglow and/or self-extinguishment are effects measured, as is length of char. Afterflame is the continued burning of the specimen after the flame is removed. Afterglow is sparking after withdrawal of the flame. Char is that area of fabric which is destroyed or degraded from face to back, not including the area which is only discolored by smoke.

Some of the cigarette ignition tests measure flammability of the fabric only, and some test a mock-up of the combined components or the piece of furniture, itself. The length of char is measured. Criteria for passing are non-ignition and a maximum char length of 1.3 to 3 inches, depending on the specific test or regulatory district.

While flame resistance of fabrics is of obvious importance, the combination of fabric, filling and furniture configuration all contribute to a fire. Tests have shown that fabrics and filling may perform well when tested separately, but the combination may have different burning characteristics.

Open Flame Ignition Tests

BOSTON FIRE CODE: The Boston test is a vertical test; the fabric is subjected to a Tirrell burner flame for ten seconds. The fabric must extinguish in three seconds after flame removal. This is repeated twice, with ten-second intervals between repetitions. Each time, the fabric must self-extinguish within three seconds. This test is considered difficult to pass, because a fabric which passes the first time may not withstand subsequent reignition, as topical flame-retardant treatments may break down during the initial test. Requirements for passing are: char length — seven inches maximum, afterflame — two seconds maximum, afterglow — forty seconds maximum, no flaming drop-off.

NEW YORK AND NEW JERSEY PORT AUTHORITY: A vertical flame test is used for coverings, linings, webbing and cushioning and padding under one-half-inch thick. A small sample is subjected to a Bunsen burner for 12 seconds. Requirements for passing are: char length — eight-inch maximum; average afterflame — fifteen seconds maximum; drip burn — five seconds maximum after falling.

NYNJPA also uses the Tunnel Test and the Radiant Panel Test to test padding and cushioning exceeding one-half-inch thickness.

CALIFORNIA BULLETIN 117, SECTION E: A small sample is held in a metal frame at a 45° angle; a flame is held to it for one second. Time of flame spread (time, in seconds, for flame to travel five inches up the specimen) and time to self-extinguish are measured. A class 1 rating signifies normal flammability. This is considered only as a test to screen out highly flammable fabrics.

CALIFORNIA BULLETIN 117, SECTION F: This is a vertical test method using five specimens in each yarn direction. Requirements are: average char length not to exceed seven inches; average afterflame not to exceed ten seconds; average afterglow not to exceed twenty seconds.

The other sections of California Bulletin 117 deal with filling materials.

NFPA 701: This is a vertical flame test sometimes applied to upholstery fabrics but more often to drapery. Char length, afterflame and drip burn are measured. It is described in Chaper Eleven, "Drapery."

Cigarette Ignition Tests

An Underwriters Laboratory fact-finding report published in 1977 states that "cigarettes and other unknown smoking materials were the ignition sources in over 85 percent of the incidents in which upholstered furniture was the first to ignite."*

Smoldering ignition, not open flame ignition, is the most frequent cause of upholstery fires. Cigarettes can smolder unnoticed in crevices at joints and in indentations formed at welts and in tufted areas. People fall asleep while smoking or they carelessly leave a lit cigarette on the furniture. Several agencies have developed testing standards for cigarette ignition on furniture samples, mock-ups or components.

CALIFORNIA BULLETIN 116: A sample seating piece is tested by burning three cigarettes in each of several locations such as on the smooth seating surface, in a depression at the welted edge and in the crevice between seat and back or seat and arm. Each furniture piece is tested until either (1) three cigarettes have burned their full length, (2) three cigarettes have extinguished without burning their full length or (3) one cigarette has resulted in failure. A piece of upholstered furniture fails to meet the provisions of the law if either obvious flaming combustion occurs or if char develops more than two inches in any direction from the cigarette.

---

*Underwriters Laboratories, File R8044, p. 4.

The California Bulletin regulating upholstered furniture was dated January 1973 and took effect in October 1975.

CPSC (CONSUMER PRODUCT SAFETY COMMISION): On a federal level, the National Bureau of Standards (NBS) had begun looking into upholstery fire resistance in 1968 when the existing Flammable Fabrics Act was expanded beyond clothing fabrics. In 1973, the Consumer Product Safety Commission was formed as the government agency responsible for administration of the Flammable Fabrics Act, including the adoption of any program or standards regulating upholstered furniture. NBS retained the responsibility for designing test methods for flammable fabrics.

Previous testing had shown that test performance of individual components such as fabrics and filling might be quite different from performance of an assembled unit. Therefore, mock-up testing was recommended. The mock-up would be of seating surface and vertical surfaces with the fabric and padding materials, and welt cord representative of the production upholstered piece. (See Fig. 13.1 for the mock-up format.)

While mock-up testing is less costly than testing the finished product or a prototype, the expense of testing a new mock-up for each fabric to be used on a furniture piece is still considerable. To make mock-up testing economically feasible, it was determined to develop a classification system for fabrics. Then, for example, a particular furniture piece meeting all the requirements in mock-up testing with one class A fabric could be produced with any class A fabric without further testing.

In an effort to produce data upon which to base a standardized code, the National Bureau of Standards working with the Consumer Product Safety Council developed a fabric classification based on resistance to ignition by a cigarette. The testing apparatus contains horizontal and vertical glass fiberboard pieces covered with the test fabric (see Fig. 13.2A). Fabrics are classified according to char length produced by a lighted cigarette as shown in Table 13.1. Certain fabric types were found to be typical of each class.

It would appear that a combination of fiber and weight of fabric makes the difference. Wool, vinyl, and the synthetics such as nylon, olefin and polyester had a char length less than 1 1/2". But when placed over the flammable cotton batting, the medium-weight synthetics were not able to maintain this. The fire resistance of synthetics seems to increase as the weight increases.

On the other hand, it would appear that fabrics with a cellulosic content, such as cotton, linen and rayon, present a greater smoldering ignition hazard which increases as the weight of the cellulosic increases.

Frame

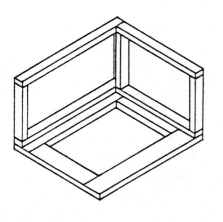

Panels

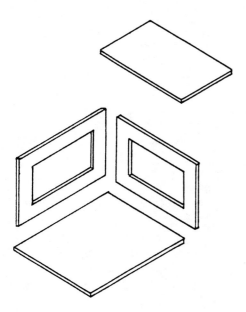

Mock-up

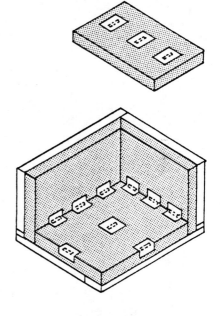

Figure 13.1. TESTING APPARATUS FOR CIGARETTE IGNITION RESISTANCE MOCK-UP TESTS. For mock-up testing, panels prepared with padding and upholstery fabric are inserted in a frame. Lighted cigarettes are placed on the assembled unit in specified locations and each is covered with a piece of sheeting material. Mock-ups such as this are used in CPSC, NFPA 260B and BIFMA tests.

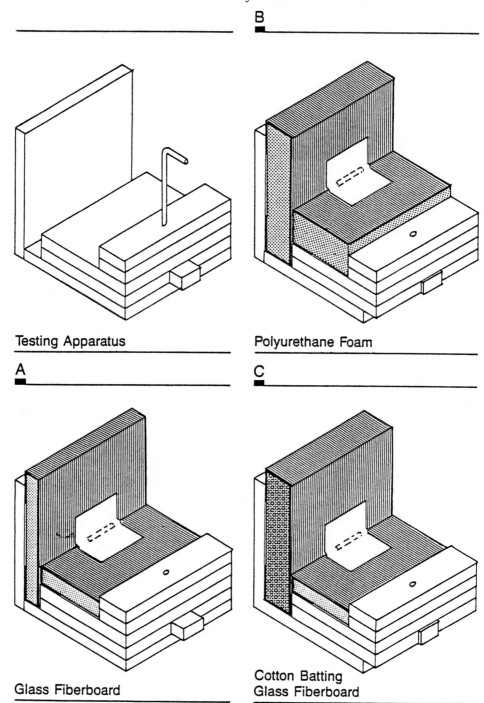

B

Testing Apparatus

Polyurethane Foam

A

C

Glass Fiberboard

Cotton Batting
Glass Fiberboard

Figure 13.2. TESTING APPARATUS FOR CIGARETTE IGNITION RESISTANCE AND CLASSIFICATION OF FABRICS. The testing apparatus used to test the fabric component of upholstered furniture pieces is similar for many agencies. The principle difference is in the padding used. Glass fiberboard and cotton batting are used by CPSC and BIFMA. Polyurethane foam is used by UFAC and the Joint Industry Committee.

Table 13.1

FABRIC CLASSIFICATION BASED ON RESISTANCE TO IGNITION
BY A SMOLDERING CIGARETTE

Class	Char Length	Typical Fabrics
A	less than 1.5"	wool, wool blends, vinyl, heavy weight synthetics
B	*1.5" or more	medium weight synthetics, light weight or tightly woven cellulosics
C	1.5" to 3.0"	medium weight cellulosics
D	more than 3.0"	heavy weight cellulosics

*fabrics showing a char length less than 1.5" are tested a second time over untreated cotton batting in the vertical portion of the apparatus. If the char length is over 1.5", a class B rating is assigned. If it remains under 1.5", the class A rating is maintained.

NFPA (NATIONAL FIRE PROTECTION ASSOCIATION): Several organizations and agencies have developed voluntary standards as alternatives to the proposed mandatory standards. The NFPA 260B standard for cigarette ignition resistance was developed subsequent to publication of the CPSC standards and utilizes NBS proposed test methodology for mock-ups.

In the initial development, separate tests for component products were considered, but the interaction among components soon became obvious. It was determined that they would need to be tested in the combination utilized for the actual furniture. The mock-up construction and testing is similar to that recommended by NBS and CPSC. At least three cigarettes are burned on each surface location. Specifications are given for precise placement and for covering each cigarette with a piece of sheeting material. The locations include crevice(s) where seat cushion and vertical panels meet, seat cushion surfaces (including welt and smooth, quilted or tufted areas), and top of upholstered back, seat deck and armrest as applicable. Char length is measured.

NFPA 260B is designed to evaluate the ignition resistance of upholstered furniture when exposed to smoldering cigarettes under specified conditions. A mock-up is used. This standard does not address any other issues such as classification of fabrics or testing of individual components.

UFAC (UPHOLSTERED FURNITURE ACTION COUNCIL): The UFAC test method is intended as a means of establishing the ignition resistance performance level of upholstery cover fabrics in contact with polyurethane foam. In accordance with the UFAC Fabric Classification Test Method — 1983:

Fabrics which meet the requirements of this test method may be labeled as UFAC Class I, (class I is similar to CPSC classes A and B) and may be used directly over conventional polyurethane in the horizontal seating surfaces of upholstered furniture bearing the UFAC hangtag. All other fabrics are UFAC Class II (class II is similar to CPSC classes C and D) and require an approved barrier between the cover fabric and conventional polyurethane foam in horizontal seating surfaces.

The test is conducted on panels of two-inch polyurethane covered with the fabric to be tested. These are placed in a test assembly so they simulate a chair seat and back junction. A lighted cigarette is placed in this crevice, covered with a piece of sheeting fabric and allowed to burn its entire length unless obvious ignition occurs. A minimum of three test specimens is required for each upholstery (see Fig. 13.2B).

The following are the test criteria:

1. If an obvious ignition of the polyurethane substrate occurs on one or more test assemblies, the fabric is a UFAC class II cover fabric.
2. If the vertical char of any of the three test specimens is equal to or greater than 4.4 cm (1.75 in), the fabric is a UFAC class II cover fabric.
3. If no individual specimen yields a vertical char of 4.4 cm (1.75 in) or greater, the fabric is a UFAC class I cover fabric.

Combination Open Flame and Cigarette Ignition

Several associations are recommending a two-part procedure. An open flame ignition test to screen out highly flammable fabrics is followed by a cigarette ignition test of fabrics passing the open flame test.

BIFMA (The Business and Institutional Furniture Manufacturer's Association): The BIFMA standard is the result of work by the BIFMA Flammability Standards Subcommittee and an in-depth study by Underwriters Laboratory, an independent research and testing firm. This standard prescribes requirements and test methods for two tests: an open flame screening test for components and a cigarette ignition test.

The BIFMA 45° materials screening procedure specifies that all upholstery covering and fillers should meet a 45° burn-rate test based on U.S. Department of Commerce Commercial Standard 191-53. By this method, component upholstery materials are classified according to their flammability in order to identify and eliminate utilization of highly flammable component upholstery materials. Time of flame spread and time to self-extinguish are measured.

The first portion of the cigarette ignition test prescribes methods for determining cigarette ignition resistance of upholstered furniture. The actual upholstered piece may be used or a mock-up constructed similar to that for CPSC or NFPA 260B testing procedures (see Fig. 13.1). For the assembly to pass, there must be no obvious flaming combustion and no char greater than three inches from the nearest point of the original cigarette location.

Portion two prescribes a method for categorizing individual upholstery fabrics using a standard glass board and cotton batting as the substrates. The apparatus and procedure is the same as for the CPSC Fabric Classification Test (see Fig. 13.2C). A fabric which qualifies as a class A fabric in this test can be substituted for the class A fabric in a furniture construction which passes the testing of end product or mock-up described for portion one. Classes of fabric are as defined by CPSC.

Table 13.2

SUMMARY OF FREQUENTLY USED TESTS FOR IGNITION
RESISTANCE OF UPHOLSTERY FABRICS

Regulatory Body or Trade Association	Type			Based on or Similar to	Specimen		
	Vert	45°	Cig		Furn	Mock	Comp
CCC-T-191, 5903	X						X
Boston	X						X
NYNJ Port Authority	X			CCC-T-191, 5903			X
NFPA 701	X						X
Cal. Bulletin 117, F	X			CCC-T-191, 5903			X
Cal. Bulletin 117, E		X		CS-191-53			X
NFPA 702		X		CS-191-53			X
Cal. Bulletin 116			X		X		
CPSC			X			X	X(a)
NFPA 260B			X	CPSC		X	
UFAC			X				X(b)
BIFMA		X		CS-191-53			X
BIFMA			X	CPSC	X	X	X(a)
Joint Industry Comm.		X		CS-191-53			X
Joint Industry Comm.			X	UFAC			X(b)

(a) Fabric is tested over glass fiberboard and over cotton batting.

(b) Fabric is tested over polyurethane.

Legend:

Vert = Vertical flame test
45° = 45° angle flame test
Cig = Cigarette ignition test
Furn = Actual upholstered furniture item
Mock = Mock-up of fabric, padding and details such as welting
Comp = Component parts, especially upholstery fabric

JOINT INDUSTRY COMMITTEE: Variations on and combinations of the described testing procedures are being investigated and recommended by several other groups and associations working on this issue. Just one more will be mentioned. The Joint Industry Committee is an effort of several furniture and manufacturer associations to develop voluntary standards for upholstered furniture. The procedure prescribed by the Joint Industry Fabric Standards Committee utilizes an open flame screening test based on California Bulletin 117, Section E, plus a cigarette ignition resistance test similar to UFAC.

Commonsense Guidelines for Patient Safety

The foregoing has been a brief discussion of some of the many standards developed by various regulatory bodies and industry associations. In many regulatory districts, one of these tests is mandated. In many other cases, however, no mandatory requirements exist. Nevertheless, there is an ethical responsibility to consider the safety of occupants. Materials that have been tested in accordance with and passed one or more of these standards should certainly be considered for use, even when not required.

In analyzing the research conducted in developing existing standards, there emerge some commonsense guidelines to improve patient safety.

Guideline 1 would recommend the use of a wool or heavy-weight synthetic textile for upholstery. An acceptable alternate fabric would be a vinyl. However, most vinyl upholstery fabrics emit toxic combustion products in stage 2 and 3 fires.

Guideline 2 would be to avoid crevices where cigarettes may lodge as follows:

1. Avoid tufting on horizontal surfaces.
2. Use welt cording only where necessary. If used, cording should be PVC.
3. Avoid seams on the seat surface. These can pull loose under heavy wear and expose the filling material.
4. Specify seating with a one-inch or greater space between back and seat.

Interestingly, **the avoidance of crevices in all these ways would be recommended for health care seating even if smoldering cigarettes were not a problem.** These crevices provide lodging for all types of soil and spills and make cleanup after accidents much more difficult than it would be with a smooth surface.

Both construction and fiber affect flame resistance. A high yarn count and tightly constructed fabric is best. If the construction is porous, trapped air within the fabric feeds fire.

Modacrylic is an inherently flame-resistant fiber. A fabric of 70 percent modacrylic with 30 percent nylon or other blend usually passes stringent flame tests. A heavy, tightly constructed nylon fabric will pass most tests. Wool is inherently flame resistant but still must be treated to pass some tests.

Flame-Retardant Treatment

To use a fabric that does not comply with applicable fire regulations, a chemical flame retardant must be used. However, some fabrics cannot be treated without harming their strength or appearance. Also, other finishes such as soil or stain repellants may combine with flame-retardant chemicals for unanticipated results. If flame-retardant treatment is planned, the designer should check with the manufacturer before treating and should have a sample processed and tested early in the planning process so that the results of treatment are known long before final fabric selection and specification.

According to the NFPA, 75 percent to 80 percent of all fire deaths result from inhalation of toxic products of combustion, not burns. BIFMA believes:

> It is in the best interest of all concerned that this standard (reference to BIFMA standard but could apply to all) be implemented without the use of possible harmful chemical flame retardants. In the absence of appropriate standards for toxicity, carcinogenic potential or other biological hazards, it is possible that new side effects that may exceed the flammability hazard may be created by widespread use of such fire retardant activities.*

Environmental Factors

The interior architecture of institutional buildings is often bland or monotonous due to a lack of architectural detailing and the use of a preponderance of smooth materials such as paint, plastic and glass. Both cost and the need for easy cleanability are contributors. It is often the furnishings which differentiate interior spaces and give them a sense of identity. These qualities can be readily and economically achieved using furniture forms and the textural attributes of fabrics.

---

*BIFMA. First Generation Voluntary Upholstered Furniture Flammability Standard for Business and Institutional Markets, p. 2.

Texture

Texture refers to the visual and tactile qualities of a surface. Cloth has an almost unlimited diversity of texture. This variety gives the designer a valuable, yet functional and economic means of defining and enlivening a space.

Texture can be tough or smooth, shiny or matte. In a **textile,** it is determined by the nature of the fiber, itself, the preparation of the yarn, the construction of the fabric and the finishes that are used. For example, the basic nylon fiber is lustrous and smooth. It becomes matte and pebbly when delustered and twisted. Crepe yarn is an example of a tightly twisted yarn. Nylon yarns can be woven into a heavily ribbed ottoman or a more evenly textured hopsacking.

In a **chemical-coated fabric,** most commonly, a vinyl fabric, the textural possibilities are more limited. The texture is achieved by some method of making indentations as the coating sheet is produced and by the luster of the applied finish. While some variety is possible, the potential for textural variation is much less than for textile-based fabrics.

Both our visual and tactile senses are satisfied by texture. Visually, it is read as the relief created by highlight and shadow. Tactually, it is rough or smooth, even or uneven. There is a sensual pleasure in touching that should not be discounted. There may also be a revulsion to prickly or sticky fabrics.

The optical quality of relief may be stimulated not by the highlight and shadow of actual unevenness but by dark and light yarns or by repetition of a small motif such as a polka dot that simulates relief.

The textural qualities of a textile are typically pleasant, both visually and tactually. Those of chemical-coated fabrics are not generally as pleasant.

There is a close texture and color relationship between the natural environment and textiles. In textiles, as in nature, color is seldom solid and unbroken but is fragmented by the juxtaposition of minute particles of color and by highlight and shadow. The softness and textured surfaces of textiles offer relief to the hard, often unbroken surfaces of paint, plastic and glass. Of all the man-made surfaces, textiles offer the greatest potential for fragmenting color.

Effects of Light

The effect of light on color and the change in apparent color brought about by a change in the source of light has been discussed in previous chapters. Light also has an effect on texture. Directional light will enhance it; non-directional light will diminish it. To prevent the visual loss of textural perception in directionless and shadowless lighting conditions, textural contrast must be intensified or directional light sources added.

Flatness and Scale

Form is an inherent part of any seating element. The relationship of the upholstery fabric to this form is an important consideration in the fabric selection. The more complex the furniture form, the more limited is the choice of fabrics. In any case, the pattern or visual configuration of the cloth should be flat and static. Excessive dimensional depth may conflict with or camouflage the form of the furniture. Large, bold patterns can overwhelm the piece or distort the form. Bold diagonals can make the furniture look lopsided or in danger of falling over. With bold contrasts, it can appear that one of the colors is jumping off the furniture.

The scale of both the cloth and any pattern should relate to that of the furniture. A large pattern or a thick, highly textured fabric will be overwhelming on a lightly scaled chair. With large-scale seating pieces, there is less limitation in pattern, but a thin weave with little textural interest may look anemic.

Comfort and Porosity

Porosity of a fabric is the extent to which air and moisture can pass through it, sometimes referred to as the ability of the fabric to "breathe." This is directly related to comfort and time. Sitting on a non-porous upholstery fabric becomes uncomfortable over time as moisture accumulates. A vinyl upholstery is non-porous and is comfortable only for short-term seating such as for some nursing stations where nurses are constantly up and down or for waiting rooms where waiting times are quite short.

Wool is the most porous of the fibers and the most comfortable in this respect. Nylon is a relatively non-porous fiber, but, because of the woven construction of a typical nylon fabric, there is air and moisture passing between the fibers. Thus, it is still fairly comfortable for long-term seating. In a very tightly woven nylon upholstery fabric, porosity and comfort would be less than with a looser weave. This is an area where there may need to be an evaluation of priorities, as the tighter the weave, the more durable and less porous the fabric is likely to be. In clerical areas where staff members are seated for many hours, porous fabrics are essential to comfort. In patient and visitor areas with long-term seating situations, they are very desirable.

The ability to breathe will also be affected by the density of the cushioning beneath the upholstery fabric.

Wear-Life Factors

Durability, appearance retention, maintenance and cost effectiveness are again the balancing factors upon which specification must be based. Durability is not enough. A material that lasts "forever" is not satisfactory if it is faded, embedded with soil, stained and uncomfortable.

Durability

Resistance to abrasion is, perhaps, the most essential durability factor. Nylon is the most abrasion resistant of the textile fibers. Resistance to abrasion is not dependent on the fiber alone; it is also related to yarn and fabric construction, fabrication of the upholstery, and style of seating, as will be discussed in Chapter Fourteen. Vinyl-coated fabrics do not perform as well as nylon or wool under severe abrasive conditions, such as when the upholstered portion of a chair is constantly rubbed against laminate-clad casework. Abrasion resistance is most often tested by the Wyzenbeek oscillatory-cylinder method in which the fabric is submitted to a rubbing action.

Extensibility and elasticity play a part in abrasion resistance, allowing the fabric to "give" under stress. Of the fibers most highly recommended for upholstery, nylon has the best extensibility and elasticity.

Strength is of somewhat lesser import in evaluating durability only, because, in most cases, where a manufacturer states that a fabric is suitable for contract work, it will have the required strength. Standard tests are commonly used for testing three types of strength: breaking or tensile strength, tear strength and seam strength.

For strength tests, a machine which grips the sample of cloth between jaws and records the applied load is used. Break strength is the capacity of a material to withstand the ultimate tensile load required to rupture the fabric. The elongation at the time of rupture is also recorded. Tear strength is evaluated on the same machine by testing a sample which has been slit from one end, and recording the force required to continue the slit. This same test method is also used to determine the force required to separate two parts of a standard-sewn seam. In each of these tests for strength, fabrics are tested in both directions; thus, two figures will be given such as 40×35.

Appearance Retention

With textiles, resistance to snagging, fuzzing and pilling are factors in appearance retention. With chemical-coated fabrics, these need not be considered.

Resistance to further tearing once a puncture occurs is generally better in a woven fabric than in a vinyl-coated fabric. The vinyl has a greater tendency to keep tearing.

Color retention in textiles depends on the dye method, the dyes, themselves, and the ability of the fiber to accept the dye. These will be discussed in Chapter 14, "Textile Upholstery Fabrics." In most vinyl-coated fabrics the color is an integral part of the vinyl, as it is a component of the initial solution. This type of color is extremely colorfast. If the color is printed or an overprint is used, it would be subject to wearing off through abrasive action in normal seating use as well as in the cleaning process.

For all upholstery fabrics, appropriate color and texture are effective in concealing slight damage and soiling. Yellow shows soil more than any other color and should be avoided in upholstery.

Extensibility and elasticity, important to durability, are even more important to appearance retention. Sagging upholstery is not very attractive.

Maintenance and Cleaning

Regular cleaning and immediate spot removal are the key factors in maintaining upholstery as is true with all other materials. The longer abrasive particles remain, the greater the damage they do; the longer stains remain, the more apt they are to become permanent.

Several manufacturers are making seating with easily removable covers. When soiling occurs, these can be removed, replaced with a cover from a small inventory maintained for this purpose, and sent out for cleaning.

The ease of fabric restoration after the fabric is torn or burned by a cigarette is another consideration in selection. Unfortunately, both occur through normal use, nervous actions and vandalism. Here, textiles have the advantage. They can be mended or rewoven so that the repair is almost invisible. Vinyl repair is more difficult and is almost always evident.

Cost Effectiveness

Of the three upholstery fabrics most recommended for health care use, wool and nylon textiles and vinyl-coated fabrics, all can be purchased in a great variety of price ranges. For each, the least expensive is rarely a good buy. It will wear out or become worn looking very quickly with no way to rejuvenate it.

Medium-priced goods can be very durable and maintain their appearance for many years. All things considered, these may be the best buy. Savings can be effected by rank ordering desired properties and allocating the budget accordingly. Careful reading of Chapters Fourteen and Fifteen should be helpful in determining the most necessary attributes for specific locations, thereby enabling a cost-effective approach.

High cost does not necessarily improve durability or appearance retention, although it may. After a certain point, increased cost is often for special effects or a more luxurious fabric. This may be well worth the cost in a special focal area but is seldom cost effective over a large area. In fact, the expensive luxury fabric is apt to need special care and not be at all suitable for health care use.

Where spillage and heavy soiling are problems, vinyls are effective, as the cleaning is easier. In all other areas, textiles, properly specified, are easy to maintain and should be considered for their appearance and comfort qualities.

Organization of Chapters on Upholstery

For each functional area of the health care facility, advantages and limitations of upholstery materials must be evaluated and balanced. The following chapters on textiles and chemical-coated fabrics are intended to help the reader make knowledgeable decisions. The information is organized as follows: properties, health and safety, construction and finishes, maintenance, fabrication, and specification notes.

Properties

Properties are the characteristics or attributes of the material. Each fabric has certain properties as a result of the components used and the way they are put together. This section examines those properties which are important to evaluate. Testing methods and performance standards are identified.

Health and Safety

With each fabric, there are associated questions of health and safety. This section seeks to respond to those most frequently asked.

Construction and Finishes

Construction includes both the component parts and the way they are assembled. Understanding the construction of a fabric will aid in assessing how the desired properties are achieved and to what extent they are possible. Seldom can all criteria be met; understanding the construction will help in setting priorities and meeting the most important needs. This is especially true with textiles, which are very complex fabrics. Appropriate finishes enhance the performance attributes achieved in the construction.

Maintenance

In this section, maintenance requirements are discussed. In evaluating any fabric, it is essential to understand the equipment and labor that will be needed to maintain it. These will profoundly affect the total cost of the product. They must be added to the initial cost to calculate the life cycle cost.

Fabrication

As previously stated, this section is not a complete guide to fabrication. Reliable manufacturers and workrooms will use fabrication methods they have developed and used successfully over time. One of the vital steps in preparing the fabrication specification is to provide a way to evaluate the quality of work of the bidders.

What will be provided in this section is assistance with matching certain fabrication details with the function of the space and other client needs.

Specification Notes

This is not a complete guide to specification. Rather, it identifies special points that are often not given the attention they deserve and details and refinements that are often overlooked.

Chapter Fourteen

TEXTILE UPHOLSTERY FABRICS

THE PROPERTIES of virtually every fabric originate with the properties of the fiber. In this chapter, the properties of textile fibers particularly important to upholstery will be examined.

However, the fiber properties are only the beginning. These may be modified, enhanced or diminished in the making of the yarn and in construction of the textile. Finishes are added at all stages of production and play an important role in determining the characteristics of any textile. They are used in the preparation of fibers and yarns for construction, to give a variety of surface effects and to enhance performance. Even when the textile is completed, external influences do not end. The fabrication of the upholstery and the construction of the furniture will make a difference in the usable life of the textile as will the maintenance it receives.

Properties

The life expectancy of an upholstery textile, as with all other finishes, is based on durability properties. For upholstery textiles, **principal durability properties are abrasion resistance, extensibility** and **elasticity, strength,** and **resistance to slippage.** However, durability is not enough.

For an upholstery to continue to be useful, it must not just hold together but retain its appearance as well. A fabric that appears worn is as detrimental to the image and perceived quality of an institution as one that actually is worn. **Principal appearance-retention properties are dimensional stability, resistance to snagging, resistance to fuzzing and pilling, color retention, texture and pattern,** and **soil resistance.**

Specification standards for plain, tufted or flocked upholstery fabrics as used in new indoor furniture are set forth in ASTM D3597. Within

ASTM D3597, certain ASTM and AATCC test methods are refer-enced. The Joint Industry Upholstery Fabric Standards Committee has also set forth specification standards for upholstery fabrics, both woven and knitted. These are identified under UFS numbers. ASTM test methods are referenced in the Joint Industry standards, and most per-formance requirements are the same as for ASTM D3597, although ASTM D3597 specifically states it is not applicable to knitted fabrics.

The following is a brief description of durability and appearance-retention factors and the principal contributors. Test methods are refer-enced where applicable. Once these life-expectancy factors have been reviewed, greater insight and understanding can be gained by reading the section "Textile Construction and Finishes." A summary of specifica-tion standards can be found in Table 14.1.

Abrasion Resistance

In the yarn, abrasion resistance is affected by the type of fiber as well as the size, twist and ply of the yarn. Abrasion resistance of nylon is ex-cellent; that of acrylic and wool is medium. Thick yarn, a tight twist and plied yarns provide the most resistant surface. In the fabric, a close-set weave provides abrasion resistance, as each yarn serves to protect adja-cent ones. A thick, soft fabric has a cushioning effect that helps minimize abrasion.

Upholstery fabrics are commonly tested by the oscillatory-cylinder method (Wyzenbeek). As with any laboratory test, results are not con-clusive predictors of performance in the field. They are, however, rea-sonable indicators and the results should be taken into consideration.

The oscillatory-cylinder method is defined in ASTM test method D4157. This may cause some confusion, as the fabric specifications published by many manufacturers reference ASTM D1175, oscillatory-cylinder method, and the ASTM D3597 specification standard also pre-scribes D1175. However, D1175 which defined two test methods was discontinued in 1982 and replaced by two separate numbers, D4157, be-ing the oscillatory-cylinder method.

In the oscillatory-cylinder method, the fabric is rubbed back and forth by an abradant-covered roller. The measure is the number of dou-ble rubs (sometimes called cycles) needed to break a yarn. To be classi-fied as heavy duty, a fabric must withstand 15,000 double rubs. There are many fabrics available that withstand 40,000 and more. These should be strongly considered for heavily used areas.

Table 14.1

SPECIFICATION STANDARDS FOR UPHOLSTERY TEXTILES

Characteristic	ASTM#	AATCC#	UFS#	Requirements
Abrasion Resistance	D4157		16	Heavy duty 15,000 cycles, min.
Tensile Strength (Breaking Load)	D1682		14	50 lbs., min.
Tear Strength	D2262		11	6 lbs., min. (a) 4.5 lbs., min. (b)
Seam Breaking Strength	D434 D4034 (c)		15	25 lbs., min. 50 lbs., min.
Yarn Slippage			18	7,000 cycles, min.
Dimensional Change (warp or filling)	D3597		13	5% shrinkage, max. 2% gain, max.
Colorfastness to: (d)				
Crocking (dry)		8	07	class 4, min.
Crocking (wet)		8	07	class 3, min.
Light (40 hrs)		16	08	class 4, min.
Water and Solvent		107	10	class 4, min.
Burnt Gas Fumes		23	09	class 4, min.

Of these standards, abrasion resistance and lightfastness are the ones most frequently listed on fabric samples.

Legend:
ASTM = American Society for Testing and Materials
AATCC = American Association of Textile Chemists and Colorists
UFS   = Joint Industry Committee Upholstery Fabric Standards

Notes:
(a) For Category 1 fabrics defined as flat, woven fabrics except lightweight printed-cotton fabrics (less than 8 oz/sq yd).
(b) For Category 11 fabrics defined as woven pile-fabrics, tufted pile-fabrics and flocked pile-fabrics. Required also for knitted fabrics by Joint Industry Committee.
(c) For knitted fabrics, D4034 is a modified version of D434.
(d) Colorfastness ratings are on a scale of 1 to 5 with class 5 being the best.

Whatever the fabric, abrasive wear can be minimized by appropriate fabric use and fabrication techniques. Arms of seating pieces are the place most vulnerable to wear. The use of non-upholstered arms is recommended for heavily used locations. The second most vulnerable wear point is the top, front edge of the seat, especially if there is a welt. Welts are points of wear, both because they extend above the surface and because the fabric covering of the welt is tightly stretched.

The furniture construction and style is also a factor in abrasion resistance. A resilient undercushioning will help protect the fabric. A tightly stretched fabric is more vulnerable to abrasion than one that is not so tightly stretched.

Extensibility and Elasticity

These properties have to do with the ability to extend when a force is applied and to recover the original size and shape immediately after stress-causing deformation. These are extremely important both in abrasion resistance, so that the fabric can "give" rather than "fight" when an abrading force is applied, and in shape retention. A fabric is expected to fit furniture without buckling, sagging or wrinkling. To do this, it must be able to expand when seating is occupied and regain its shape when the occupant leaves.

Nylon has excellent extensibility and elasticity. In the man-made yarns, those that are crimped and heat-set have the greatest extensibility and elasticity. These two properties are present to a greater extent in knit than in woven constructions.

Strength

Tensile Strength: The tensile strength of a fabric refers to its ability to resist breaking under tension. It is a result of the tenacity of the fiber, the spinning of the yarn and the construction of the cloth. Of the natural fibers, silk and linen have outstanding tensile strength. Of the synthetics, nylon and polyester are outstanding. Tightly twisted yarns are stronger than less twisted ones and tightly woven fabrics are stronger than loosely woven ones.

However, low tensile strength which results in tears and splits is not a common hazard in fabrics designated by the manufacturer as appropriate for institutional or contract use. The biggest factor about which one should be aware is the possibility that flame retardants and some other chemical finishes can lower the inherent tensile strength of the fiber. Tensile strength as well as elongation or stretch is measured using ASTM D1682, Test Methods for Breaking Load and Elongation of Textile Fabrics.

Tear Strength: Resistance to further tearing once a slit or tear develops is measured by tear·strength tests. D2262, Test Method for

Tearing Strength of Woven Fabrics by the Tongue Method, is the method prescribed under ASTM D3597. The Joint Industry Committee prescribes a modified 2262 for knitted fabrics.

SEAM BREAKING STRENGTH: The ability of a fabric to hold a secure seam is essential for long life of any upholstery. Several factors enter into this and there is further discussion in the next few paragraphs on seam slippage. Seam slippage and seam breaking strength are tested in accordance with test method D434 as specified in ASTM D3597. The Joint Industry Committee uses the same test method but requires a higher minimum force to rupture the seam.

Resistance to Slippage

Slippage occurs when the warp or filling yarns slide over one another. Smooth yarns tend to slip more than rough ones. This action will not only speed abrasion but mar the appearance. The weave will become uneven and, in case of poor dye penetration in piece-dyed goods, non-colored yarn segments will be revealed. The best guards against slippage are tightly woven, balanced (equal yarn count in warp and weft) constructions and the use of back coatings when a fabric may be susceptible.

The most troublesome form of slippage is seam slippage when seaming stitches hold firm and adjacent yarns pull away. Yarns can also ravel out at the cut edge. Back coatings will help prevent these problems.

The Joint Industry Committee recommends the Dynamic Seam Fatigue (Schnadig) method for testing seam slippage. In this test, a specimen with the type of seam to be tested is mounted over polyurethane foam simulating a seat cushion. A fatiguing load is applied through a freely moving, rubber-faced wheel which is dropped onto the specimen from a constant height. The circumference of the wheel impacts the mounted specimen parallel to and one inch from the seam. Continuous impact cycling is begun and continued at a constant rate until failure is observed or 7000 cycles have been completed.

In the fabrication of the upholstery, workroom procedures that will help prevent seam slippage and raveling include:

1. Seam allowances of at least 1/2"–3/4".
2. Machine stitching the outline of the pattern before cutting.
3. Double-stitching seams.
4. Muslin reinforcement of seams.

Dimensional Stability

For a fabric covering to maintain its fit, it must maintain its initial size, neither shrinking nor gaining. Exposure to water, either in the laundry or by spillage, is the major reason for dimensional change. Dimensional change is tested by subjecting a specimen to soaking and drying under controlled conditions. Wool is particularly susceptible to shrinkage; nylon, being non-absorbent, is not likely to shrink.

Resistance to Snagging

A snag occurs when a yarn is caught and pulled out of the fabric surface. Loosely constructed fabrics and fabrics with long floats are the most susceptible to snagging. (Floats are explained in later sections on "Twill Weave" and "Satin Weave.") Backings tend to reduce snagging. A very tight construction is the surest way to prevent it.

While many snags are caused by an accidental brush with a sharp object, others are caused because people tend to pick at a fabric when they are idle or nervous. This is often the case in hospitals and nursing homes where people may be apprehensive and nervous and where long hours may be spent waiting with little of interest to occupy one's time.

Resistance to Shedding and Pilling

Shedding results from fibers working out of the fabric and onto the surface. Pilling results when these fibers collect in little balls or pills. Both conditions, besides being unsightly, provide places for dirt to collect. There is no acceptable test method for shedding or pilling of upholstery fabrics.

Wool fabrics sometimes pill, but this is not considered to be serious. Wool fibers are relatively weak and the pills eventually fall off. It is much more serious when a spun nylon pills, as the fibers are so strong that they do not fall off. About the only solution for restoring the appearance of a pilled, spun nylon is to actually cut off the pills. This can be done by shaving the fabric with a safety razor. A better answer, of course, is to avoid the problem by using a filament nylon in locations subject to heavy wear. (The difference in a spun and filament nylon will be explained in a following section, entitled "Yarn.")

Color Retention

COLOR ABRASION: Where there has been poor dye penetration, abrasive action can cause loss of color. This is most frequent with linen but can happen with cotton and synthetics as well.

It is most common in piece-dyed goods but can also happen in yarn-dyed ones. Portions that rise above the surface, such as nubs in a nubby fabric and welts, are the most susceptible.

CROCKING: Crocking is the rubbing off of excess dyestuff onto some other surface. The color of the fabric itself is not changed. It is the other surface such as a wall or people's clothing that is affected.

There are two kinds of crocking: wet and dry. These refer to the crocking of a wet fabric or a dry fabric. While neither is common, dry crocking sometimes occurs in wools as residual oils containing dyestuffs rub off. Certainly, one should be aware of the possibility of wet crocking where incontinent patients may be seated. It is easy enough to test for crocking: simply wipe a clean white cloth across the fabric surface, both wet and dry.

Crockfastness is measured under AATCC test method 8. The test measures the degree of color transfer from the textile to a white cloth rubbed across its face.

FADING: Dyes are subject to attack from chemicals, atmospheric contaminants and sunlight. Some fibers and colors are more vulnerable than others. Nylon fibers will deteriorate in the sun. Reds and rusts, in particular, should not be selected for areas where they will be constantly exposed to the sun.

Many manufacturers are testing their upholstery fabrics for lightfastness under AATCC 16A which measures colorfastness to light in a carbon arc fadeometer and under AATCC 16E which measures colorfastness to light in a xenon arc fadeometer. AATCC tests also include those for atmospheric fading and colorfastness to water and to solvents.

Texture and Pattern

The effectiveness of texture and pattern in concealing wear is discussed in Chapter Two, "Carpet." Many of the comments are relevant to upholstery, also. In specifying an upholstery textile, care should be taken to select a texture that does not have small portions extending above the overall surface, as these are especially subject to abrasion.

Soil Resistance

The most soil-resistant fabrics are those which present the least surface area and are the least absorbent. Thus, smooth, non-absorbent fibers in a tightly constructed textile would be the most soil resistant.

However, fibers which are non-absorbent toward one class of chemicals often readily absorb another. Polyester is an excellent example; while it resists water-borne soil, it readily absorbs oil-borne soil. In addition, fibers that are low in moisture content tend to generate static electricity which, in turn, attracts soil particles. Generic nylon is an example of this.

Modifications to the fiber itself may be made to aid soil resistance. More often, various finishes are used to enhance soil resistance. Soil-release agents are also useful in maintaining a new appearance.

Other Requirements

Under ASTM D3597, retention of hand, character and appearance shall not change more than in the limitations set by prior agreement between purchaser and seller. Also, durability of back coating should be compatible with the recommended cleaning method. These are properties which are visually observed after undergoing tests for dimensional change and colorfastness to water and to solvent.

Health and Safety

Flammability

An extensive discussion was presented in Chapter Thirteen, "Introduction to Upholstery Fabrics."

Biogenic Factors

Places where people sit for long periods of time can become warm and moist, providing a breeding ground for microorganisms. Various chemicals are used in the finishing process to counteract this. This can also be minimized by selecting seating constructed with as few crevices as possible. Minimizing crevices prevents soil accumulation and provides for easy cleanup when accidents happen such as those with incontinent patients. For many locations, it is important to select fabric that can withstand frequent cleaning with antimicrobial solutions.

Electrostatic Propensity

Under conditions of reasonable humidity, this is not likely to be a problem in most patient, visitor or staff seating. It is only when using sensitive electronic equipment that static in upholstery factors is likely to be a problem. Wool can be used or, if a synthetic such as nylon is desired for other reasons, one with appropriately modified fibers or finish treatment can be used.

Textile Construction and Finishes

Fibers are the basic component of textiles. The properties of the fibers are a major contributing factor to the final characteristics of a textile. However, fiber selection is only the beginning. The fiber, the yarn, the method of textile construction and the finishes are all interdependent. Together, they determine the characteristics of the finished textile. In order to understand what a particular fiber will contribute to the textile, it is necessary to understand the basic properties of fibers.

Fiber Classification

It would be impractical to remember the properties of each individual fiber. For easier reference, a classification system has been devised. Within each class many properties are similar. This classification system was introduced in Chapter Eleven, "Drapery."

To review, fiber classification is based on:

1. Origin of fiber—natural or man-made
2. General chemical type—cellulosic, protein, mineral or synthetic
3. Generic term—e.g. wool is a generic protein, nylon is a generic synthetic.

For further review on the classification of fibers, turn back to Chapter Eleven, "Drapery."

Table 14.2

CLASSIFICATION OF FIBERS

Natural Fibers		Man-made Fibers		
Cellulosic	**Protein**	**Regenerated Cellulosic**	**Synthetic**	**Mineral**
Cotton	*Wool	Rayon	*Nylon	Fiberglass
Linen	Silk	Acetate	Olefin	
		Triacetate	Saran	
			Acrylic	
			Modacrylic	
			Polyester	

*indicates the fibers used most often for upholstery textiles for health care use.

Fibers used most often for upholstery in institutional settings are **wool** and **nylon**. These are often combined to obtain the best properties of each.

Modacrylic fibers which are inherently flame resistant are sometimes used where fire codes are most strict.

Olefin has many good performance characteristics but is not inherently flame resistant, is more subject to abrasion and less resilient than nylon and has limited aesthetic possibilities. These limit its application, but for very tight budget jobs it is a viable choice.

Cotton, rayon, acrylic and polyester are each sometimes used in combination with wool for special effects or budget purposes.

Fiber Properties

In evaluating fibers for use in upholstery, there are certain properties that could be judged to be most important. These are **tensile strength, dimensional stability, absorbency, reaction to chemicals,** and **reaction to the environment.**

STRENGTH: The tensile strength of a fiber is a measure of its ability to withstand tension without breaking. The strength or **tenacity** of a fiber is expressed in grams per denier (GPD) as follows:

> 5–8 GPD, exceptionally strong
> 2.5–4 GPD, strong
> 1.5–2 GPD, weak

Flexibility is also a part of strength. This is the ability of a fiber to resist breaking under repeated flexing.

DIMENSIONAL STABILITY: The ability of a fiber to be dimensionally stable is dependent on a number of contributing properties. **Extensibility** is the ability of the fiber to be extended. **Recovery** is the percentage of return to the original length after extension. **Elasticity** is the ability to recover its original size and shape after extension. **Resiliency** is the ability to return to its original shape after bending, compressing or crushing.

ABSORBENCY: **Moisture regain** indicates the normal moisture level at standard conditions. **Absorption** indicates the amount of water the fiber is capable of holding. Absorbency influences effectiveness of some finishes and dyes. Highly absorbent fibers may be subject to shrinkage when fabrics are heated for drying or pressing. Absorbency is important to comfort. Non-absorbent fibers tend to feel hot and sticky when sat upon for any length of time.

REACTION TO CHEMICALS: Fibers react differently to different classes of chemicals. Reactions of most interest in the health care environment are those to alkalis, acids and solvents.

REACTION TO ENVIRONMENTS: This would include resistance to microorganisms and insects, sun and fire. In general, natural fibers, including man-made regenerated cellulosics, are subject to degradation by microorganisms and insects; synthetics are not. Resistance to sunlight may or may not be important, depending on the building orientation and the furniture placement. Fire code compliance will often require a particular flame-resistance rating. Responsible designers may wish to take precautions beyond those required, especially when requirements are minimal or non-existent.

Advantages and Limitations

The following paragraphs briefly state some important advantages and limitations of fibers typically used in upholstery textiles. (See Table 14.3 for a summary evaluation of properties.)

WOOL:

Advantages
Excellent flexibility
Exceptionally good resiliency and elasticity
High resistance to solvents
Slow burning and self-extinguishing

Limitations
Low strength
Low resistance to alkalis
Poor solar resistance
Susceptible to insects

While the dimensional-stability factors of the wool fiber are good to exceptionally good, the dimensional stability of the yarn and the fabric made of wool are not good. Wool is highly absorbent, about 30 percent. Moisture absorption and subsequent drying will cause shrinking in fibers that, because of their good extensibility, have been stretched in the spinning and weaving process. The absorbed moisture appears to release the tension of prolonged extension. It is the elastic recovery after exposure to moisture that causes shrinkage. While the fiber has all the characteristics of dimensional stability, the fabric turns out to be not dimensionally stable.

Table 14.3

EVALUATION GUIDE: PROPERTIES OF FIBERS

Property	Wool	Nylon	Modac	Olefin	Cotton	Rayon	Acryl	Poly
Strength	2	4	3	*	4	*	3	*
Flexibility	5	3	3	4	3	3	3	4
Resiliency	4	5	5	4	2	2	5	3
Extensibility	4	4	4	*	2	2	4	4
Recovery	3	5	3	3	1	1	3	5
Elasticity	4	4	3	3	2	2	3	4
Absorbency	4	2	2	2	4	4	2	1
Resistance to:								
Alkali	2	4	4	4	4	3	3	3
Acid	3	2	4	4	2	3	3	4
Solvents	4	4	4	2	4	4	4	4
Sun	1	1	5	3	3	1	5	3
Micro/Insects	1	5	5	5	1	1	5	5
Reaction to:								
Flame	BS	BS/M	M	B/M	BQ	BQ	BQ/M	BS/M
Flame removal	SE	SE	SE	CB	CB	CB	CB	SE

Abrasion resistance is a function of strength, flexibility and resiliency.

Dimensional stability is a function of resiliency, extensibility, recovery, elasticity and absorbency.

Legend:

* = dependent on formulation   Modac = modacrylic
5 = excellent or very high   Acryl   = acrylic
4 = very good or high   Poly   = polyester
3 = good or medium
2 = fair or low
1 = poor or very low

B = burns, S = slowly, Q = quickly, M = melts,
SE = self extinguishing, CB = continues burning

NYLON: Nylon's strength, flexibility and resiliency combine to give it excellent abrasion resistance.

Advantages

High strength
Good flexibility
Very high resiliency
High to excellent dimensional stability factors
High resistance to alkalis and solvents
Excellent resistance to microorganisms and insects
Slow burning and self-extinguishing

Limitations
Low resistance to acids
Poor solar resistance
Accumulation of static electricity in unmodified fiber
May be flammable in sheer and brushed pile fabrics

Nylon has low moisture absorbency, about 8 percent at 95 percent relative humidity. The advantage of this is that nylon fabrics tend not to stain with water-borne soil and maintain their dimensional stability. Limitations are that it can be uncomfortable against the skin, it is difficult to dye, and static electricity problems are magnified in unmodified fibers.

MODACRYLIC: This is an inherently flame resistant fiber. A fabric with a modacrylic content of at least 70 percent usually passes stringent flame tests.

Advantages
Good flexibility
Good to high dimensional stability factors except elasticity
High resistance to alkalis, acids and solvents
Excellent solar resistance
Excellent resistance to microorganisms and insects
Flame resistant
Antistatic

Limitations
Medium strength
Medium elasticity

Modacrylic has good bulking properties and can be made to resemble wool in appearance.

ACRYLIC: The properties of acrylic are the same as those of modacrylic except that it is not flame resistant. Acrylics burn quickly and continue to burn after the flame is withdrawn.

OLEFIN: Like modacrylic, olefin is a synthetic and has many similar properties. The differences are:

1. Strength and extensibility dependent upon formulation
2. Low resistance to solvents
3. Poor resistance to solar radiation
4. Not flame resistant
5. Low melting point

POLYESTER: Like nylon, polyester is a synthetic; it has many similar properties. The differences are:

1. Only medium resilience
2. Only medium resistance to alkali
3. High resistance to acids
4. Good solar resistance

Special features are that polyester has excellent wrinkle resistance and good dye affinity. However, it also has an affinity for oil-borne stains and they are very difficult to remove.

COTTON AND RAYON: These fibers are both cellulosics and have many properties in common.

Advantages

High strength (cotton — rayon varies with formulation)
Good flexibility
High resistance to alkali (cotton only)
High resistance to solvents
Good solar resistance (cotton only)

Limitations

Low to poor dimensional stability factors
Low to medium acid resistance
Poor solar resistance (rayon)
Poor resistance to microorganisms and insects
Burns quickly and continues to burn when flame is withdrawn

Cotton and rayon are both highly absorbent.

Modification of Fibers

Natural fibers can be modified by chemical or mechanical treatments of the yarn as will be discussed later in the section on "Finishes."

Man-made fibers can be modified in almost limitless ways. Some of these are: modification of the cross section, modification of the chemistry, delustering, texturizing and the making of fiber combinations.

MODIFICATION OF CROSS SECTION: Originally, man-made fibers were extruded through round holes in a spinneret and had a round cross section. By changing the shape of the orifice, fibers with shapes such as tri-lobal, rectangular and pentagonal are produced. Hollow tubes through the center are another modification. These modifications change the sheen, texture and opacity of the fiber.

MODIFICATION OF THE CHEMISTRY: The chemical composition may be modified to enhance the dyeing, soil-release, flame-resistant, solar-resistant and anti-static properties.

DELUSTERING: A high degree of luster or sheen is an inherent property of man-made fibers. When this is an undesirable property, chemicals added to the solution can produce a pitted surface that will dull the reflectivity and thus the sheen of the fiber.

TEXTURIZING: Bulkier and loftier fibers are produced by incorporating air spaces in the fiber. Fibers can be crimped by chemical or mechanical methods. Crimped fibers are used to produce thicker, more resilient yarn.

FIBER COMBINATIONS: Fibers are combined or blended in many different ways. Methods of blending and the proportion of each fiber to use are subjects of much study. The concept is to produce a new fiber which has the best properties of the component fibers.

Some of the dependable fibers used for blends and their functions are:

1. *Acrylic:* contributes bulk and texture, provides dimensional stability.
2. *Nylon:* adds strength; as little as 15 percent will improve strength of a wool fabric. Also adds abrasion resistance, durability and dimensional stability.
3. *Polyester:* provides wrinkle resistance and press retention as well as strength and abrasion resistance.
4. *Rayon:* provides an easy way to add decorative effects and color. Gives the fabric an improved "hand" or tactile quality.

Yarn

Before most fabrics can be constructed, the fibers must be made into yarn. Yarn is the general name for the linear elements employed in fabric construction. It is an assemblage of fibers that are laid or twisted together to form a continuous strand.

Types of yarn construction are based on the length of the fiber. Fibers come in two basic lengths: staple and filament.

STAPLE FIBERS: These are short fibers that are measured in inches or centimeters. They range from 3/4"–18" (2 cm–46 cm). All natural fibers except silk are in staple form.

FILAMENT FIBERS: These are long continuous strands measured in yards or meters. All man-made fibers are produced as filaments. Silk is the only natural fiber in filament form. Silk filaments may be 1600 yards long.

Based on the fiber from which it is formed, yarn is of two types. **Spun yarn** is made from staple fibers. **Filament yarn** is made from filament fibers. Filament fibers can be cut into staple length and spun into yarn. When filament fibers are cut into staple and spun, the word spun is included in the yarn description, for example, spun nylon. When yarns are formed from the original fiber, the type of yarn is assumed and would not be mentioned. Yarn formed from filament nylon is simply called nylon; yarn spun from staple cotton is called cotton.

Spun Yarns

Staple fibers are normally spun by one of three systems: the cotton system, the woolen system or the worsted system. Each is designed to:

1. Clean and parallel staple fibers.
2. Draw fibers into a single strand.
3. Twist the fibers to hold them together and give them strength.

The three systems differ, in that each is specialized to deal with the length, cohesiveness, diameter, elasticity and surface contour of the natural fiber for which it was designed. Staple cut from filament is also spun on these systems as appropriate. The resulting yarns differ not only because of fiber characteristics but also because of variations in the total spinning system.

COTTON SYSTEMS: The cotton system is the basic system. Five steps are involved.

1. Opening and loosening of the fibers
2. Cleaning — removes leaves and other impurities
3. Carding — separates fibers, lays them in one direction and begins to draw them out
4. Drafting or roving — continues drawing out, adds twist to hold the fibers together
5. Spinning — adds additional twist to strengthen

This system produces **carded** cotton which has a rough matte texture. Examples of fabrics made with carded yarns are muslin and gingham.

Smoother and more lustrous fabrics are made from **combed** cotton. Combed cotton is made by adding a combing step, after step 3, carding. Shorter fibers are combed out; only the longer fibers remain. Smoother yarns result from spinning these longer fibers. Fabrics with the sheen of organdy and percale are the result.

WOOLEN SYSTEM: This system is similar to the carded cotton system. Fuzzy wool yarns with a soft surface are produced. Tweed and hopsack are examples of fabrics woven from woolen yarns.

WORSTED SYSTEM: The worsted system is similar to the combed-cotton system. Long wool yarns are used and a tight twist is obtained in the spinning step. Fabrics produced with yarns from the worsted system are smooth, crisp and typically tightly woven. Examples are gabardine and serge.

Filament Yarns

Filament fibers are already continuous strands and may be used as is to create monofilament or multifilament yarns. Monofilament yarns are one filament which may be thick as used for monofilament fishing line or thin as used for nylon hosiery. Multifilament yarns are composed of many fine filaments twisted to form one strand of yarn. Most are only lightly twisted, as little twist is needed to hold the filaments together. A tight twist may be used for special effects.

Comparison of Spun and Filament Yarns

Yarns spun from staple will more easily pull apart under stress. Spun yarns have a rougher surface due to the many fiber ends. Shedding and pilling are apt to occur in spun yarns as some of the short fibers pull loose from the yarn.

The strongest yarns are composed of strong filament fibers. Filament yarns are smooth and typically shiny unless modified. Due to their smooth surface, there may be yarn slippage in a fabric.

Plied Yarns

After twisting, the yarns are one-ply or singles yarns. Two or more singles yarns twisted together increase tensile strength, uniformity and abrasion resistace, especially in spun yarns. Filament yarns do not need plying, as these same benefits are derived from the number and size of the filaments. However, filament yarns may be plied for special effects or to achieve a mixture of yarns.

Twisting of most ply yarns is in the direction opposite to the twist of the singles from which they are made.

Varieties of Yarn

CREPE: Crepe yarns are very tightly twisted ply yarns. They are pebbly, elastic and matte textured.

CORD OR CABLE: These are thick yarns made of multiple-ply yarns twisted together.

SLUB: Slub yarns are spun yarns which have the twist interrupted at intervals. This leaves soft, bulky sections along the length of the yarn.

NUB: In a nub yarn, dense fibers are incorporated along the length of the yarn. These form enlarged segments or nubs.

RATINÉ: A ratiné yarn is made up by twisting one heavy ply back and forth across a thread-like core.

BOUCLÉ: This is a variation of ratiné which appears looped and curly.

SEED OR KNOT: These are another version of ratiné with knots at regular intervals along the length.

SPIRAL OR CORKSCREW: Two yarns of different diameters are twisted together. The unevenness forms the spiral or corkscrew.

CHENILLE: Chenille yarns are cut from a leno woven fabric. (A leno construction is one in which two or more warp ends twist between insertions of weft, providing resistance to slippage.) The fabric is constructed and then cut between the warp yarns. The soft filling yarns form the fuzzy pile of the chenille.

ELASTIC OR STRETCH: These are made in two ways, either from yarn wound around a spandex or latex core, or from highly crimped, heat-set fibers.

Fabric Construction

A fabric is a planar structure produced by interlaced or interlocked fibers or yarns. Most fabrics for upholstery are constructed by weaving. When a stretchable fabric is needed, a knit construction is often used.

Woven Fabrics

Woven fabrics are made by the interlacing of two or more sets of yarns at right angles to each other. Lengthwise yarn is called the warp. These are the yarns that are strung onto the loom. They are usually the stronger of the two sets of yarns. Warp yarns are sometimes called ends. Filling yarns interlace the warp to form the fabric. They are also called picks, weft or woof.

All woven fabrics are based on one of three constructions: **plain** weave, **twill** weave and **satin** weave. The extraordinary variety that can be produced is the result of the variety of yarn groupings, sizes, and density and the interrelationship of all of these in addition to the great variety in yarn types, sheen and color.

Plain Weave

Of all textile constructions, plain weave is the most universal. In a plain weave, each filling yarn passes alternately over and under one warp yarn. Likewise, each warp yarn passes over and under each filling yarn. Homespun and chintz are simple plain weaves.

GROUPING: The simplest variation of plain weave is grouping. Basket weave is produced by doubling yarns in both the warp and the weft. Hopsacking is a fabric using coarse yarns in a basket weave. In further variations, the yarns may be doubled in one direction only.

MIXING YARN SIZES: To produce many other variations, yarn sizes can be mixed. Taffeta is a plain woven fabric in which the filling is heavier than the warp, producing a fine crisp rib. Canvas, duck and sailcloth are all basket weaves where two warp ends interlace with a heavier singles filling.

CHANGING THE DENSITY: The density of construction will modify the weave. The importance of density becomes clear with the realization

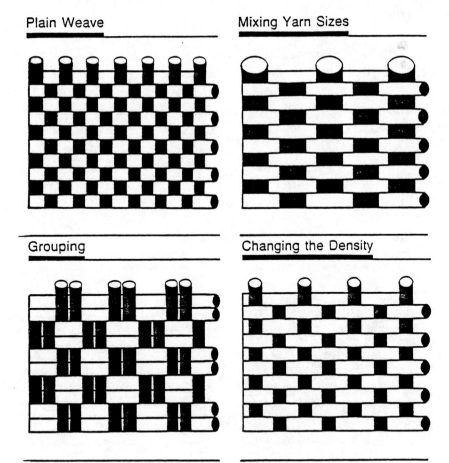

Figure 14.1. PLAIN WEAVE AND VARIATIONS. An incredible variety of fabrics can be constructed by employing simple variations of the plain weave such as grouping several yarns as one, using two or more yarn types or sizes, and changing the yarn density.

that cheesecloth and muslin are woven using yarns of approximately the same size and type. As increasing the density increases both the quantity of yarn used and the production time, it becomes a key factor in textile cost. High-density upholstery fabrics are the most durable and also more costly than lower-density textiles.

Most plain weaves are more or less balanced; that is, they have an equal yarn count in warp and weft. By cramming in extra yarns in one direction, a rib is formed. Rep, grosgrain and ottoman are plain weaves with crammed or closely set warp yarns. These all have a horizontal rib. When the filling yarns are crammed, a vertical rib results. Bedford cord is an example.

Twill Weave

Twill weaves are characterized by the diagonal ridges exposed on the surface. They are formed by the systematic floating of yarns in one direction. A float is a portion of a yarn that floats or passes over two or more adjacent, opposing yarns.

Twills may be balanced with an order of interlacing, such as over two warp yarns and under two. A fabric constructed with a balanced twill is the same on both sides.

An uneven twill such as over two, under one, will have a warp face and a filling face that differ. If, as in denim, the warp and filling yarns are a different color, the colors of the face and back of the fabric will differ.

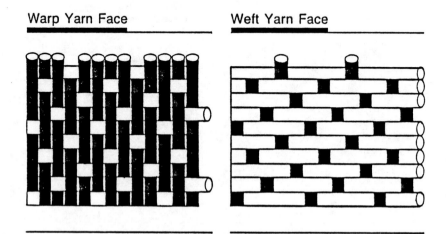

Figure 14.2. WARP AND WEFT YARN FACES. In uneven twills, either the warp yarn or the weft yarn will predominate on the face of the fabric. If the warp and weft yarns are of two different colors, the face color will vary in accordance with the predominant yarn.

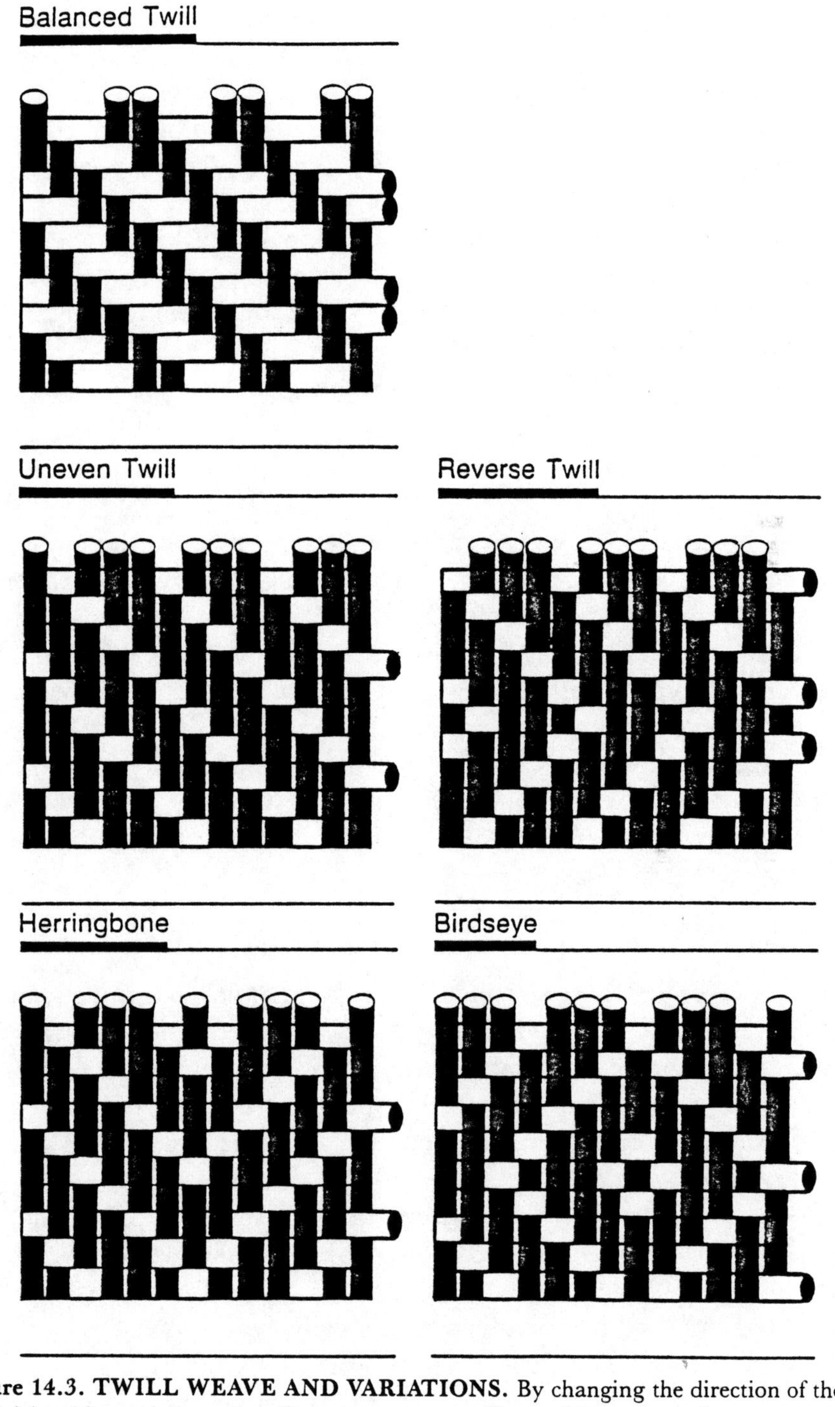

Balanced Twill

Uneven Twill

Reverse Twill

Herringbone

Birdseye

Figure 14.3. TWILL WEAVE AND VARIATIONS. By changing the direction of the diagonal in either a balanced twill or an uneven twill, a wide variety of patterns can be achieved.

Twill constructions enable a denser, more tightly crammed construction than do equivalent plain weaves. For stability, this is required, as the longer the float, the denser the construction must be.

REVERSE TWILL: The direction of the diagonal can be from right to left or from left to right. A combination of the two along the length of the fabric is a reverse twill.

HERRINGBONE: If the reversal of direction is across the width of the fabric, the twill weave is known as a herringbone.

BIRD'S-EYE: A combination of reverse twill and herringbone produces a diamond shape, called a bird's-eye.

HOUNDSTOOTH: Still another variation of twill weave is a broken check pattern known as houndstooth.

Satin Weave

The third basic weave is a satin weave. Satin is also the name of the cloth constructed. This is an extension of twill weave with a longer float and a staggered progression of floats rather than a regular one. The simplest type of satin weave is five-point satin, where each warp yarn floats over five weft yarns and under one. This is a warp face textile, because the warp yarns predominate on the face of the fabric.

A variation of satin is a filling-faced fabric where it is the filling or weft yarns that float on the face. This is called sateen.

Satin weaves are seldom suitable for upholstery fabrics, as the long floats are vulnerable to snagging.

Pile Weaves

Pile weaves are those in which an extra set of yarns is introduced into a ground fabric of plain or twill weave. The extra set of yarns forms raised loops which can be cut or left uncut. Most of the pile fabrics used in upholstery are woven with a supplementary set of warp yarns which is raised over a rod or wire to form the pile. A few are made with a supplementary set of weft yarns.

FRIEZE AND GROSPOINT: For frieze and grospoint fabrics, the warp yarns are raised over a round wire, which is then withdrawn leaving horizontal rows of uncut loops. The yarns used for a frieze are very tightly twisted and the result is a very sturdy, warp pile cloth.

VELVET, VELOUR AND PLUSH: These warp pile fabrics are woven with the warp raised over sharp wires rather than round wires. As these wires are withdrawn, the loops are cut forming the familiar cut pile fabrics. Velvets are made from various fibers and have a low dense pile. Velours

Weft Pile

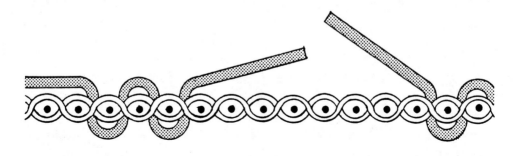

Warp Pile

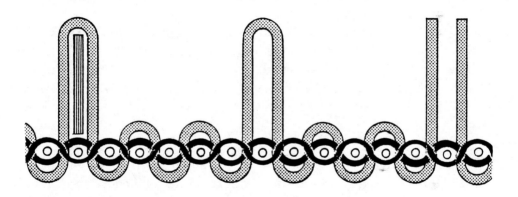

Figure 14.4. PILE WEAVES. In weft pile weaves, the supplementary yarns are woven into the fabric with long floats. After weaving, these floats are cut to form the pile. In warp pile weaves, the supplementary yarns are raised over a wire to form a loop. If a cut pile is desired, the wire used is sharp on the upper edge. It cuts the loops as it is withdrawn.

are usually of linen or cotton and have a somewhat higher pile. They may be calendered flat in a panné finish or crushed. Plush, usually of worsted or mohair yarns, has a still higher pile. Sometimes, plushes are crushed or embossed.

VELVETEEN AND CORDUROY: The pile fabrics discussed so far all have warp piles. There are also cut pile fabrics with a weft yarn pile. Two of these are velveteen and curduroy. Where the supplementary element is a weft yarn, the pile is created after weaving by cutting weft floats. Curduroy comes in many variations, some with large-ribbed, wide wales and some with cables and other patterns.

The quality and durability of pile fabrics depends on the fiber and yarn used and the density of the pile. Long, thin yarns woven in a low density are subject to matting down and are easily abraded. For durability, the pile must be very dense.

Jacquard Fabrics

Jacquard fabrics also have extra sets of yarns. They are produced on looms equipped with a special overhead mechanism. This employs punched pattern cards similar to computer-punched cards to control and place individual yarns which are woven into the ground cloth to form a pattern.

The invention of the Jacquard loom by Joseph Marie Jacquard revolutionized weaving and made possible a new range of multicolored, intricate patterns. It is possible to produce extremely elaborate patterns on the Jacquard loom. Brocade and tapestry are examples.

These fabrics may have long floats as the supplementary yarns are alternately exposed and removed from view. Long floats on the face of the fabric are not suitable for upholstery in locations that will receive heavy wear. Long floats are not a problem on the fabric back where they are not exposed to snagging or picking.

Dobby Weaves

Fabrics with small figures such as dots and geometric shapes are produced on a loom with a dobby attachment, usually called a dobby loom. In this loom, multiple warp yarns are also controlled by punched cards.

Knitted Construction

At present, a very small portion of upholstery fabrics are of knitted construction. However, potential for increased use is high. Knitting is faster than weaving with resulting economy. New machinery and techniques have made possible greater fabric stability and more variety than previously possible. Along with excellent resilience, knitted fabrics have an inherent stretch capacity and good recovery. These properties make them an excellent choice for upholstering contoured furniture, as less time and skill are required to obtain a tailored appearance than with woven fabrics.

Knitted fabrics are constructed using needles that form a series of interlocking loops from a single yarn or set of yarns and connect rows of loops into a continuous cloth. Knits are basically classified according to the method of knitting: weft knit or warp knit. In weft knitting, the structure is formed by horizontal passes of the needles and yarn similar to hand knitting. In warp knitting, loops are formed vertically. As they are simultaneously formed across the width of the fabric, each is interlocked with an adjacent warp yarn. In both weft and warp knits, a horizontal row of loops is called a course; a vertical column is called a wale.

Knit Fabrics

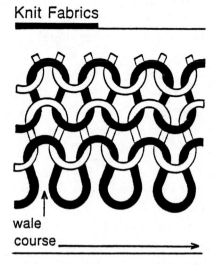

wale

course ⟶

Figure 14.5. KNIT CONSTRUCTION. In all types of knitted fabrics, the horizontal rows of loops are called courses and the vertical columns are called wales.

WEFT KNITS: Weft knit goods are produced as single or double knits. Single-knit fabrics are seldom used for upholstery, as they are prone to "runs" in the event of snagging. Double knits are run resistant and can make a durable upholstery fabric with excellent dimensional stability. They are firmer, less stretchable, have more body and are more resilient than single knits.

Double-knit fabrics are produced using two sets of needles, resulting in a double thickness of fabric. A Jacquard attachment for individual needle control can be used to produce a variety of patterns.

WARP KNITS: Warp knits are classified by the machine used to produce them. The most important of these are the tricot and the raschel. Tricot knits are generally lightweight and not used for upholstery. Although raschel machines mainly produce lacy casement drapery fabrics, they are capable of producing dense sturdy fabrics as well. Pile yarns can be inserted so that plush fabrics and even carpeting are possible.

The amount of elasticity can be varied as can the texture. A Jacquard attachment can be used for the production of patterns.

VARIATIONS OF KNITS: Warp knit machines can be adapted so that weft yarns can be inserted. This gives greater stability across the width of the fabric than with a standard warp knit fabric. Likewise, weft knit machines can be adapted for warp insertion, giving greater stability in a lengthwise direction than would otherwise be the case. In the knit-weave process, machines have been adapted to insert both weft and warp yarns into the basic structure. Weft or warp insertion in knits can produce fabrics that are stronger and have greater dimensional stability than either knits or weaves.

Knit-sewn fabrics, also called stitch through or stitch bonded, are also strong and dimensionally stable fabrics. These are constructed using a variety of techniques, with the basic concept being that of needles knitting a yarn through warp and weft yarns or through a web of fibers.

Finishes

There are hundreds of finishing processes and treatments that make the textile suitable for its end use. Virtually all textiles have finishes of several kinds. Finishes can be described in three categories: (1) standard finishes make the product ready for use; (2) special finishes affect the appearance and hand of the textile; and (3) functional finishes affect the performance of the fabric.

Color applied after fabric construction can also be considered a finish. Many woven or knitted fabrics are produced as "greige" or grey goods. They are not literally grey but some degree of off-white. These grey goods are dyed near the end of the production process.

Standard Finishes

Fabrics as they come from the loom or knitting machine, particularly those made from natural fibers, contain many impurities. They may be too stiff or too loose. Finishing for natural fibers involves more different processes than for man-made fibers. For all fibers standard finishes make a fabric usable.

Following are some of the many standard finishes for use with upholstery textiles constructed from natural fibers.

BOILING, SCOURING: Impurities are removed by boiling cotton and linen and by scouring wool. Scouring is simply washing in an alkali or solvent solution.

PRE-SHRINKING: Pre-shrinking provides control of shrinkage in the finished textile. It is accomplished in different ways with different fibers, with wool being the most difficult and the most complex.

CARBONIZING, SHEARING, SINGING: Wools are carbonized in acid to remove vegetable matter. They may then be sheared or singed to remove surface fibers. Cottons are also singed.

FULLING: This is a technique in which wools are soaked in warm soapy water to shrink the fibers together and soften the fabric.

TENTER DRYING, CRABBING: Tenter drying for cotton and crabbing for wool are techniques used to set the grain. Tenter drying involves a tenter frame which exerts tension on the fabric as it is passed over a heat source. In crabbing, the wet wool fabric is passed through pressing rollers.

The most used finishing processes for synthetic fabrics involve desizing, scouring and dry heat setting.

DESIZING: Sizing is often added to the warp yarns to stiffen them for the weaving process. (This is also done to cotton and linen.) In the desizing treatment, special enzymes are used to convert the sizing to compounds that are easily washed out.

SCOURING: This is the same as the process for wool.

DRY HEAT SETTING: This is the process used for synthetics to set the fabric configuration and enhance dimensional stability. Carefully controlled temperatures are used which promote fiber flow or melt. The physical characteristics of the polymer are changed and the fabric is set.

Special Finishes

There are the chemical and mechanical treatments which change the surface appearance and hand of the textile.

NAPPING: Napping is the brushing of the textile surface with wire bristles mounted on rollers to form a nap or very low pile. Wool broadcloths and flannels are typical napped fabrics.

SUEDING: In sueding, a nap is formed by abrading with emery cloth. This produces cotton or wool suede cloth.

CALENDERING: In an ironing process, the fabric is pressed under heavy steel rollers which have been heated. Various degrees of luster are produced.

EMBOSSING: By using one roller with an engraved design, embossing is produced. The effect can be made stronger by using a positive and a negative roller.

ADDING RESIN: Various synthetic resins are used to give sheen or crispness to a fabric. These may also produce such functional attributes as dimensional stability and resistance to wrinkles.

Functional Finishes

Although all finishes are functional to a degree, the term functional finishes is used here to describe those finishes that enhance performance. They typically involve immersion in chemicals. Most are relatively new as compared to the standard and special finishes.

MOTHPROOFING: In mothproof finishes, a chemical agent is added to protect protein fabrics from moths and carpet beetles. These are added during fulling or dyeing.

ANTIBACTERIAL, ANTIMICROBIAL: These finishes inhibit the growth of bacteria and other microorganisms. They are very important for health care institutions and in tropical climates.

Some are soluble and some are durable. Soluble finishes must be renewed after each cleaning. Even the durable finishes do not have an infinite life. The number of laundering or dry cleaning treatments the finish will tolerate is usually specified by the manufacturer.

FLAME-RETARDANT FINISHES: Some fabrics as those made from modacrylic fibers are inherently flame resistant. Most textiles will burn. Flame retardants will inhibit burning. Some flame-retardant chemicals are water soluble and must be renewed after each cleaning. Others are durable and will withstand washing and dry cleaning. However, the label should be carefully read to understand what the treated fabric will withstand and the life span of the finish.

There are some problems with using flame-retardant finishes. The chemical must be carefully matched to the fiber; blends are particularly troublesome, as the fibers cannot be treated in the same way and treatments of the different fibers in one textile may be incompatible. Flame-retardant chemicals can also change the texture or color of the fabric.

It is generally preferable to use inherently flame-resistant fibers where possible. Textile chemists are constantly working on ways to design molecular changes in fibers to provide inherent flame resistance. Some nylons and polyesters have been modified to be inherently flame resistant.

ANTI-STATIC: Anti-static finishes are used to control the buildup of electrons. Chemical treatments have been developed for some synthetics such as nylon and polyester. Much remains to be done.

Soil and Stain Repellant: These finishes enable improved soil resistance in fabrics but are by no means soilproof. Fabrics treated with these must still receive regular care.

Silicone finishes tend to repel water and thus resist water-borne soil. Fluorochemical finishes such as Scotchguard® and Zepel® resist both oil-borne and water-borne soil.

Soil Release: The release of soil and stains during laundering is facilitated by soil-release finishes. They work in two different ways. Some attract water, enabling it to lift out soil. Others coat the fibers so that soil will not penetrate. Some provide other benefits such as anti-static properties, lessening of shedding and pilling, and a softer hand.

Coloring

Coloring may be added before fabric construction or after. (See Chapter Two, "Carpet" to review the stages at which color may be introduced.) Piece dyeing, adding color after fabric construction, is essentially a finishing process.

The following discusses some implications for upholstery textiles which result from the stage at which the dye is introduced.

Solution Dyeing: Fabrics of solution-dyed fibers have excellent colorfastness to laundering, dry cleaning, light, and crocking. The yarns are uniform in color.

To be economic, runs must be large. Therefore, large inventories are produced. There is less flexibility for response to changing color trends than with methods later in the process and a limited range of colors is typical.

Fiber Dyeing: This being the natural fiber equivalent to solution dying is the earliest stage at which a natural fiber can be dyed. There is good color penetration and colorfastness. Again, a long lead time is required. Fiber dying is expensive and used mostly for woolen fibers in heather spun yarns. Heather yarns are yarns composed of a mixture of fibers of different colors.

Yarn Dyeing: Most colored yarns are dyed in yarn rather than fiber form. This method is commonly used for upholstery fabrics with various-colored yarns such as checks, stripes and other geometric patterns. It is also used for Jacquard and dobby-produced fabrics.

Piece Dyeing: This is the most efficient and least expensive method of dyeing. It is the most responsive to color trends, as it comes near the end of the production cycle and closest to the point of sale.

Because upholstery fabrics are subject to considerable abrasion, it entails the most risk. With dense constructions or hard, tightly twisted yarns, there may be poor dye penetration. Undyed fibers or yarns can be revealed at the yarn crossings as yarns move slightly in use. Dye penetration can easily be tested by unraveling the fabric and examining the yarns. Cut pile fabrics typically do not have dye penetration problems.

Solid color fabrics are most often produced by piece dyeing. In some instances, a fabric with two or possibly three colors is produced by piece dyeing. This is accomplished using the cross-dyeing process where different fibers or modifications of the same fiber are used in one fabric, with each accepting the dye differently.

Types of Dyes

For colorfastness, a dye must bond to the fiber. When a dyestuff will combine with a fiber, it is said to have an affinity for the fiber. Specific dyes are used for the various classifications of fiber. These dyes have been developed so that the chemical characteristics of the dye match the chemical properties of the fibers.

Table 14.4 summarizes the more commonly used dyes and their colorfastness. Unless otherwise described, cf (colorfastness) refers to colorfastness to light, laundering and dry cleaning.

Maintenance and Cleaning

Small tears and snags should immediately be repaired before they become large ones. An advantage of textiles is that they can be inconspicuously repaired with simple sewing techniques. Small tears can be stitched, a snagged loop can be pushed through to the back of the fabric, and broken yarns can be darned into the fabric. In more serious cases, holes can be rewoven.

Maintenance is concerned with the day-to-day care. It includes regular vacuum cleaning to prevent surface buildup of soil and immediate attention to spills and other accidents. Prompt attention is necessary to prevent spots and stains. Delayed action increases the possibility that spots and stains will not be able to be removed.

Solid or semisolid matter should be scraped with a dull blade and the residue blotted with tissue or a clean cloth. Liquids should first be soaked up with a clean, absorbent cloth. A blotting action should be used, with care taken not to rub the soil into the fabric.

Table 14.4

DYES AND FIBERS

Dye	Fiber						Comments
	Cel	Pro	Acr	Nyl	Poly	Ole	
Acid		X	X	X	X	X	cf varies
Basic (Cationic)			X	X	X		cf good, exceptional on acrylic. Brilliant colors.
Direct	X	X		X			cf good to light, need resin finish for cf to laundering. Used for low to medium cost fabrics.
Disperse			X	X	X		cf good, also to perspiration
Metallized Acid		X					cf good
Naphthol (Azoic)	X		X	X	X	X	cf good to excellent, also to chlorine, acid and alkali. Brilliant color at low cost but tends to crock.
Reactive	X	X	X	X			cf excellent to laundering and light, good to excellent to dry cleaning, fume fading, crocking and perspiration.
Sulphur	X						cf good to laundering, varies to light, perspiration, acids, and alkalis, poor to chlorine. Can weaken fabric.
Vat	X						cf good to excellent

Legend:

Cel = cellulosic fibers   cf = colorfastness
Pro = protein fibers
Acr = acrylic and modacrylic
Nyl = nylon
Poly = polyester
Ole = olefin or polypropylene

The most important aspect of upholstery fabric cleaning is the matching of the cleaning solution to the fabric. This means that the fabric fiber and finishes must be known. Care instructions are given by all textile manufacturers. The designer must be sure that the client has the fabric information and care instructions. These must be used to successfully direct maintenance and professional cleaning.

Most stains can be categorized in one of three categories: water-borne, oil-borne or a combination.

WATER-BORNE STAINS: Clean water should be used to sponge off stains. Warm water can be used for most stains, but cold water should be used for blood, as warm water will coagulate the protein in blood. If the stain persists, a mild detergent solution should be used.

OIL-BORNE STAINS: These should be sponged off with the manufacturer's recommended spot-removing solvent, carefully following the recommended application method. The solvent should always be applied with a clean cloth, never directly to the fabric. Excess solvent should be soaked up with a clean, absorbent cloth.

COMBINATION STAINS: These should first be treated as water-borne stains. If this is not sufficient, they should then be treated as oil-borne stains.

In all cases, work should proceed from the edges to the center. Neither water or solvents should be used in soaking quantities. This can cause release of chemicals or dyes in the fabric backing or in the cushioning, staining the fabric anew. Too much moisture can also bring the crayon marks used as cutting guides to the surface. Any cleaning agent should be carefully tested in an inconspicuous place on the furniture before proceeding with its use.

Fabrication

Selection of furniture and the selection of options such as corded welts or no welt should be made in accordance with the recommendations for fire safety, endeavoring to have as few crevices and indentations as possible.

Unless the fabric is completely non-directional such as some plain weaves, the direction must be specified. For example, stripes can run vertically or horizontally. Vertically means that the warp will run up and down on vertical sections of seating and front to back on the cushions. This is the standard practice. Horizontally means that the warp runs from side to side on the seating, i.e. the weft runs vertically. When a fabric is applied to furniture so that the weft runs vertically, this is called railroading. The term is most frequently used with stripes.

Matching of stripes, end to end, is generally unsatisfactory. The direction should be specified so this does not occur if it is not intended.

Cut pile and napped fabrics are standardly fabricated with the pile direction slanting down on the vertical planes and toward the front on the horizontal planes.

Fabrics with a rib are generally most satisfactory when the rib runs vertically on the seating. This increases comfort and wear life.

The placement of any large pattern should be specified. State whether it should fall randomly or at a specific place on each cushion and back section.

Specification

All fabrication information such as welts and fabric direction must be clearly stated.

Fabric must be identified by name, color and number. Samples should be requested to verify the fabric and retained as the standard for the project.

Shop drawings should be requested for any fabrication detail that is not the manufacturer's standard.

Directions must be given for delivery and packaging for extra fabric required by the client and for disposition of scrap pieces. Size of scrap pieces to be retained by the client should be identified.

Copies of maintenance and cleaning instructions in the quantity needed by the client should be requested in the specification documents.

Certification of flame resistance to meet the requirements of the regulatory district should be requested in the specification documents.

Chapter Fifteen

CHEMICAL-COATED UPHOLSTERY FABRICS

CHEMICAL-COATED upholstery fabrics are an alternative to textiles when a water-resistant upholstery fabric is needed. They are appropriate where fluids such as urine or blood may be a problem, as absorption is minimized and fluids can be easily removed. In cases where accumulation of soil can be substantial, their easy cleanability with common cleaning solutions is an asset. However, some liquids and soil contain staining agents which do penetrate the fabric and are difficult to remove.

Vinyl is one of several chemical-coated fabrics used to upholster furniture. This chemical-coated fabric classification includes vinyl, urethane, acrylic and polyesters. Vinyl is the most frequently used, as it is lower in cost and more durable than the others which are typically softer and more supple.

Treating and coating fabrics has a long history. The Egyptians used resin-treated flax for wrapping and preserving their dead. Greased animal skins were used at a very early date to protect against cold and rain. Oil, natural rubber and, later, synthetic rubber, pyroxylin and cellulose nitrate have all been used as coatings. In 1938-39, Germany produced the first plasticized PVC (vinyl) coated fabrics. During World War II, vinyl was developed by the military because of the rubber shortage. After the war, it gained immediate acceptance in consumer markets for items such as wall coverings and upholstery.

Easy cleanability, good durability and good fade resistance make vinyl a serviceable upholstery fabric with good appearance retention. Vinyl, as an upholstery fabric, also has its limitations. From a maintenance viewpoint, tears and cigarette burns cannot be suitably repaired as they can with textiles. From an environmental perspective, vinyls have a more institutional look than textiles. Water resistance which is a maintenance advantage is a comfort disadvantage, as the non-absorbent vinyl is consequently hot and sticky for long-term seating.

Properties

Many of the properties to be evaluated in a vinyl upholstery material are the same as those for textiles; for example, the durability properties of **abrasion resistance** and **strength** and the appearance-retention property of **color retention.** In addition, some are peculiar to chemical-coated fabrics such as **adhesion, cold crack resistance, flex resistance, volatility** and, for those with non-woven backings, **button-pull-through resistance.**

CFFA (Chemical Fabric and Film Association) has set performance standards for these properties for vinyl-coated and other chemical-coated fabrics. A summary is presented in Table 15.1. CFFA has classified the fabrics by backings and further classified each as class A or class B, with class A having, in general, higher minimum performance standards than class B.

Similar standards are set in ASTM D3690 where finishes are classified as class A—heavy duty, class B—medium duty, and class C—light duty. In general, the CFFA standards are the same as or slightly more stringent than the ASTM standards.

Abrasion Resistance

The ability of the chemical coating to resist surface wear when rubbed by other surfaces is a prime contributor to durability. To measure the abrasion resistance of chemical-coated fabrics, CFFA test method 1 utilizes the Wyzenbeek test method using wire screen as the abradant and two pounds of pressure on the specimen. It is recommended that the fabric sustain a minimum of 3000 double rubs or cycles. This cannot be directly compared with recommended abrasion-resistance standards for textiles, as a different abradant and load are used.

As with textiles, abrasive wear can be minimized by appropriate fabric use and fabrication techniques. It is recommended that in heavily used locations, furniture arms not be upholstered. Welts are vulnerable to wear because they extend above the overall surface. They should be avoided where rubbing or abrading conditions are most frequent.

Strength

The backing has particular relevance in the determination of the various strength attributes of a vinyl upholstery fabric. Strength is determined principally by the type of backing and the weight of the fabric.

Table 15.1

CFFA MINIMUM PERFORMANCE STANDARDS FOR VINYL-COATED AND
OTHER CHEMICAL-COATED UPHOLSTERY FABRICS — INDOOR

Test	Test Method	Knits		Non-Wovens		Wovens	
		Class A	Class B	Class A	Class B	Class A	Class B
Abrasion Resistance min. cycles	CFFA 1	3000	3000	3000	3000	3000	3000
Accelerated Light Aging 200 hours	CFFA 2a	No color change		No color change		No color change	
Ahesion lbs	CFFA 3	3.0	3.0	4.0	3.0	4.0	3.0
Button Pull Resistance	CFFA 5	NA	NA	80 lbs	60 lbs	NA	NA
Cold Crack Resistance	CFFA 6	0°F −18°C	0°F −18°C	0°F −18°C	0°F −18°C	0°F −18°C	0°F −18°C
Crocking Resistance	CFFA 7	Good	Good	Good	Good	Good	Good
Flex Resistance cycles	CFFA 10	25,000	25,000	25,000	25,000	25,000	25,000
Seam Strength lbs	CFFA 14	40x40	30x25	45x45	35x35	50x50	25x25
Tongue Tear lbs	CFFA 16b	5x5	4x4	NA	NA	6x6	4x4
Trap Tear lbs	CFFA 16c	NA	NA	20x20	15x15	NA	NA
Tensile Strength lbs	CFFA 17	70x70	50x50	75x75	50x50	80x80	40x40
Volatility 220°F, 104°C	CFFA 18	8%	8%	8%	8%	8%	8%

Figures are from Chemical Fabrics and Film Association, Inc.

TENSILE STRENGTH: Tensile strength is a measurement of the force required to rupture or break the chemical-coated fabric. ASTM D 751-79 is the reference used by CFFA. This is noted as CFFA test method 17 and measures the force necessary to break the fabric in each direction.

SEAM STRENGTH: Splitting of seams is a fairly common occurrence when poor-quality vinyls are used. Seam strength, therefore, could be an important criteria in the selection of vinyl upholstery fabrics. The use of a backing is the first step in minimizing seams splitting. The type of backing will also make a difference as can be assumed from the figures in Table 15.1

The CFFA test method for seam strength is a modified ASTM D 751-79, Tack-Tear Resistance. The test machine consists of a straining mechanism, holding clamps and load testing mechanism. Specimens are tested sewn along the length of the fabric and across the fabric. The load necessary to tear the fabric in each direction is recorded; thus, two figures will appear in the test results.

TEAR STRENGTH: The tear strength is the measurement of the force required to continue or propagate a tear in a coated fabric. CFFA recommends a number of different methods to measure tear strength. These are:

1. Elmendorf Method, ASTM D 1424-81, Tearing Strength, Pendulum Impulse Method.
2. Tongue Method, Federal Specification No. 191A—Method 5134, Tearing Strength, Tongue Method.
3. Trapezoid Method, ASTM D 1117-80, Trapezoid Tearing Strength.

Both the tongue method and the trapezoid method use a testing method consisting of a straining mechanism, holding clamps and load-recording mechanism. Principal differences in the tests are the length of the cut and the position of the clamps. The load necessary to tear the fabric in each direction is recorded; thus, two figures will appear in the test results.

Color Retention

COLOR ABRASION: Where pigments have been integrally introduced into the vinyl solution, color abrasion is not a problem, as the color extends through the full thickness of the vinyl coating. With printed vinyls, loss of color through abrasive action can be a problem, particularly where a raised pattern has been overprinted with a second color.

CROCKING RESISTANCE: Crocking is the transfer of color from one surface to another by rubbing action. CFFA utilizes federal standard No. 191A—Method 5651, Colorfastness to Crocking, to determine resistance of chemical coatings to crockings. Ratings may also be made in accordance with AATCC Chart for Measuring Transference of Color as recommended by ASTM D 3690. Resistance to crocking is usually rated as:

Good: No appreciable staining to the transfer cloth.
Fair: Appreciable but not objectionable staining.
Poor: Objectionable staining.

RESISTANCE TO FADING: Color retention is important if the appearance of a fabric is to be maintained. CFFA test method 2a determines the resistance of chemical-coated fabrics to prolonged exposure to sunlight. A carbon arc fadeometer is used for testing. There should be no change in color after 200 hours in the fadeometer.

Adhesion

As with all fabrics made up of face components and a backing, the adhesion of one to the other is extremely important. CFFA test method 3 utilizes ASTM D 751-79, Adhesion of Coating to a Fabric, to determine the force or pull necessary to separate a chemical coating from its fabric backing. The testing machine consists of a straining mechanism, holding clamps and a load-recording mechanism. Test results are reported in pounds of load. Recommended minimum force is 3 or 4 pounds, depending on the backing and class.

Cold Crack Resistance

The purpose of CFFA test method 6 is to determine the temperature at which cracks may appear if chemical-coated fabrics are left in the cold and then folded sharply. This property may not be highly relevant for health care application, as upholstery fabrics are seldom submitted to below-freezing temperatures in the health care environment.

Flex Resistance

This is the resistance to change in surface appearance when a chemical-coated fabric is subjected to repeated flexing. The unit of measurement is the number of cycles at which the fabric shows visual evidence of cracking, whitening, crazing or separation of the coating from the fabric backing.

Volatility

The measurement of the weight loss of a chemical-coated fabric when subjected to an elevated temperature is its volatility. The reference used for this test identified as CFFA test method 18 is ASTM D 1203-81 E1, Loss of Plasticizer from Plastics (Activated Carbon Method). The test is conducted in a forced-air laboratory oven and the percentage of weight loss after twenty-four hours of treatment is recorded. Loss of plasticizers, whether due to an elevated temperature or simply through aging, can cause blocking or surface tack.

Button-Pull-Through Resistance

This property would be relevant when buttons are used to affix tufting in furniture in construction. Standards for button pull through are given for non-wovens only, because button-pull-through problems rarely occur with woven or knit substrates. Tufting is not recommended on horizontal surfaces of seating for health care, because indentations and crevices where dirt can accumulate are created. Vertical surfaces are not likely to receive the hard wear that would lead to button pull through.

Cleanability and Resistance to Alkalinity

Any fabric used for seating is highly subject to ground-in soil due to the constant rubbing action of people getting up, sitting down and shifting position. Vinyl is non-absorbent and quite durable. However, as with vinyl wall coverings, a top finish will enhance the cleanability of the upholstery fabric. Also, as with vinyl wall coverings, resistance to alkalinity is important, as many of the commonly used cleaning solutions are alkaline.

Health and Safety

Flammability

An extensive discussion is presented in Chapter Thirteen, "Introduction to Upholstery Fabrics."

Biogenic Factors

Biogenic factors are similar to those for textiles. Minimizing crevices diminishes places where soil can collect and enables easy clean up. Selection of fabrics which can withstand frequent cleaning with antimicrobial solutions is important for many locations.

Chemical-coated fabrics are somewhat more vulnerable to mildew than textiles. Protection against mildew requires fungicide treatment for both the vinyl face and the backing.

Electrostatic Propensity

Vinyl-coated fabrics tend to be insulating or marginally antistatic. For locations where static can be a problem, specialty grades are available in a static dissipative range.

Construction and Finishes

To make vinyl upholstery fabric, vinyl resins are applied on one face of a backing of natural or synthetic fibers to provide a durable protective surface. (As noted above, chemicals other than vinyl are sometimes used.)

Vinyls can be plain or expanded. Plain vinyls are dense and firm. Expanded vinyls are manufactured with thousands of tiny air holes formed through addition of a chemical blowing agent to the solution.

These cells, which make the vinyl light, spongy and pliable, provide softness and comfort. Expanded vinyls are easier to tailor and tend to be more leather-like in appearance.

Face Components

As with other vinyl products, the vinyl face is made up of PVC resin, plasticizers, pigments, stabilizers, fillers and perhaps some other additives. The function and properties of these components are much the same as in vinyl wall coverings and will not be repeated here. While color is usually integral, imparted by pigments in the mixture, it can be printed on the surface, or a pattern may be printed over a base color.

Top finishes are used for upholstery-grade, vinyl-coated fabrics to provide protection against staining, scuffing and abrasive wear. These are usually a solvent blend of PVC or a water emulsion of polyurethane and/or acrylic.

DiversaTech General, makers of Boltaflex® vinyl upholstery fabrics, has introduced a finish called Prefixx which they compare with solvent PVC finishes. (The formulation is a trade secret.) The major advantage appears to be that it is resistant to more stains for longer periods (24 hours) than solvent PVC finishes, and solvent cleaners can be used to remove stubborn stains. Solvent-based cleaners generally cannot be used on finishes of solvent PVC, as they might remove part of the finish and damage the vinyl coating.

Before specifying any vinyl upholstery fabric, it is important to read the manufacturer's instructions for stain removal and to select the upholstery material accordingly. It is also an excellent idea to test samples for removal of stains which occur frequently.

Backings

There are considerable differences in the quality of vinyl fabrics. In fact, the cheapest grades are made as sheets without the support of a backing. These sheets are called "unsupported" vinyl. For durable upholstery fabrics, textile backings are fused to the vinyl to provide "supported" sheets.

The Chemical Fabrics and Film Association, Inc. (CFFA) lists three categories of backings: knits, wovens and non-wovens. Vinyl-coated fabrics with knit backings tend to have the greatest degree of extensibility and recovery.

Methods of Manufacture .

Chemical-coated fabrics used for upholstery are manufactured using three methods: calendering, extruding and cast coating.

CALENDERING: The coating ingredients are first mixed and blended on heated rolls called mills. They are subsequently passed through one or more sets of rolls or calenders from which they emerge as continuous sheets. A fabric backing is laminated to the vinyl sheet during the process. The last roll may be embossed, sandblasted or highly polished to produce textured, matte or gloss finishes.

EXTRUDING: The PVC resins, plasticizers and pigments are blended together and fed to an extruder. The extruder heats the ingredients and then forces the homogeneous mass through a thin slit which is the width of the sheet to be extruded. The vinyl coating is then nipped to a fabric by pressure rolls and cooled.

It is extremely difficult to produce a perfectly smooth sheet in the extrusion process; fine ridges and valleys will show on the surface. These can be smoothed by flame polishing or burnishing rolls. On the other hand, the extruder die can be appropriately machined to produce ribbed or corduroy-like sheets.

Extruding tends to orient the long-chain polymers in the direction of the extrusion. The result is a gain in strength in the extrusion direction but a loss in the opposing or transverse direction.

CAST COATING: In the cast-coating process, the liquid plastic (plastisol in the case of flexible PVC-coated fabrics) is deposited onto a paper-carrier webb. It passes under a knife or "doctor" blade held a distance above the webb equal to the thickness of the sheet desired. The liquid solidifies as it cools and the paper is removed and reused. The vinyl surface which was next to the paper carrier webb becomes the finished surface, its texture being determined by that of the paper. For a supported sheet, the vinyl is bonded to fabric in a subsequent process.

Maintenance

Chemical-coated fabrics are very resistant to scuffing and soiling; most cleaning can be accomplished with warm soapy water and several clear rinses. If soil becomes embedded in depressions of embossed surfaces, a medium bristle brush can be used to loosen the soiling agent from the depression.

A regular cleaning program of washing all vinyl upholstery with warm water and mild soap should be established. Once a month may be sufficient for medium-use locations. Heavy-use areas may require more frequent washing.

The principle underlying a regular cleaning schedule is to prevent buildup of substances which can cause deterioration such as hardening or embrittlement of the surface. In addition to soil, some common but harmful agents are: body oils, hair oil, harsh detergents and furniture polish.

Furniture is also subject to stains from ink, tar, chewing gum and other substances used or tracked in by persons using the facility. All stains should be removed as soon as possible. Certain stains become set if not removed immediately. If the stain persists after using soapy water and a clear rinse, other remedies can be tried. These should be in accord with the cleaning instructions given by the manufacturer of the chemical-coated fabric. Full-strength rubbing alcohol, a dilute bleach solution, or mineral spirits are often recommended.

After scraping off any solid residue and cleaning with soap solution and after verifying approval of use in the manufacturer's instructions, use full-strength rubbing alcohol for gum, shoe polish and ink; use dilute bleach solution for mildew and mineral spirits for tar, asphalt and grease. Call in a professional cleaning service if stains persist.

Do not use cleaners that are not recommended by the manufacturer. In particular, do not use powdered abrasives, steel wool or industrial-type cleaners. They will cause dulling of the surface. Dry cleaning and lacquer solvents will attack the chemical coating, remove printed patterns and in general disturb the surface.

Fabrication

Selection of furniture and the selection of options such as corded welts or no welts should be made in accordance with the recommendations for fire safety, endeavoring to have as few crevices and indentations as possible.

Vinyl-coated fabrics are much more difficult than textiles to shape to fit curves or complex shapes. Seating intended to have vinyl upholstery should have straight lines and simple forms.

Matching of stripes, end to end, is generally unsatisfactory. The direction should be specified so this does not occur if it is not intended.

Fabrics with a rib are generally more satisfactory when the rib direction runs vertically on the seating. This increases comfort and wear life.

A strong upholstery thread is needed. Nylon thread is generally recommended by manufacturers. However, some designers believe that nylon has a tendency to cut the fabric and recommend a heavy cotton thread.

A larger stitch length is used than that for textiles. Seven to eight stitches per inch is typically satisfactory.

Specification

Specification notes for vinyl-coated fabrics are essentially the same as those for textiles.

All fabrication information such as welts and fabric direction must be clearly stated.

Fabric must be identified by name, color and number. Samples should be requested to verify the fabric and retained as the standard for the project.

Shop drawings should be requested for any fabrication detail that is not the manufacturer's standard.

Directions must be given for delivery and packaging for extra fabric required by the client and for disposition of scrap pieces. Size of scrap pieces to be retained by the client should be identified.

Copies of maintenance and cleaning instructions in the quantity needed by the client should be requested in the specification documents.

Certification of flame resistance to meet the requirements of the regulatory district should be requested in the specification documents.

Part V

FURNITURE AND CASEWORK

Chapter Sixteen

PLASTIC COATING MATERIALS FOR FURNITURE AND CASEWORK

ADVANCING plastics technology is continuously leading to new materials and to improvements to existing ones. Throughout this book it can be seen that, in many cases, the most durable materials are plastics in one form or another. These are replacing natural materials in locations where finishes are subjected to heavy use and, often, abuse. For example, nylon is used for carpet and upholstery fabrics, vinyl for resilient floor coverings, wall coverings and upholstery, and modacrylics and polyester for drapery fabrics. Plastic resins have largely replaced natural resins in paints and other coatings.

Perhaps it would be helpful to have a very brief explanation of plastics. What they are can be understood by looking at their common characteristics; they are organic and synthetic polymers having plasticity.

ORGANIC: Plastics are organic materials; that is, they are based on carbon chemistry.

SYNTHETIC: Plastics are products not found in a natural state. They are converted from raw materials into new and radically different forms.

POLYMERS: Polymer is derived from the words "poly" meaning many and "mer" meaning unit. A polymer is a giant molecule made up of many repetitions of a small molecule or monomer. It is a long chain of like units.

PLASTICITY: Plastics are called plastic because at some stage they have plasticity; the material can be formed into desired shapes. They may be plastic only once (thermosetting) or they may be capable of becoming plastic many times (thermoplastic). The term plastic is used to refer to materials which have plasticity in addition to the other attributes—organic, synthetic and polymeric.

Thermoplastic and Thermosetting Plastics

There are two broad categories of plastics: thermoplastic and thermosetting. In a thermoplastic material, the linear molecules or polymers are not connected to each other. They are free to slide past one another when an appropriate external force is applied. Thus, sufficient heat can cause a thermoplastic material to become plastic again after it has hardened. The distinguishing characteristic of thermoplastic materials is that, because of the unconnected chain structure, they can be repeatedly softened and hardened by heating and cooling. Some thermoplastic finish materials are vinyl, acrylic, nylon and some polyesters.

In thermosetting plastics, the linear molecules are connected to one another. The polymers link together as curing takes place. Adjacent chains are chemically bonded and are no longer free to move among each other. The hardening is irreversible. This type of linking in which the material goes through a plastic stage once and then hardens or sets irreversibly is called thermosetting. The name was given when it was thought that the application of heat was necessary to cause the reaction. Heat beyond room temperature is not necessary with all materials but the name remains. Epoxy, polyurethane, some polyesters and melamine formaldehyde are some thermosetting plastics used in finish materials.

Coatings

The discussion on the structure and properties of wall coatings in Chapter Six serves as a foundation for this discussion of coatings for furniture and casework. The section on the contribution of the resin to the coating is particularly relevant and review may be desirable.

Plastic resins are developing as appropriate heavy-duty finishes for the hard wear sustained by items in constant use. Many of the finishes for furniture and casework involve plastics.

Furniture and casework can, of course, be painted just as walls can. It is seldom, however, that furniture or casework will be coated on site. The coating process will take place under factory conditions where there is more control than at a construction site and more possibility for enhancement of the inherent properties of the coating material. For example, a baked enamel applied at the plant where heat treatment is possible is more durable than a site-applied enamel.

This chapter will not belabor the application to furniture and casework of coatings, previously discussed in Chapter Six. It is sufficient to say that there is the potential for enhancement of properties because the coatings are factory applied.

The subjects of this chapter are powder coatings, an emerging technology utilizing plastic resins; and transparent finishes, the most durable of which employ plastic resins.

POWDER COATINGS

Powder coatings are emerging as a significant finishing technology in furnishings as well as in building components. Although powder coating is not new, it is only recently that it is beginning to be broadly known. A powder coating is, essentially, dry paint. Instead of resins and pigments being dissolved or suspended in a liquid medium such as a solvent or water, they are applied as a dry powder directly to the surface to be finished.

The resins used for this process are synthetic resins. Many are the same as those used in liquid coatings. However, even a coating using the same resins will generally have better performance properties. Because the resins do not need to be dissolved, higher molecular weight resins can be used to increase the density of the film. Powder coatings generally have superior chipping resistance; a majority of formulations withstand 160 inch-pounds of impact without cracking or chipping. Many liquid paints will not withstand 30 inch-pounds by the same test. They also tend to have superior scratch resistance, with a film toughness greater than that of most liquid paints.

Powder coatings also tend to have a more consistent and uniform surface than liquid coatings. Runs, sags and drips do not occur, edge coverage is good, and fewer imperfections occur because there is no chance of solvent entrapment in the cured film.

Advantages of this process accrue to both user and manufacturer. The absence of a solvent means no pollution fumes, little odor, and greatly reduced fire hazard in the plant. It is also economical, as one coat can give adequate coating thickness and overspray can be recovered and reused.

Structure and Properties

A powder coating is a fine powder which fuses into a continuous film under heat. The powder is composed of synthetic resins and pigments. The resins and pigments contribute properties as described in Chapter Six, "Wall Coatings." Other ingredients may be heat and light stabilizers, plasticizers and reinforcing fillers, and, if it is a reactive or thermo-setting system, curing agents.

The majority of powder coatings being used today are thermosetting powders based on resin systems of epoxy, polyurethane or polyester. When heated in the presence of a curing agent, resins assume a liquid state, fuse into a continuous film and chemically react to form a smooth and uniform finish. Once cured, the finish is permanently set. The curing involves the cross linking of polymer chains, and the finish will not soften with further application of heat.

The different resins exhibit functional properties of hardness, impact resistance and chemical resistance to a greater degree in these thermo-setting powder systems than in analogous liquid systems. This is be-cause the heat-cured systems develop a higher degree of cross linking of the synthetic resins and, thus, enhance the resin properties.

Thermoplastic powders do not chemically cross link upon application of heat but melt and flow over the part in the oven. As the part cools af-ter leaving the oven, the film hardens but will remelt upon application of sufficient heat.

Powder coatings are assessed in accordance with properties which in-clude: hardness, impact resistance, abrasion resistance, flexibility, adhe-sion and chemical resistance.

HARDNESS: Pencil-hardness tests measure hardness. Under procedure ASTM D-3363, tests are performed using Eagle Turquoise drawing leads to determine at which lead category the hardness of the coating is exceeded by that of the lead. Results are stated in terms of the familiar vocabulary of pencil hardness from the softest at 6B through B, HB, F, H to the hardest at 6H. Typical hardness measures of powder coatings are H through 4H.

IMPACT RESISTANCE: A material that has good impact resistance will re-sist both cracking and loss of adhesion. Under procedure number CGSB1-GP-71, method 147-1, a Gardner variable-impact tester drives a 5/8" hemispherical punch into coated panels. The highest impact which does not cause breaking in the sample is recorded. The highest impact that can be delivered by the test is 160 inch-pounds.

ABRASION RESISTANCE: The finish is tested with a Taber abrader using CS 27 wheels with a 1000-gram load for 1000 cycles. The measure is the weight of coating removed in the test.

FLEXIBILITY: Flexibility is measured under ASTM D-522. The mate-rials to be tested are applied at uniform thickness to flat sheet metal panels. After the coating has dried or cured, the panels are bent over a conical mandrel which has a minimum diameter of 1/8" at one end. The smallest diameter at which the panel withstands a 180° bend without cracking or loss of coating adhesion is recorded. For example a 2-mm thick coating of urethane on a 0.032" thick steel panel might withstand a 180° bend over a 1/4" diameter mandrel.

ADHESION: There should be no lifting of 1/8" squares of coating between scribe lines in cross hatch adhesion testing using pressure sensitive adhesive backed tape.

CHEMICAL RESISTANCE: Chemical resistance tests are generally conducted by each manufacturer on their own materials. In Table 16.1, Evaluation Guide: Powder Coatings by Resin System, ratings are given in the broad categories of acids, alkalies, detergents, strong solvents and oils. The ratings are averages and it should be noted that a specific substance could be quite different from the average. For example, vinyl has only a poor rating for resistance to strong solvents. However, what does not show in the table is that it has excellent resistance to two solvents: gasoline and alcohol. The table can be used for general information. When making an evaluation of a specific product, the manufacturer's test results should be obtained.

Table 16.1

EVALUATION GUIDE: POWDER COATINGS BY RESIN SYSTEM

Property	Thermosetting			Thermoplastic			
	Epoxy	Urethane	Poly	Poly	Nylon	Vinyl	Acrylic
Abrasion Resistance	5	4	4	5	5	3	3
Impact Resistance	4	4	4	3	5	5	4
Hardness	5	4	4	3	3	3	3
Flexibility	5	4	4	4	5	5	5
Adhesion	5	5	5	5	5	3	3
Resistance to:							
Acids	3	5	3	2	2	4	3
Alkalies	5	1	1	1	2	4	3
Detergents	5	4	4	2	4	5	3
Strong Solvents	4	3	3	2	5	1	3
Oils	5	5	4	3	5	2	3

Legend:

5 = Excellent   Poly = Polyester
4 = Very good
3 = Good
2 = Fair
1 = Poor

Classification

Powder coatings are classifed by their resin systems as already explained and as illustrated in the table. Some of the resins have special attributes for which they might be selected. Special strengths or weaknesses are noted in the following text.

EPOXY: Epoxy is known for its excellent abrasion and chemical resistance. It also has excellent adhesion to metal without the use of a primer. Limitations are that it has poor resistance to ultraviolet rays and poor weathering qualities. Gloss retention is poor outdoors and less than that of some of the other resins indoors.

POLYURETHANE: This resin is also known for its very good abrasion and chemical resistance. It has excellent adhesion to metal without the use of a primer. In contrast to epoxy, ultraviolet rays will have little effect and polyurethane has good weatherability. It does not darken or yellow with age.

POLYESTER, THERMOSETTING: This resin has very good impact resistance, good weatherability and excellent adhesion to metal without the use of a primer.

POLYESTER, THERMOPLASTIC: The thermoplastic formulation of polyester has outstanding abrasion resistance, second only to nylon. It also has exceptionally good gloss and color retention.

NYLON: Nylon is particularly tough and has excellent abrasion resistance. Resistance to strong solvents is the best of all the resin systems. Nylon also has a low thermal conductivity which makes it a comfortable choice for the coating of metal parts that people may be touching such as chair arms.

VINYL: Vinyl has excellent impact resistance and the most flexibility of all. It has superior toughness and high tear strength, good outdoor weatherability and corrosion resistance. It is also economical. It should not, however, be used where it may come in contact with strong solvents.

ACRYLIC: Acrylic is the clearest of all the synthetic resins and can be dyed in pure, strong colors. It does not yellow or darken under prolonged exposure to light.

Maintenance

Color-matched touch-up compounds are sometimes available for repairing damage that may result from abuse of the coating while in service. These are usually of a paste-like consistency which air dries at room temperature and closely approximates the color of the factory-applied finish. Application is variously by artist's brush, spatula, small caulking gun, air dispenser or squeeze bottle.

Cleaning is generally as simple as wiping with a cloth moistened with the cleaning solution recommended by the manufacturer of the furniture. It should be emphasized that the manufacturer's instructions are important. While all of the powder coatings being used on furnishings are relatively hard, durable and stain resistant, some are nevertheless more vulnerable to one particular class of solvent or detergent solutions than to another.

Application

Powder coatings are all factory applied. Application is most often by electrostatically charging the powder particles and applying them to a grounded part. This takes place in a coating chamber. The charged powder adheres to the coated part by electrostatic charge until it enters the curing oven. Under heat, the powder melts over the surface of the part. Coatings are uniform, because the charged particles envelop and adhere evenly to objects regardless of corners, perforations, direction of spray, or uneven surfaces.

Several other methods are used, most frequently the fluidized bed process. This involves a fluidized bed tank in which the powder is suspended by an upward stream of air passing through a diffuser plate in the bottom of the tank. As parts are dipped into the bed, the powder particles flow like a liquid to cover all the surfaces. Before dipping, the part is preheated to a temperature above the melting point of the coating powder. As the particles contact the heated surface, they melt, adhere and flow out to form a smooth continuous film.

TRANSPARENT COATINGS

Transparent coatings utilize the same materials as paints except for the pigments. Oils and resins are used alone or in combination with a solvent when needed as a transfer agent.

The simplest finish, in terms of materials, is an oil finish. Oil finishes are not often used today, as it is a long slow process to obtain a good oil finish on wood.

Except for the oils, all the transparent finishes are built around a resin dissolved in a solvent. Like paint, the type of resin and the various additives give each its own characteristics. Plastic resins, particularly urethane, are often the choice for furniture and casework finishes in locations subject to harsh use.

The most abundantly used transparent coating is varnish. The word varnish, however, embraces a wide range of coatings. There are two broad categories of varnish:

1. Oleoresinous varnish consists of oil, resin and a solvent. This is the transparent coating commonly meant when people use the word, varnish.
2. Spirit varnish is made up of resin and a solvent. Dammar varnish, a crystal clear but brittle varnish used to coat paintings, is a spirit varnish; so are several other finishes that are not usually thought of as varnishes. Danish oil is not an oil at all but a spirit varnish of phenolic resins dissolved in a slow-evaporating mineral solvent. Shellac is also a spirit varnish consisting of resin produced by the lac bug and dissolved in alcohol.

These transparent coatings vary along a spectrum, from all resin at one end of the spectrum to all oil at the other, with coatings containing varying proportions of oil and resin between. This is illustrated in the diagram below. (All are assumed to be dissolved in some amount of solvent.)

ALL RESIN

Coating	Resin/Oil	Examples
Spirit Varnish	all or mostly resin	Dammar varnish, Danish oil, shellac
Short Varnish (Oleoresinous)	5–15 gallons oil to 100 pounds resin	Japan varnish, rubbing varnish
Medium Varnish (Oleoresinous)	15–30 gallons oil to 100 pounds resin	Furniture, interior and floor varnishes
Long Varnish (Oleoresinous)	35–50 gallons oil to 100 pounds resin	Spar (moisture resistant) varnish
Fortified Oil	all or mostly oil	Cable dressing, rubbing oil

ALL OIL

It can be seen that the varnishes used for furniture and other interior components are near the center of the range. There is good reason for this. By altering the proportion of oil to resin, the properties of the varnish are changed. Varnish short on oil tends to be hard, brittle and very clear. As oil is added to the mixture, the varnish becomes softer, more durable and more weather resistant. So the center of the range represents an optimum combination of hardness, clarity and durability for interior furniture and architectural elements.

The other major finish used in furniture finishing is lacquer. Originally, lacquer was the resin of the lac tree dissolved in camphor. Today's lacquers are best thought of as a fortified spirit varnish. They are made up of nitrocellulose, resins, solvents, and plasticizers.

Spirit varnish and lacquer finishes are often very beautiful on furniture. They are hard and clear and can be rubbed to a high polish. However, for the most durable transparent coating in conditions of hard use, an oleoresinous varnish, usually simply called a varnish, is probably the best choice.

Many manufacturers are using varnish with urethane resins for a very durable finish. Urethane has an ideal combination of abrasion resistance, skin flexibility, good adhesion and chemical resistance. It is a transparent resin with good resistance to yellowing. It also has the advantage of being fast curing. Overall, a urethane varnish is a very satisfactory transparent finish for wood furnishings that will be utilized in areas of heavy use.

Chapter Seventeen

PLASTIC SURFACING MATERIALS FOR FURNITURE AND CASEWORK

F URNITURE and casework in health care facilities are subjected to abuse beyond the amount received in less demanding environments. Plastic laminate is a durable surfacing material and the one that is almost always used for casework. It is frequently used for tabletops and sometimes on other furnishings such as wide arms of seating pieces. The first part of this chapter is an examination of plastic laminates.

In nursing homes and in hospitals, countertops around sinks are subjected to a high degree of activity. Stain and impact resistance are particularly important in these locations as is abrasion resistance. An excellent countertop material is Corian® produced by Dupont. The second part of this chapter is a discussion about Corian.

PLASTIC LAMINATE

Plastic laminate has emerged from a workhorse product to an increasingly attractive material with more and more functional attributes. Laminated plastics were initially developed for use in electrical insulation. The first "decorative" plastic laminates were in black and dark wood patterns. They were used on the black and dark wood radio cabinets popular in the 1920s.

Most of the beginning uses of this material were as a durable and economic substitute for wood, marble and other natural materials. Advances in technology have spurred exploration of plastic laminate as a material with its own aesthetic rather than as an imitation for a more expensive material and have made possible the enhancement of the already good qualities of the material.

New patterns, sheens and colors plus three-dimensional surfaces and metal surfaces have become possible with new technology. Some of the new designs are formulated for increased functional performance. Others emphasize visual attributes and are only appropriate for vertical surfaces where they do not receive the type of wear inherent to a horizontal surfacing material. It is important to follow the manufacturer's directions regarding recommended locations, as those with special visual features may not be functional nor retain their appearance in heavy-duty applications.

Structure and Properties

Plastic laminate is a composite material of layers laminated together under heat and pressure. The core layers are of heavy kraft paper impregnated with phenolic resin. Over this is applied a decorative layer impregnated with melamine formaldehyde, commonly called melamine. The top layer is a protective finish of melamine.

In the fabrication process, the core sheets are run through a phenolic resin solution, dried and cut to size. The decorative layer is similarly prepared with a melamine resin. (In the color-through products, melamine is used for all sheets.) An appropriate number of sheets of phenolic paper is laid up in a hot-plate press. The decorative sheet is laid over these and a thin veil of melamine-impregnated cellulose is placed on top. A stainless steel sheet or caul which will impart the desired gloss, matte or other finish is laid over the entire assemblage. This is then pressed between the platens of the hot plate press at 800 to 1200 psi and temperatures of about 275°–325° F where the resin melts, cures and fuses the layers together. The back is sanded to maintain a uniform thickness and to facilitate bonding.

Layers

DECORATIVE: The decorative layer is typically a printed, heavy, kraft paper. Any type of motif, from abstractions to photographic simulations of other materials such as wood, can be printed on the paper. Sometimes, instead of paper, the decorative layer is a thin piece of material such as a wood veneer or woven fabric.

MELAMINE: Hardness, clarity, stain resistance and freedom from yellowing make melamine formaldehyde resin an excellent material for furniture, countertops, and other working surfaces that must be both decorative and functional. It is resistant to water and most solvents and stains. It is also heat resistant to temperatures as high as the original curing temperature.

Layers

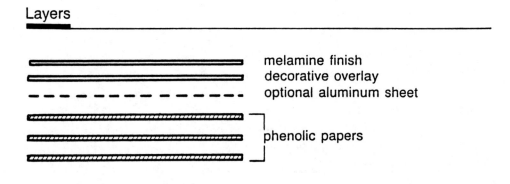

melamine finish
decorative overlay
optional aluminum sheet

phenolic papers

Figure 17.1. STRUCTURE OF A PLASTIC LAMINATE. Layers of plastic-impregnated materials are laminated to form plastic laminates. Specific attributes are present in accordance with the number of layers and their composition. For example, the number of layers is increased to achieve high impact strength or the formulation of the top layers may be adjusted to achieve high wear characterstics.

Fabrication Process

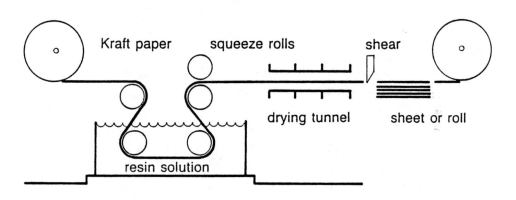

Figure 17.2. FABRICATION OF PLASTIC LAMINATE. Illustrated is the preparation of the resin-impregnated kraft paper. Layers of this prepared paper are assembled and pressed between the platens of a hot-plate press to form a plastic laminate sheet.

PHENOLIC RESINS: Good thermal and chemical resistance and dielectric strength are attributes of phenolic resins. Products made with these resins also have good flammability ratings, creep resistance, and low water absorption. Phenolic resins give physical strength to the core layers, provide impact resistance and help hide irregularities in the substrate.

Performance Standards

Formal performance standards for plastic laminates have been set by an industry trade association, NEMA (The National Electrical Manufacturer's Association). NEMA was formed many years ago when plastic laminates were made exclusively for electrical insulation. These are now called industrial laminates.

When melamine resins and decorative laminates came on the scene, NEMA formulated separate standards for high-pressure decorative laminates (HPDL). To conform to NEMA standards, the HPDL must meet or exceed criteria for each of fifteen categories. Test methods are described in NEMA Standards Publication LD3-1980. Requirements may vary according to type and grade or may be the same for almost all. Types and grades are discussed in a later section.

The following is a very brief explanation of the test methods and the minimum requirements. Table 17.1 shows those properties where NEMA values vary according to type and grade. Paragraph numbers and quotations are from the NEMA Standards Publication, LD3-1980.

3.01 WEAR RESISTANCE: The test sample is rotated between two rubber wheels to which sandpaper is attached. The decorative face of a class 1 laminate must resist 400 cycles of abrasion. (See Table 17.1 for others.)

3.02 SCUFF RESISTANCE: Defacing by an object rubbed across the plastic laminate is called scuffing. To test scuff resistance, a heavy metal pendulum, shaped like a shoe heel, is swung against the sample and allowed to drop, rubbing against the test sample after impact. To meet this standard, the plastic laminate face must show no visible change.

3.03 IMPACT RESISTANCE: An eight-ounce, stainless steel ball is dropped onto the test sample consisting of an HPDL sheet bonded to a 45-pound particleboard substrate simulating a typical application. The ball is dropped from increasing heights until the sample sustains permanent damage. For satisfactory performance, standard, general-purpose plastic laminate must show no damage up to a drop distance of 50 inches. (See Table 17.1 for others.)

3.04 DIMENSIONAL CHANGE: The paper from which plastic laminates are made is a cellulosic product. Cellulose fibers tend to absorb and release moisture and are consequently subject to dimensional change. The extent of this change is tested by exposing test samples to humidity extremes: 24 hours in an oven at 70° C (158° F) and then seven days in a high humidity chamber. Expected percentages of changes in both direc-

Table 17.1

NEMA MINIMUM PERFORMANCE REQUIREMENTS
FOR PLASTIC LAMINATE TYPES

Type	Grade	Nominal Thickness	Wear Resis.	Impact Resis.	Dimensional Change		Radiant Heat Resis.
			Cycles min.	Inches min.	%MD max.	%CD max.	Seconds min.
General Purpose	GP 50	0.050	400	50	0.5	0.9	125
General Purpose	GP 38	0.038	400	35	0.6	1.0	100
General Purpose	GP 28	0.028	200	20	0.7	1.2	80
General Purpose	GP 20	0.020	200	15	0.8	1.3	60
Post-forming	PF 42	0.042	400	30	1.1	1.4	100
Post-forming	PF 30	0.030	300	20	1.1	1.4	80
Cabinet Liner	CL 20	0.020	50	10	1.2	2.0	--
Backer	BK 20	0.020	--	--	--	--	--
Backer	BK 50	0.050	--	--	--	--	--
Specific Purpose	SP 125	0.125	400	75	0.3	0.7	200
Specific Purpose	SP 62	0.062	400	55	0.5	0.9	150
High Wear	HW120	0.120	3000	75	0.3	0.7	200
High Wear	HW 80	0.080	3000	40	0.4	0.8	175
High Wear	HW 62	0.062	3000	35	0.5	0.9	150
Fire Rated	FR 62	0.062	400	55	0.5	0.9	125
Fire Rated	FR 50	0.050	400	45	0.5	0.9	75
Fire Rated	FR 32	0.032	300	20	0.7	1.2	50

tions are stated in the manufacturer's literature. With this information, detailing with proper tolerances can be designed.

3.05 BOILING WATER RESISTANCE: This is the first of four heat criteria. For this test, water is heated in a flat-bottomed pot until it comes to a full boil. A small amount is spilled onto the HPDL and the hot vessel containing the rest of the water is set in the puddle where it remains for twenty minutes. To perform satisfactorily, the HPDL must exhibit no visible change in color or texture after drying. Post-forming types may show a slight effect.

For this and the following categories involving heat, stain and light resistance, cabinet liner may show a moderate effect. Backer type is not evaluated.

3.06 HIGH TEMPERATURE RESISTANCE: To perform this test, bath wax is heated to 180° C (365° F) in a flat-bottomed pot. The hot wax-filled pot is placed on the HPDL for twenty minutes. The NEMA standard is "slight effect" meaning "a change in color or texture which is difficult to perceive."

3.07 RADIANT HEAT RESISTANCE: In this third test for heat, the plastic laminate is subjected to direct contact with a heating element at temperatures reaching 205° C (400° F) until the laminate fails. Failure is evidenced by "blistering, charring, permanent discoloration or crazing."* Average resistance time is measured in seconds. The NEMA criteria for standard, general purpose HPDL is 125 seconds.

3.08 CONDUCTIVE HEAT RESISTANCE: This test measures the effect of continued exposure to heat conducted by an aluminum plate at a temperature of at least 174° C (345° F). This fourth test involving heat resistance simulates an iron or other appliance resting directly on the HPDL. To meet NEMA criteria, the specimen should show no perceptible surface damage after five minutes.

3.09 STAIN RESISTANCE: Twenty-nine reagents in two categories are tested. Each is placed on the face of the plastic laminate for 16 to 24 hours with part covered with a watchglass and part exposed.

To meet NEMA criteria for category one, reagents must be completely removed without abrasive action. Qualifying reagents include mustard, washable ink, vinegar, amyl acetate, lipstick, coffee, tea and other common reagents.

To meet NEMA criteria for category two, reagents may show a moderate affect; that is, they "require the use of an abrasive for removal, resulting in a decrease in gloss."† This category includes merthiolate, wax crayon, shoe polish, supermarket ink, ball-point pen ink and solvent, felt-tip pen ink.

3.10 LIGHT RESISTANCE: HPDL is manufactured for interior applications; it must be stable in interior lighting conditions. In this test procedure, the specimen is exposed to forty-eight hours of direct, continuous

---

*Pub. No. LD-3, Part 3, p. 33.
†Pub. No. LD-3, Part 3, p. 33.

ultraviolet light. To satisfy NEMA criteria, the plastic laminate may show only a slight effect.

3.11 APPEARANCE: In this test, a full sheet of HPDL is visually inspected under direct light from a distance of seven feet. The surface is considered unsatisfactory if any one of the following three categories of defects is apparent:

1. Type A: Smudges, smears, fingerprints or streaks.
2. Type B: Any visible foreign particle with an area of 0.60 sq mm or larger.
3. Type C: Any visible group of three or more foreign particles within a 12" diameter circle, each having an area of 0.30 sq mm or more.

3.12 CLEANABILITY: To test cleanability, NEMA prepares a soiling agent from potting soil, Portland cement, carbon black, red iron oxide, several fatty acids and several other ingredients. After mixing these with water, the resulting paste is rubbed over the test surface and left to dry for sixteen hours. Then the surface is washed with a cellulose sponge moistened with Formula 409®. The sponge is attached to the arm of a machine which moves it across the dirty area. The unit of measure is the number of strokes needed to return the plastic laminate surface to its pretest condition. A maximum of twenty-five is allowed by the NEMA standard.

3.13 SURFACE FINISH: This test is not to establish a standard for satisfactory performance but to supply interpreted data. By NEMA definition, gloss is "determined by the smoothness of the surface and is measured by the amount of light that is reflected when the angle of incidence is equal to the angle of reflection."* Measurements are made using the Hunter glossometer. There is a wide range of sheen extending from 0–100, matte to mirror-like.

Sheen is selected by the designer as appropriate to the application and the lighting conditions. It should be noted that **the higher the sheen and the darker the color, the more subject the plastic laminate will be to visible smudge and grease marks.**

3.14 FORMABILITY: This is one of two tests designed for plastic laminate sheets intended for post-forming. Six specimens are cut from the HPDL sheet, heated and formed to the smallest radius recommended by the manufacturer. This test is scored as "pass/fail," with "pass" meaning that the

---

*Pub. No. LD-3, Part 3, p. 35.

test specimen withstood forming to the manufacturer's minimum recommended radius without cracking, blistering, crazing or discoloring.

3.15 BLISTER RESISTANCE: This is the second test designed for plastic laminate sheets intended for post-forming. Samples are put through the actual post-forming process. Measurement is made of the time required to meet the proper post-forming temperature and the time interval beyond that point until the samples react to the heat by blistering. The NEMA test result is expressed in seconds. Two measurements are given: time to reach post-forming temperature and blister-resistance time.

Health and Safety

Flammability

Plastic laminates are tested in accordance with the Steiner Tunnel Test. Both unbonded laminates and laminates in combination with typical adhesives and substrates are tested. The substrate and adhesive can significantly change the fire rating from that of the unbonded material, either raising or lower it. Since plastic laminates are never used apart from the substrate, it is the test of the actual combination intended for use that is of practical importance.

To make fire-rated plastic laminate, a fire-retardant chemical is added to the phenolic resins used to impregnate the core sheets. The substrates generally used are fire-resistant particleboard or asbestos cement board.

A majority of the laminates and combinations have a class B or class 2 rating. A class A or class 1 rating can be achieved using a fire-rated plastic laminate in combination with a fire-rated substrate and a nonflammable adhesive. Some code districts allow surfacing materials less than 0.036" thick to be exempted. Some plastic laminates intended for vertical surfaces are within this dimension.

In most building codes, interior finish requirements are set forth in a separate "interior finish" section. Once the maximum flame spread index permitted by the building code is determined, an appropriate assembly can be selected using test results of various recommended assemblies of laminate, adhesive and substrate as provided by the manufacturer.

Biogenic Factors

Plastic laminate has a water-resistant surface which means that soil and microorganisms remain on the top of the surface where they can be easily removed.

Post-forming, which will be discussed shortly under types of plastic laminates, is directly related to health. A curved surface instead of a corner seam where the countertop meets the backsplash means easier cleanability and one less seam where microorganisms can escape routine cleaning.

Safety

Post-forming also means the opportunity to eliminate pointed corners and sharp rims that people can bump against and injure themselves. This is an important consideration in designing for the elderly, the handicapped and children.

Sometimes, wood or vinyl edges are used on plastic laminate tables or countertops to prevent the chipped edges that result from use in heavy-duty locations. These softer, rounder edges also protect the people who bump into them.

Types and Grades

Plastic laminates come in several types and grades designed to meet specific performance and economic needs. Virtually every manufacturer of plastic laminates produces four types: general purpose, post-forming, cabinet liner and backing sheets. Each type is made in several grades designated by thickness. For example, GP50 is general-purpose HPDL that is 0.050" thick. NEMA performance standards have been developed for grades of these four types plus for specific purpose, high wear, and fire-rated plastic laminates which are made by some manufacturers. (See Table 17.1 for the different types of HPDL and minimum performance requirements for each.)

Other special-function products for which there are not yet NEMA performance standards are antistatic and chemical-resistant plastic laminates.

A relatively new type of plastic laminate is a product where the color is the same through the total thickness of the material rather than being limited to the surface. This product has not yet acquired a commonly used generic name. The name that will be used in this book is "color through."

Most types are made in several thicknesses; the thicker plastic laminates generally have the higher performance. Each type (except backer and cabinet liner sheets) is made in a number of finishes. These may run the gamut from matte to high gloss in the most used types. In the special-purpose plastic laminates the range of finishes is more limited.

General Purpose

These are the plastic laminates most frequently used for horizontal and vertical surface finishes. They are made for durability, appearance retention, resistance to stain, ease of cleaning and resistance to heat up to 275° F. General-purpose HPDL is made in a number of thicknesses; there are NEMA standards for four thicknesses. The thinner ones are for vertical use only.

Thin plastic laminates, recommended for vertical surfaces only, have the same stain resistance and ease of cleanability as thicker laminates, but abrasion resistance and impact resistance are less. For many locations they are appropriate, but where impact from carts is likely, their lesser resistance to impact can be detrimental.

A thinner plastic laminate has fewer phenolic-impregnated plies and is less dimensionally stable. For this reason, it is not recommended on surfaces exceeding 24 inches wide.

General-purpose HPDL is available in a wide variety of colors, patterns and finishes. All of these are not always available in the vertical grades.

Post-formable

This is a special type of HPDL with a thickness and chemical composition that allow permanent bending while substantially retaining the characteristics of general-purpose HPDL. In the manufacturing process, special resins are used and the sheets are only partially cured. Because of this undercure, the flat sheets can be reheated and softened enough to be bent or post-formed to simple curves suitable for coved backsplashes and rounded edges for countertops and cabinet doors.

Post-forming was first developed for a radiused edge on a horizontal surface. The reverse bend was then developed to form a coved, seamless connection between countertop and backsplash. Other post-formed edge treatments include no-drip, double-radiused and 180° wrap edges.

In the post-forming process, the laminate is held in a machine designed to prevent any unplanned movement. Heat is applied to raise the temperature of the laminate to 312°–325° F. At just the right moment, the bending force is applied. For a period of 20 to 40 seconds, the shape of the plastic laminate can be permanently altered without damage to the laminate. If the heating period is too long or the temperature too high, blistering will occur. After forming, the plastic laminate is held in position until the temperature cools and the new shape is fixed.

No Drip

Radiused

Double Radiused

180° Wrap

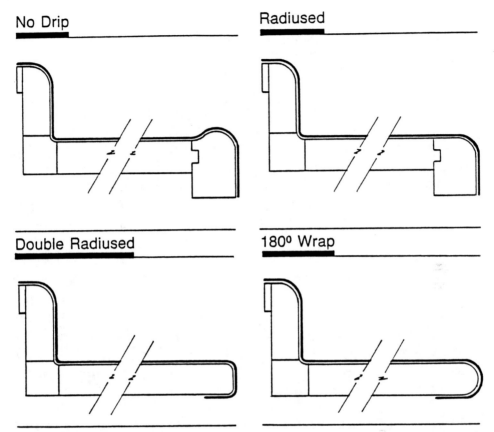

Figure 17.3. POST-FORMED EDGE TREATMENTS. The curved edges made by post-forming give a softer look to casework and are safer than the traditional sharp edge. However, the HPDL used in the post-forming process is less impact resistant than standard HPDL. In locations where impact resistance is important, this limitation should be carefully balanced against the advantages of the curved form.

Success in forming is dependent on the skill of the operator, the radius of the bend and the thickness of the sheet. The thinner the plastic laminate sheet, the tighter the radius possible. An inside radius can be formed smaller than an outside radius in the same plastic laminate. All manufacturers give product information on the radius obtainable with their post-formable products. It is the manufacturer's claimed possible radius that is subjected to NEMA testing.

To meet the NEMA performance standards, the impact resistance of PF42, the thickest of the post-formable laminates, is not required to be as high as that for the thicker, general-purpose laminates, GP50 and GP38. In locations where impact resistance is important, this limitation should be carefully balanced against the advantages of the curved form.

Cabinet Liner

Cabinet-liner-type laminate is for use only in cabinet interiors. It is a thin sheet designed for a smooth, easily cleanable, economic surface inside cabinets. It is neither very durable nor impact resistant compared to the laminates designed for the wear surfaces of cabinets. Color selection is usually limited to white, black and a few neutral, solid colors.

Cabinet-liner types may also be used for the backing of cabinet doors if this is desirable for budget reasons. **Cabinet doors and any other long, unsupported spans must be balanced with plastic laminate on both faces. If the laminate is on one face only, warping will occur.** It is also best, though not always necessary, to have both faces of the same-thickness laminate.

Backer

When laminate is bonded to any substrate, warping can result. To prevent this, either the substrate must be firmly supported or be laminated on both faces. Backer sheets without a decorative surface are available to inhibit moisture absorption through the back or concealed surfaces and to balance the construction in locations where the backing laminate will be unseen. A backer of approximately the same thickness as the face sheet will provide the greatest stability.

Specific Purpose

Specific-purpose type is a general-purpose HPDL with increased thickness. Important attributes which are enhanced in specific-purpose plastic laminates are impact resistance, heat resistance and dimensional stability. SP125, a specific purpose, 0.125" thick HPDL, must have a minimum impact-resistance rating of 75 inches and a minimum heat-resistance rating of 200 seconds. This compares with 50 inches and 125 seconds as the minimum requirement for the best general-purpose plastic laminate.

HPDL with heightened impact resistance is manufactured for doors to be used in heavy-impact areas, especially doors likely to be bumped by heavy carts. It is also useful for service elevator walls and vertical surfaces of nursing stations located in areas of high cart traffic.

One of the techniques used to produce a heat-resistant HPDL is the insertion of a metal sheet in the core. A burning cigarette lying on a surface may char a plastic laminate. A thin sheet of aluminum placed under the decorative surface sheet will conduct heat away from the heat source and prevent charring. Metal core plastic laminates carry a class 1 or class A fire rating.

The addition of this metal sheet, usually aluminum or steel, also has the beneficial effects of increased impact resistance, heightened electrical resistance and static dissipation qualities and excellent dimensional stability.

This and other techniques are used to manufacture plastic laminates that will meet all the NEMA requirements for the specific-purpose type. However, sometimes one attribute is enhanced, but overall, the laminate does not qualify for this more demanding category.

The most significant attribute that need not be improved for an HPDL to quality as specific-purpose quality is wear resistance. This can be the same as with a general-purpose HPDL.

High Wear

High wear is the designation for plastic laminates with increased surface-wear resistance. High-wear plastic laminates are formulated with special resins. To merit classification as high wear, abrasion resistance must be sufficient to withstand a minimum of 3000 cycles. This can be compared to the 400 cycles required for general-purpose HPDL.

There are some plastic laminates on the market which have greater abrasion resistance than that required for a general-purpose HPDL but do not qualify as a high-wear HPDL. One of these is a product by Nevamar called ARP® (acronym for abrasion resistant product) which withstands 1200 cycles. Increased abrasion and scuff resistance in this product is achieved by the use of a very thin deposit of microscopic particles of aluminum oxide on the melamine layer.

The construction of ARP is based on the theory that abrasive action is caused by silica (sand) particles found in most dust and dirt and many of the objects that are slid across counters. Since silica is much softer than aluminum oxide, the ARP surface increases resistance to abrasive action.

Any increase in abrasion resistance will increase the wear life of the plastic laminate and also increase appearance retention by decreasing changes in gloss and color and resisting scuff marks. With the high-wear products there is an increase in cost to obtain this. While ARP is not a high-wear product, some increased abrasion resistance is obtained at no cost increase over other general-purpose products made by the same manufacturer.

Antistatic

Antistatic HPDL is intended for interior surfaces where there is a need to minimize the accumulation of electrostatic charges. This would include such horizontal surfaces as hospital monitoring and testing facilities and electronic data processing work surfaces. It could also be used for vertical surfaces of work station dividers.

To make this antistatic HPDL, the decorative paper is impregnated with a specially formulated melamine resin and the core is of an electrically conductive sheet and kraft papers impregnated with phenolic resins. This is made in a limited number of colors and matte finishes. There are no industry standards for antistatic laminates.

To be effective, grounding of antistatic HPDL is necessary. This can be achieved by using terminals and grounding cords securely attached to the laminate and to a suitable ground. There should be periodic verification of electrical continuity between laminate and grounding point. Waxes must not be used, as they will impair the electrical characteristics.

Chemical Resistant

Chemical-resistant HPDL is formulated for use in intermediate laboratories where resistance to relatively harsh acids, alkalies, corrosive salts, solvents and staining substances such as reagents is required. They can be appropriate for chemical, medical and pathology laboratories and clinics and might be used for nursing stations where staining is a problem.

The light weight of the plastic laminate and substrate assembly when correctly fabricated is an advantage when compared to the traditional slate, stone or marble lab top.

There are no industry standards for chemical-resistant laminates. Those available are substantially different from each other. Certainly, one should obtain complete testing results, including those on chemical and stain resistance, before specifying a chemical-resistant HPDL.

All those available can be post-formed. Wilson Art's Chemsurf® is available in a wide variety of colors. Formica's laboratory grade is available only in matte black due to inherent physical properties of the components.

Chemical-resistant laminates are also apt to show increased resistance to wear, impact and heat as well as better cleanability.

Color-through

Plastic laminates with the color extending through the total thickness of the laminate are made in the same way as other HPDL products. The difference is that all of the paper layers are impregnated with the melamine resin. Thus, all the core layers are the same as the surface layers with no phenolic resin being used.

The visual advantages of this type of HPDL have been extensively advertised by Formica with Colorcore® and Wilson Art with Solicor®. Many attractive edge treatments can be achieved that are impossible

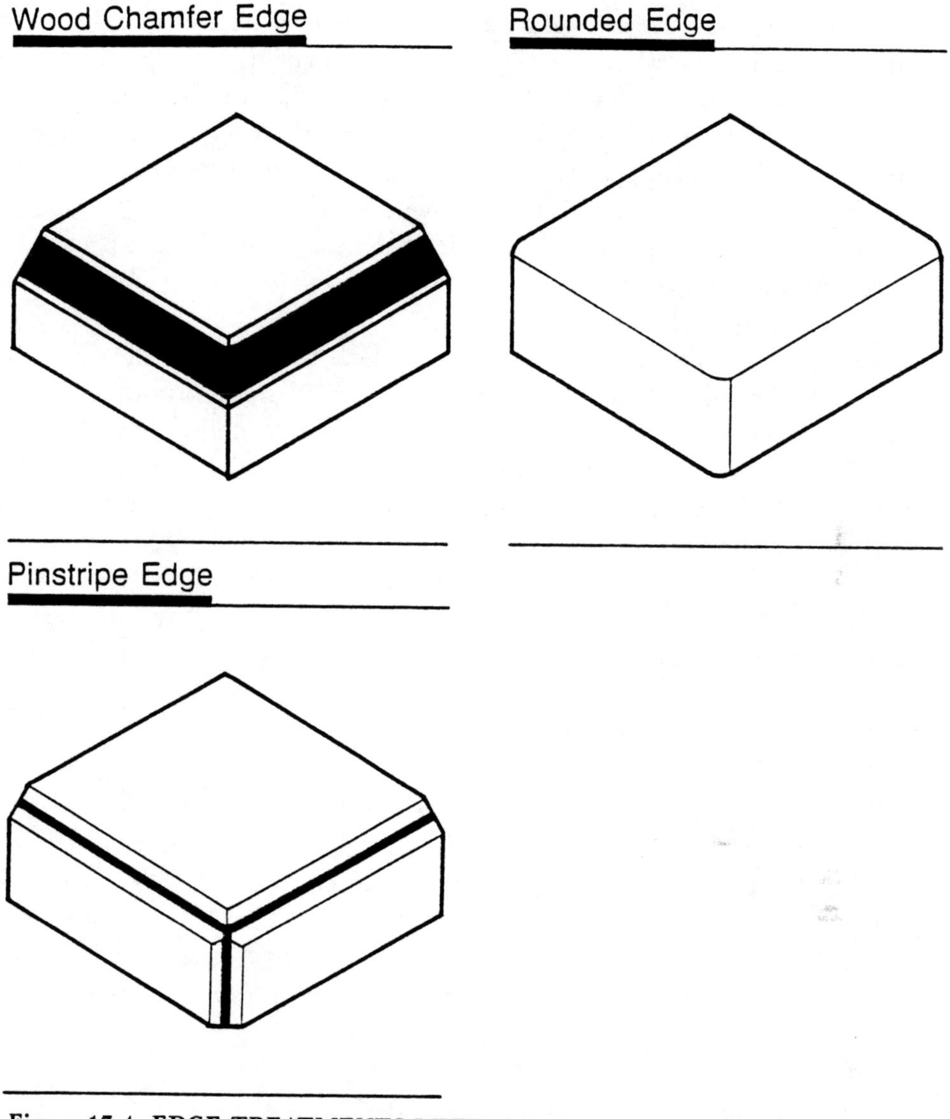

Wood Chamfer Edge

Rounded Edge

Pinstripe Edge

Figure 17.4. EDGE TREATMENTS WITH COLOR-THROUGH PLASTIC LAMI-NATE. Because all the layers of the laminate sheet are the same color, the appearance is that of a homogenous sheet suitable for many different fabrication designs. Directions for constructing a wide variety of edge treatments are provided in the manufacturer's literature. The creative designer will think of many more.

when color is confined to the surface. The way to achieve some of these is illustrated in Figure 17.4. Also, many handsome or unusual effects can be achieved by routing or sandblasting.

The main disadvantage of this material is cost. Melamine is a more expensive material than phenolic resin. This is reflected in the cost of the material.

There are other possible disadvantages. The phenolic resin is the more flame resistant of the two resins. Therefore, the color-through product generally has a higher flame spread rating than an otherwise similar general-purpose product on the same substrate. This is not a serious problem, as appropriate fire ratings to meet the various codes can be achieved with proper combination of laminate, adhesive and substrate.

The color-through plastic laminates are more brittle and stiffer than the traditional plastic laminate and require more careful handling in transporting and fabricating.

The adhesive line is not masked by a dark edge. While the elimination of the dark line at corner seams of plastic laminate products is generally considered an advantage, proper adhesive choice and careful fabrication are essential to achieving the desired result.

While the Formica and Wilson Art products have many similarities, they are quite different types. Colorcore conforms to HW62 except for thickness; it is 0.05" thick versus 0.062". It is not produced as a post-forming material, although it can be bent to a rather generous radius. Solicor which is made for post-forming closely conforms to standard type PF42.

Surface Finishes

The surface finish is determined by the nature of the cauls used in pressing the HPDL. These can be highly polished or minutely etched stainless steel or aluminum. Laminate surfaces also may be buffed or polished after pressing.

The finishes impart various degrees of sheen to the surface. NEMA defines this as levels of gloss and identifies five according to degree of gloss in the machine direction (MD) and cross-machine direction (CD). These are textured-low gloss, textured-high gloss, satin, furniture and gloss.

The degree of sheen or gloss is measured on a glossometer. To clarify confusion about what gloss is, NEMA describes it in NEMA standard 11-14-1985 as follows:

> Gloss should not be confused with reflectance or apparent reflectance. Gloss is determined by the smoothness of the surface and is measured by the amount of light which is reflected when the angle of incidence is equal to angle of reflection. Reflectance is the ratio of the total quantity of light reflected from a surface to the total quantity of incident light on the surface regardless of direction. Reflectance is determined by color and shading of the opaque laminate and is independent of surface finish. Apparent reflectance, of which gloss is a special kind, refers to a specified condition of view or reflection.

Table 17.2

STANDARD PLASTIC LAMINATE FINISHES

Sheen	MD	CD	Description
Textured-low gloss	1-20	21-40	Low profile textures given
Textured-high gloss	21-40	21-40	Clarity and depth to color, soften pattern without obscuring pattern
Satin	15-34	5-19	Semi-gloss, but lower sheen than furniture finish
Furniture	35-60	21-35	Smooth semi-gloss for smooth, low glare finish
Gloss	70-100	70-100	Maximum smoothness and luster

Legend:
MD= machine direction
CD = cross machine direction

When selecting finishes, one should realize that **both high-gloss finishes and solid colors tend to highlight surface scratches and abrasion. Fingerprints, handprints and other types of imprints accumulated in everyday use also are very visible, especially when the color is dark.**

Cleaning and Maintenance

Plastic laminate is an easy finish to keep clean, especially when compared to transparent or opaque coatings traditionally used as casework finishes. It can be cleaned with a damp cloth using mild soap or household ammoniated solutions. It must be rinsed with clear water and dried with a clean cloth or soft paper towel to prevent streaking.

Commercial liquid cleaners can be used for removal of stains that were not removed by soap and water. Undiluted household bleach (5% solution hypochlorite) can be used. It should stand no more than 1.5 minutes before rinsing. Stubborn stains can be removed with organic solvents such as alcohol, acetone, lacquer thinner, paint solvent or contact adhesive solvent. Solvents can attack the glue line at seams and edges. They are also flammable, so that great care must be taken when using them.

Do not use harsh abrasives or cleaners containing them. They may scratch the surface. Agents containing strong acids or alkalies should not be permitted to remain in contact with plastic laminate. If they are spilled on the laminate, they should be washed off immediately.

Sometimes, it is desirable to use cleaner waxes. These leave a thin protective film on the plastic laminate. The manufacturer of the particular plastic laminate should be asked to recommend the appropriate wax to use.

While a very durable and resistant material, plastic laminate, when seriously scratched, gouged, chipped, blistered or burned, is impossible to repair. It will need to be replaced. Precautions that should be taken in everyday use are: Never use as a cutting or chopping board, do not expose to intense radiant heat, and do not expose to constant sunlight.

Fabrication

Because plastic laminate is a surfacing material rather than a structural material, choice of substrate is of the utmost importance. It must be stable, warp resistant, and of sufficient density and internal bond strength to restrain movement of the laminate. It must also have a clean, smooth face over the total surface so that a good bond can be obtained.

A laminate-clad panel is a "plywood-like" assembly consisting of laminate face and back, core or substrate, and the glue lines necessary to hold it together. If the laminate is glued to one surface only, the unbalanced assembly will warp with changes in the humidity and temperature unless it is firmly restrained. Therefore, a sheet of laminate is usually bonded to the back side to form a balanced structure. If this backing sheet does not show, it can be a less expensive paper-phenolic utility laminate.

It is also recommended that the machine direction of the face sheet and the back or balancing sheet be the same to minimize panel distortion. Machine direction is determined by the way in which the paper is made, treated and assembled. It is usually the same as the direction of the sanding scratches on the laminate back. The reason this is important is because the expansion and contraction factor is always greater perpendicular to machine direction than parallel to it.

Substrate

Suitable substrate materials are plywood, particleboard (minimum 45# density), and medium- and high-density fiberboard. These will all supply the rigidity and good face needed. Other suitable substrates include honeycomb core, foamed plastic, metal and asbestos cement board.

For fire-rated assemblies, the substrates commonly used are fire-rated particleboard and asbestos cement board. These are expensive and difficult to bond but must be used when fire codes demand.

Certain properties of the assembly are influenced by the density of the substrate. For example, thinner laminates require higher density substrates to achieve end properties similar to thicker laminates on lower density boards.

Products that do not make suitable substrates are plaster board, gypsum board and plaster. Their internal bond is insufficient for this purpose. However, because metal-core HPDL is so dimensionally stable, it can be installed over these substrates. This is particularly useful in remodeling work.

In remodeling work, it may also be desired to use HPDL over old laminate. This is possible as long as the old laminate is smooth, even and completely free from defects. It should be sanded to create a "tooth" for the new adhesive.

Adhesives

The third component in the assembly is the adhesive which bonds the laminate to the substrate. Adhesives are selected for their intended use and in accordance with the equipment needed for fabrication. There are three types of adhesives used: thermosetting, polyvinyl acetate and contact types.

1. Thermosetting types are rigid glues applied under pressure. They cure at room temperature or can be heat cured. They develop a rigid glue line and result in maximum bonding effectiveness and heat resistance. These require the greatest care in the selection of a balancing sheet so that both faces will act in unison, minimizing panel distortion. Use is limited to flat, pre-assembled pieces.

   Urea formaldehyde is satisfactory for most conditions.

   Resorcinol and phenol resorcinol have high heat and water resistance. They are used in the fabrication of fire-rated HPDL.

   Epoxy has low shrinkage properties. It is used mainly for bonding laminate to impervious substrates such as steel.

2. Polyvinyl acetate is used for bonding laminate to wood when resistance to water and high heat are not required.

3. Contact types have high immediate bonding strength. Pressure may be applied by hand rolling or by passing the assembly through a pinch roller. They are the least demanding to use and typically selected for on-site fabrication. They are used for application of laminates to curved surfaces. However, they do not resist

laminate movement due to varying humidity conditions as well as the thermosetting types. Heat-resistant types are available.

Each manufacturer has recommendations for substrate and adhesive combinations and for fabrication procedures. These should be carefully studied and the appropriate combination selected for the specific job conditions.

Fabrication

In addition to selecting the proper components, conditioning and workmanship are key factors in a successful job.

CONDITIONING: Laminates and most substrates are cellulosic products which experience dimensional changes in varying humidity conditions. Conditioning of the laminate and substrate in the same environment prior to fabrication is essential. They should be brought to an equilibrium at room temperature (70° F) and at a relative humidity of 45%–55%. This can avoid problems arising after fabrication and installation due to differences in contraction and expansion between laminate and substrate.

WORKMANSHIP: Close attention to the manufacturer's instructions and good technique are necessary for a neat and lasting job. Key points are:

1. Adhesive of the correct thickness and evenly spread. Spot gluing is not acceptable.
2. Proper curing time for thermosetting and polyvinyl adhesives and proper drying time for contact adhesives.
3. Proper bonding pressures for the adhesive that is used.
4. Proper fabrication techniques as recommended by the plastic laminate manufacturer. These include:
   a. Rounded inside corners with a minimum radius of 1/8".
   b. Wide connecting strips between and around cut-out areas.
   c. Appropriate weight backer sheets.
   d. Alignment of grain or backer sheet parallel to that of face sheets.

Most problems are caused by improper conditioning and poor bonding. These can be prevented by using uniform glue lines and pressure on smooth, clean, conditioned laminates and substrate. Sturdy framing and balanced construction will help in achieving dimensional stability. Rounded inside corners and thick backer sheets will help prevent stress (corner) cracking.

STANDARDS: There are two organizations involved in setting standards for fabrication.

The National Association of Plastic Fabricators (NAPF) sponsors and publishes an American National Standard, "Performance Standards for Fabricating High Pressure Decorative Laminate Countertops," ANSI A161.2-1979. This publication outlines approved methods for lamination, adhesion, cut-outs and other fabrication details.

The Architectural Woodworking Institute (AWI) publishes *Architectural Woodwork, Quality Standards, Guide Specification and Certification Program* for specification of quality by grade of casework. There is a complete description of the quality of detail for grade levels. Once the decision about the grade desired is made, specification is easily accomplished by referencing AWI standards.

Types of Casework

AWI also publishes *Architectural Casework Details* which illustrates standard details for each of three types or styles of casework. These types are defined by the relationship of the cabinet door and drawer to the frame as: exposed face frame, flush overlay and reveal overlay. A variation of exposed face frame is the lipped overlay. A plan section showing the relationships is shown in Figure 17.5.

FLUSH OVERLAY AND REVEAL OVERLAY: When using a plastic laminate finish, the most practical design is one in which the doors and drawers overlay the case body, such as the flush overlay and reveal overlay. While the doors and drawers do require edging, the fitting requirements are less rigid than with exposed face frame. With these construction types, flush joints in the case body can be covered. This coverage is desirable with laminated casework, as true flush joints are difficult to achieve due to permissible thickness tolerances of laminates.

The reveal overlay has less demanding fitting tolerances than the flush overlay and the reveal between door and drawer fronts reduces the problem of alignment. Heavy-duty hardware is required for overlay types, especially those with the added weight of plastic laminate.

EXPOSED FACE FRAME: The type of cabinet least adaptable to plastic laminate covering is exposed face frame. The exposed flush joints are difficult and costly, since sanding to even out the joint is not possible. Doors and drawers which fit within the frame are difficult to fit, especially if the edges are finished with laminate.

Reveal Overlay

Flush Overlay

Exposed Face Frame

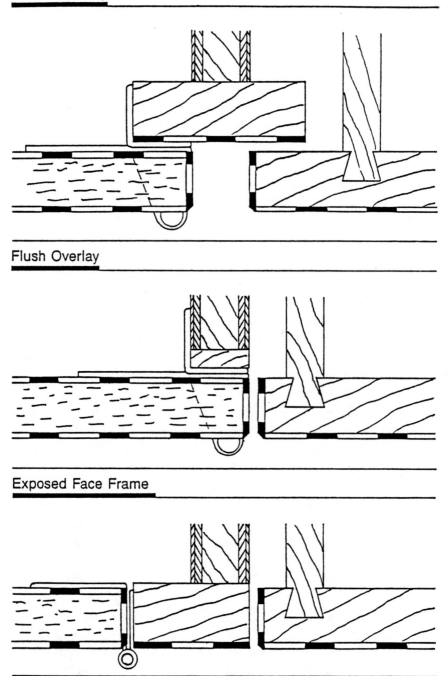

Figure 17.5. TYPES OF CASEWORK. The reveal overlay casework design has the least demanding fitting requirements and is, therefore, well suited to plastic laminate finishes. Flush overlay casework is also an appropriate type to be used with plastic laminate finishes. With an exposed face frame design, fitting requirements are such that a plastic laminate finish is very difficult to achieve and impossible where economic efficiency is important. (Adapted from materials published by Architectural Woodwork Institute.)

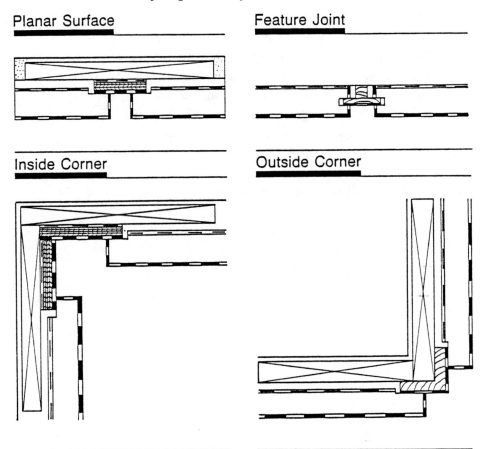

Planar Surface

Feature Joint

Inside Corner

Outside Corner

Figure 17.6. REVEAL JOINTS IN PLASTIC LAMINATE CONSTRUCTION. The use of reveal joints is a technique often used to accommodate the expansion and contraction of plastic laminates. Careful design will incorporate this functional feature to enhance the aesthetic appearance of the casework, wall paneling and other constructions. (Adapted from materials published by Architectural Woodwork Institute.)

Reveals

The reveal is an important detail when using a plastic laminate. Potential contraction and expansion of the laminate must be accommodated; this is accomplished using the reveal as a feature detail on corners and along plane surfaces.

Edge Details

Squared edges at the counter edge may be applied in two sequences:

1. By application of the edge laminate to the substrate prior to that of the top face. Because this requires that face and substrate mate-

rials be individually cut, it is the more expensive method. It tends to withstand more wear than the second method.

2. By application of the edge laminate after the face laminate has been applied to the substrate. This method is more economical, as substrate and face laminates are all cut at once. It is also aesthetically desirable, especially when a very thin edge laminate is used.

The edge is the most vulnerable part of the casework, and for greatest durability and easier repair when chipping does occur, it is probably better not to laminate the edge at all. Instead, use a solid wood strip which is more resilient and can be sanded and refinished (See Fig-

Laminate Edge

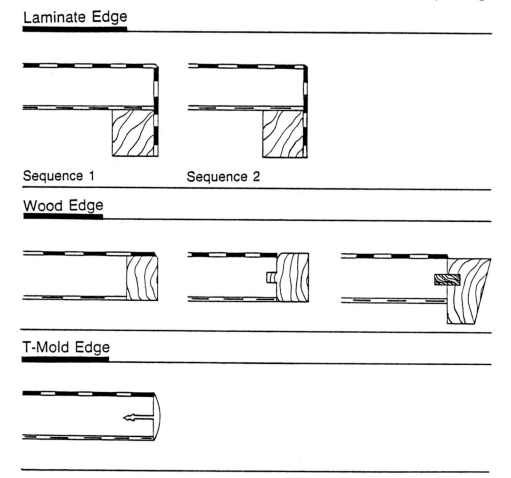

Sequence 1   Sequence 2

Wood Edge

T-Mold Edge

Figure 17.7. EDGE DETAILS. The edge of a laminated surface can be treated in a number of ways. For a uniform appearance, the edge can be covered with the same plastic laminate used on the horizontal surface. A more durable edge is one made of wood. Probably, the most durable edge treatment of all is a vinyl T-mold.

ure 17.7 for some details that can be used.) A wood surface flush with the laminate should be avoided.

The best treatment of all may be a vinyl T-mold. This is the same material as that used in vinyl corner guards. It is very resilient and will withstand severe impact without being defaced. The T-mold fits into a groove formed in the substrate and is difficult to jar loose.

Specification

AWI specification standards and formats will save a great deal of time in preparing the specification.

The specification should state the following with regard to building codes:

1. Flame spread, fuel contribution and smoke emitted data required by the codes applicable to the building site.
2. Whether data need be for the laminate, substrate, adhesive assembly or for the unbonded laminate.
3. The type of certification needed; UL label, independent laboratory letter or self-certification by the manufacturer.

In selection of the laminate, remember that a high gloss finish will show surface blemishes and is not intended for heavy service areas such as countertops. It will also be more difficult to maintain the appearance of solid dark colors than that of any others.

It is necessary to specify clearly or detail on the drawings exactly which surfaces are to be finished with HPDL. It is clearer when drawn and easier to confirm that all surfaces have been identified. The type of HPDL for each finished surface should be identified, especially with regard to backing, cabinet liner and facing types.

CORIAN®

An excellent product for horizontal surfaces is Corian manufactured by Dupont. This product has been especially successful in patient rooms and lavatories. It is also used in operating rooms and public lavatories and for window sills in all locations. There are some vertical locations, as well, such as tub and shower walls and toilet partitions in public restrooms.

Structure and Properties

Corian is a solid non-porous surfacing material homogeneously composed of mineral fillers and high performance acrylic (methylmethacrylate polymer). Certain properties inherent in acrylics contribute to its good performance as a countertop and vanity top material. It has extremely low permeability and good stain, chemical and environmental resistance. It does not yellow or darken under prolonged exposure. In addition, maintenance and fabrication are very easy.

Color and graining extend through the full depth of the material. In this way, it is different from similar-appearing products. Unlike gel-coated cultured marble products or plastic laminates, Corian can be effectively repaired when scratches, cigarette burns, and other surface blemishes do occur. Abrasive cleaners and pads and even sandpaper can be used to renew the surface. Since even the most abrasion and scratch-resistant surface will eventually be scarred in some way, this repairability is a valuable asset.

The structure and color-through properties of Corian contribute to its ease of fabrication. It can be cut, shaped, drilled, routed and sanded much like wood. Edges can be given a variety of sculptural treatments. If desired, combinations with metal, wood and other materials can be fabricated.

Three colors are available: cameo white, almond and a beige, with veining that extends through the depth of the material. More colors are in development. The surface is smooth and hard, with a gloss reading of 5-20 on the 60° Gardner glossometer.

Corian is available in sheet and shaped products. Standard sheet thicknesses are 1/4", 1/2" and 3/4". The 1/4" thick sheet is not suitable for horizontal applications. Shaped products include lavatory bowls and one-piece vanity tops with an integral bowl. The one-piece vanity and bowl is particularly advantageous, as there are no soil-catching seams or joints.

The Corian technical bulletin available from Dupont lists performance properties and test data. A bulletin with detailed information on stain and chemical resistance is also available.

When Corian is being considered for use, it is often as an alternative to plastic laminate. Therefore, it is probably desirable to evaluate it against similar performance standards. Performance standards for plastic laminates have been addressed by NEMA (National Electrical Manufacturers Association) and are described in the first part of this chapter. Corian has been tested in accordance with some of these. It has also been tested under a number of ASTM procedures.

Performance Properties

Minimum performance requirements for types of plastic laminates were summarized in Table 17.1. The performance properties of Corian shown in Table 17.3 can be compared with those of plastic laminates.

Table 17.3

PERFORMANCE PROPERTIES OF CORIAN®

Property	Typical Result	Test
Impact resistance	No fracture 1/4" slab — 36" drop, 1/2 lb ball 1/2" slab — 36" drop, 1 lb ball 3/4" slab — 36" drop, 2 lb ball	NEMA LD3-3.03
Boiling water resistance	No visible change	NEMA LD3-3.05
High temperature resistance	No visible change	NEMA LD3-3.06
Conductive heat resistance	No visible change	NEMA LD3-3.08
Light resistance	No change when subjected to 200 hours; NEMA requires 48	NEMA LD3-3.10
Gloss, 60° Gardner	5-20	NEMA LD3-3.13
Abrasion resistance	No loss of pattern, maximum wear depth 0.008" — 10,000 cycles	CS-221-76
Water absorption	24 hours Long term 0.04 (3/4") 0.4 (3/4") 0.09 (1/4") 0.8 (1/4")	ASTM-D-750

Although Corian has greater temperature resistance than plastic laminate, hot cookware should not be set on the surface.

The resistance to light and weathering is such that Corian could be used on outdoor furniture for dining terraces or courtyards. While there may be some loss of surface gloss and slight color change, physical properties will not be affected. By the very nature of the material, it will not suffer rot, rust, delamination or surface peeling.

Stain and Chemical Resistance

Exposure to a reagent for sixteen hours (uncovered and covered by glass) is a generally accepted test of chemical resistance. A class 1 rating is assigned to those reagents having little or no effect; a class 2 rating is assigned to reagents having an adverse affect on appearance or properties. Because Corian can be sanded, stains occuring from exposure to class 2 reagents can often be removed.

While Corian is extremely stain resistant, it can be stained or the surface etched by some chemical families. These chemicals include strong acids (like concentrated sulfuric acid), ketones (like acetone), chlorinated solvents (like chloroform), and strong solvent combinations (like paint removers). Length of contact will affect the extent of the damage. Except for paint remover, brief contact will not generally be severely detrimental. Acid drain cleaners should not be used in Corian sinks.

Health and Safety

The Tunnel Test, ASTM E-84, "Standard Methods for Surface Burning Characteristics of Building Materials," is used for measuring flammability of Corian. This is the flammability test most frequently required by building codes and is described in Chapter Two.

Results of the Tunnel Test with Corian are:

| | *Standard Colors* | | | | *Designer Colors* | |
| | 1/4"* | | 1/2" | 3/4" | 1/2" | 3/4" |
	Masonry	*Gypsum*	*Sheet*	*Sheet*	*Sheet*	*Sheet*
Flame Spread	15	25	5	5	15	15
Smoke Developed	20	25	10	10	25	30
Class	1	1	1	1	1	1

*Quarter-inch results reflect material adhered to both masonry surfaces and standard grade one-inch thick gypsum board using panel adhesives for Dupont Corian and tested as a composite.

Note that smoke development is very low. This is of importance as large amounts of smoke can reduce visibility and consequently the ability to exit. Smoke can also hamper fire fighting activity.

It may be desirable to compare these ratings with the flammability ratings of plastic laminate assemblies consisting of laminate, adhesive and substrate. A conventional plastic laminate assembly would commonly be a class 3. With a substrate of fire-rated particle board or asbestos cement board, a class 2 can be achieved. The use of fire-rated plastic laminate, resorcinol adhesive and a fire-rated substrate can produce a class 1 rating.

Biogenic Factors

The non-porous surface of Corian prevents absorption. Soil and microorganisms do not penetrate and can easily be removed with washing. The material will withstand strong cleaning chemicals when their use is indicated.

Safety

Rounded edges are easily made with standard carpentry tools. With the elimination of pointed corners and sharp rims, there is greater safety, especially for the elderly, handicapped and children.

Cleaning and Maintenance

Because Corian is solid and non-porous, washing with soap and water is sufficient for most cleaning. For any stains that remain, household and commercial cleaners such as powdered cleansers, ammonia, strong detergents, oxalic acid solutions, dilute hydrochloric acid and dilute trisodium phosphate can be used. Abrasive cleansers and pads are recommended to remove more stubborn stains; even cigarette burns.

Paint removers and acid drain cleaners should not be used. If detrimental chemicals are spilled on Corian, the surface should be immediately flushed with water.

Repair is also relatively simple. Surface cuts and scratches can be repaired with fine sandpaper (400 grit). If the damage is deep, a coarse sandpaper (240 or 110 grit) should be used first. After sanding, gloss levels can be adjusted by rubbing with a Scotch-Brite® pad, Type A or similar type pad. Use of an orbital sander, wet sandpaper and water can speed these repairs.

Fabrication and Installation

Detailed information can be found in the manufacturer's manuals for countertops and wet walls. Some of the main points are:

1. Corner joints should be made square rather than mitered. This uses factory-cut edges, and minimizes material and labor costs.
2. Cutouts should be made with a router equipped with a sharp 3/8" diameter carbide bit. Corners of a cutout must be rounded and all edges must be smoothed.

3. Countertops should be installed on perimeter framing support without added substrate. Corner joints should be supported by framing.
4. Vertical surfacing may be installed over substrates such as water-resistant gypsum board, exterior-grade plywood and ceramic tile.
5. Joint adhesive and caulking sealant are available to match Corian colors.
6. The recommended expansion clearance for uncaulked joints is 1/32" for every eight feet in length. Joints to be caulked should be 1/16" to 1/8" wide to allow for satisfactory caulking penetration.

Specification

Certain considerations should be incorporated in the design when specifying Corian:

1. Corian is produced in a variety of standard lengths and widths which should be considered in the design for most efficient use. This includes panels and standard trim kits for tub surrounds and shower walls. A limited number of special sizes are available for large jobs on a quotation basis. A variety of standard vanity tops with integral bowls are available. Alternate bowl locations, faucet drillings, top dimensions and shapes can be ordered on a quotation basis.
2. One-quarter-inch sheet is restricted to vertical applications.
3. Three-quarter inch has greater impact resistance and allowable overhang than one-half inch; other than these, selection is an aesthetic decision.
4. Maximum unsupported and unloaded overhang is twelve inches for three-quarter inch and six inches for one-half-inch sheet.
5. Care should be taken to avoid designs where moisture can be trapped behind Corian.
6. Required submittals should include shop drawings and product-installation data.
7. Samples should be submitted for approval and retained as a standard for the job.

Chapter Eighteen

AFTERWORD

COLOR AND texture are major influences in a person's sense of environment. If the sensuous importance of finish materials is ignored, the relationship of people to the building environment suffers. It has been demonstrated that the quality of our environment affects our well-being; where could this be more important than in a facility dedicated to health care? The orchestration of colors and textures of materials determines in large measure the affinity or hostility people will have for the care environment.

However, psychological and aesthetic benefits are not enough in this demanding environment. Physical function is critical. Materials must endure, retain their appearance, be easy to maintain, and give good economic value. It is by knowing materials that the designer is able to select those that function appropriately and respond to human sensitivity. Understanding the attributes of a material enables one to use it well. If one is to go beyond the accepted use, it is essential to have a thorough understanding of the essence of the material.

Uncommon utilization of materials is well suited to the unique situation of the nursing station. In most health care facilities and especially in hospitals, the nursing station is a special case where everything comes together. It is the hub of the facility, defining and bringing together inside and outside zones and providing the focus for patient, visitor and medical personnel interaction.

At the core of the care system, the nursing station is the expression of purpose; the visual image communicates the quality of care. Located at the heart of all that is happening, this is a very busy place subjected to innumerable types of abusive wear. It is all too easy to project a tattered or dingy image. To avoid the unmaintained look of chips, gouges, stains and other disfigurement, there is temptation to "armor-clad" the station and ignore the psychological and aesthetic attributes that are a vital part of the desired image.

The nursing station is the ideal place for the creative coordination of elements. In this chapter, some previously learned principles about materials are recalled and then applied in some uncommon applications. In the nursing station, there is the opportunity to start themes from which elements will flow throughout the facility, as there is also the opportunity to bring elements together in new ways as an exclamation point at the focus.

In thinking about materials that would qualify for use as unusual but appropriate finishes for the vertical surfaces of nursing stations, several come to mind. Durable finishes that could make attractive, impact-resistant surfaces are rubber flooring, carpet, and semi-rigid plastic wall finishes. Wall protective devices such as bumper guards and handrails could also be imaginatively used.

Rubber Flooring

Rubber resilient floor covering can be very durable and attractive as a casework finish. It comes in 36 1/2" wide sheets that are easy to use in this application. Joints can be butted and very little is needed for the finishing of raw edges. The molded rubber comes in a variety of motifs which give a textural surface with visual interest. The stripe pattern is particularly effective and can be used vertically or horizontally for directional emphasis. (Information regarding rubber flooring can be found in Chapter Three.)

Semirigid Plastic Wall Covering

PVC/acrylic alloy, a heavy-duty wall covering material, is a dent-, gouge- and abrasion-resistant finish that is well suited to this vulnerable location. The integral color helps conceal any blemishes that do occur. Design details for this material are not difficult, as the complimentary joint and corner strips can be used at material edges. Corners can also be formed by bending the plastic alloy as discussed in the Chapter Eight section on semirigid plastic wall coverings. For vertical surfaces of counters, the material would be handled in essentially the same way.

Carpet

Carpet shows little effect from the bumps and knocks of cart traffic. It will also cushion the sound of impact. It is psychologically soft and contributes to a warm, hospitable atmosphere. The criteria for the selection of carpet are similar to those identified in Chapter Eight, "Heavy-Duty Wall Surfaces." However, because the surface to be covered is relatively small, heavier carpets can be used and are probably more effective in resisting the effects of severe impact.

One concern in using carpet as a casework finish is the tendency of cut edges to ravel. In fitting the carpet to the casework, there will be more seams and edge conditions than in floor or wall installations. This leads to a major consideration in using carpet as a casework facing, that is the design of the detail where the carpet meets other finishes. A raw carpet edge is not a satisfactory detail.

A vinyl edge mold, trim strip or corner mold strip can be used as can an oak trim mold. These molds are impact resistant and can be strategically located to enhance the formal design.

A change in surface planes of the substrate to enable butting the carpet to the adjacent surface finish is also a possible detail. Careful workmanship and proper acclimation are necessary to avoid gaps between the two materials. One must also make sure that the design is such that any adjoining, more vulnerable surface will be in a location where impact is not apt to occur.

Bumpers and Rails

In the design of the form of the station, one objective is to make most durable the surface that receives the initial impact. For example, if the main vertical plane with its highly durable finish is topped with a more vulnerable overhanging countertop, the value of the high-durability vertical finish will be partially negated. Thought must be given to encasing the countertop edge with the same degree of protection.

Countertops are most generally of plastic laminate, and the various edge finishes recommended in Chapter Seventeen can be employed. Very often, the overhang is not a thin edge. Instead, an enclosed work counter with a 15"–18" high exterior vertical surface is used. This requires a different treatment. Bumpers and rails of all kinds can be carefully integrated in the design. Semirigid vinyl, flexible vinyl, or wood rails can be effectively used.

One design firm has developed an oak rail with a flexible vinyl insert. This is a highly functional and elegant solution. The resilient vinyl is the first line of resistance, backed by sturdy oak. The oak is not only functional but has the warm aesthetic of wood that is appealing and comfortable to most people.

In Closing

People experience the near environment through materials and details. Buildings are enclosures where our senses are strongly affected by the color and texture of materials. The administrator who acknowledges the influence of the environment and supports the effective use of materials will likely enjoy the benefits of a serviceable and attractive facility. The designer who understands the essence of materials can use them appropriately and creatively to design an enduring and enriching environment.

APPENDICES

Appendix A

REFERENCE TO ORGANIZATIONS

ORGANIZATIONS ASSOCIATED WITH STANDARDS AND TEST METHODS

Agencies of the Federal Government

Consumer Product Safety Commission   CPSC
1111 Eighteenth Street NW
Washington, DC 20207

Federal Standards   FED-STD
Navel Publications and Forms Center
5801 Tabor Avenue
Philadelphia, PA 19120

Federal Specifications   FS
Navel Publications and Forms Centers
5801 Tabor Avenue
Philadelphia, PA 19120

National Bureau of Standards   NBS
Gaithersburg, MD 20899

Industry Associations and Testing Societies

General

American Association of Textile Chemists   AATCC
and Colorists
PO Box 12215
Research Triangle Park, NC 27709

American National Standards Institute   ANSI
1430 Broadway
New York, NY 10018

American Society for Testing and Materials   ASTM
  1916 Race Street
  Philadelphia, PA 19130

National Fire Protection Association   NFPA
  Batterymarch Park
  Quincy, MA 02269

Underwriters Laboratories   UL
  333 Pfingsten Road
  Northbrook, IL 60062

Flooring Materials

Carpet and Rug Institute
  PO Box 2048
  Dalton, GA 30722

Ceramic Tile Institute of America
  700 N. Virgil Avenue
  Los Angeles, CA 90029

Methods and Materials Standards Association   MMSA
  c/o H.B. Fuller Co.
  315 Hicks Road
  Palatine, IL 60067

Resilient Floor Covering Institute   RFCI
  1030 Fifteenth Street NW
  Washington, DC 20005

Rubber Manufacturers Association   RMA
  1901 Pennsylvania Avenue NW
  Washington, DC 20006

Tile Council of America, Inc.   TCA
  PO Box 326
  Princeton, NJ 08542

Wall Finishes

  For information about carpet and ceramic tile, refer to organizations
listed under "Flooring Materials."

Chemical Fabrics and Film Association   CFFA
  1230 Keith Building
  Cleveland, OH 44115

National Paint and Coatings Association   NPCA
  1500 Rhode Island Avenue NW
  Washington, DC 20005

Painting and Decorating Contractors of America
  7223 Lee Highway
  Falls Church, VA 22046

The Society of the Plastics Industry   SPI
  355 Lexington Avenue
  New York, NY 10017

Wallcovering Manufacturers Association   WMA
  66 Morris Avenue
  Springfield, NJ 07081

Window Treatment

The Aluminum Association, Inc.   AA
  818 Connecticut Avenue, NW
  Washington, DC 20006

Architectural Aluminum Manufacturers Association   AAMA
  35 East Wacker Drive
  Chicago, IL 60601

National Association of Architectural Metal   NAAMM
Manufacturers
  221 North LaSalle
  Chicago, IL 60601

U.S. Venetian Blind Association
  355 Lexington Avenue
  New York, NY 10017

Upholstery

Business and Institutional Furniture   BIFMA
Manufacturers Association
  2335 Burton SE
  Grand Rapids, MI 49506

Chemical Fabrics and Film Association, Inc.   CFFA
  1230 Keith Building
  Cleveland, OH 44115

Upholstered Furniture Action Council   UFAC
  Box 2436
  High Point, NC 27261
The Wool Bureau, Inc.
  360 Lexington Avenue
  New York, NY 10017
       or
  930 South Robertson Blvd.
  Los Angeles, CA 90035

Furniture and Casework

Architectural Woodwork Institute   AWI
  2310 South Walter Reed Drive
  Arlington, VA 22206
Business and Institutional Furniture   BIFMA
Manufacturers Association
  2335 Burton SE
  Grand Rapids, MI 49506
National Electrical Manufacturers Association   NEMA
  2101 L Street NW
  Washington, DC 20037
The Society of the Plastics Industry
  355 Lexington Avenue
  New York, NY 10017

ORGANIZATIONS AND RELATED CODES

Building Officials and Code Administrators,   BOCA
International
  4051 Flossmer Road
  Country Club Hills, IL 60477
     Basic Building Code
     Basic Fire Prevention Code

International Conference of Building Officials   ICBO
  5360 South Workman Mill Road
  Whittier, CA 90601
     Uniform Building Code
     Uniform Fire Code

National Fire Protection Association   NFPA
  Batterymarch Park
  Quincy, MA 02269
    Life Safety Code
    National Fire Prevention Codes

Southern Building Code Congress, International   SBCC
  Birmingham, AL 35213
    Standard Building Code
    Standard Fire Prevention Code

PROFESSIONAL ORGANIZATIONS

The American Institute of Architects   AIA
  1735 New York Avenue, NW
  Washington, DC 20006

The American Society of Interior Designers   ASID
  1430 Broadway
  New York, NY 10018

The Construction Specifications Institute   CSI
  601 Madison Street
  Alexandria, VA 22314

The Institute of Business Designers   IBD
  1155 Merchandise Mart
  Chicago, IL 60654

Appendix B

SAMPLE WINDOW TREATMENT
MASTER SPECIFICATION

THE FOLLOWING sample window treatment master specification can be edited for a specific project. Information not pertinent to the specific project should be deleted and following items renumbered. Other editing instructions include:

1. Where paragraphs are included in two versions, they are identified by the same number or letter. The one that is in accordance with the project is to be kept; the other is to be deleted.
2. Words appearing in brackets refer to the type of information that is needed. Brackets and information cues should be deleted and the appropriate information inserted in the specification.
3. NTS = Note to Specifier. The note should be deleted after appropriate action is taken.

Neither the author or the publisher has any liability or responsibility for the use of this sample specification. Specifically, its use is at the user's own risk.

Division 12 Furnishings   Section 12500

Job #   Window Treatment, Drapery

Part 1 — GENERAL

1.01 DESCRIPTION OF THE WORK

A. Drawings, applicable portions of bidding requirements, Contract Forms, Conditions of the Contract, and Division 1 — General Requirements apply to the work in this section.

B. Reference to materials or systems herein by name, make or catalog number is intended to establish a standard of quality and not to limit competition; the words "or approved equal" are implied following each brand name. See Instructions to Bidders for substitution requests during the bidding period.

B. This specification is based on drapery track systems and drapery fabrics as specified herein, which have been carefully chosen to meet the owner's specific requirements. No substitutions will be considered.

C. Provide labor, material, facilities and administration which are required to furnish, fabricate and install all work covered by this Section.

D. The extent of each type of drapery track and drapery is indicated on the drawings and by specification.

E. Work included:
   1. Provide and install drapery track.
   2. Provide material, fabricate and install draperies.
   3. Provide accessories needed to install and operate.

F. Related Work:
   1. Window Framing and Blocking, Division 8
   2. Drapery Track Pockets, Division 5
   3. Blinds and Shades, Division 12

1.02 QUALITY ASSURANCE

A. The work under this section shall be by an experienced drapery specialist. Each bidder may be requested to submit a statement describing financial resources, organization, plant facilities and a detailed list of experience on projects of similar size and scope. If the bidder does not operate his own workroom, and an outside workroom or installation service is to be used, the name and address of the outside workroom or installation service shall be included in a separate letter which details their experience.

B. Provide track units which are complete assemblies produced by one manufacturer for each type required, including hardware, accessory items, mounting brackets and fasteners.

C. Provide each fabric from the same dyelot; colors shall be uniform throughout. Colors shall match Designer's sample.

D. Fabric shall be inspected for flaws and pattern alignment prior to cutting.

E. Drapery fabric shall meet flammability requirements and other provisions of city, state and federal laws as applicable.

F. Fabric shall be tested to provide fenestration data.

1.03 SUBMITTALS

A. Samples:
   1. Upon determination of the apparent low bidder and prior to award of contract, the apparent low bidder shall submit a sample drapery (20" pleated width by 24" finished length) made from the specified fabric(s).
   2. Prior to ordering fabrics, submit two (2) 12" square samples of each fabric type and color for comparison with the Designer's samples.

B. Product data:
   1. Submit manufacturer's product data and installation instructions for each type of drapery track required.
   2. Submit manufacturer's instructions for specified fabrication of drapery.

C. Shop drawings: Indicate at large scale, installation of track at window, method of attachment, clearance and operation.

D. Certification:
   1. Accompanying each type of fabric shall be the manufacturer's written certification that the fabric meets or exceeds the flammability requirements and other provisions of the city, state and federal laws as applicable.
   2. Submit certification of shading coefficient for each type of fabric.

E. Maintenance data:
   1. Submit three (3) copies of manufacturer's written instructions for operation and maintenance of drapery hardware.

2. Submit three (3) copies of fabric mill's written instructions for recommended maintenance, including recommendations for stain removal and cleaning procedures.

F. Extra stock: Deliver stock of maintenance materials to owner. Package in protective covering for storage. Identify with appropriate labels.

NTS Quantity of extra stock must be identified here or in the schedule.

G. Make all submittals in accordance with Division 1 — General Requirements.

1.04 PRODUCT DELIVERY, STORAGE AND HANDLING

A. Materials shall be delivered to the site and installed in accordance with a schedule approved by the [Designer, Owner].

B. The Contractor shall thoroughly investigate and resolve all access restrictions, including elevator size, capacity and accessibility, to assure proper delivery of materials.

C. Deliver drapery track wrapped in a manner to prevent damage to components or marring of surfaces. Mark clearly with installation location.

D. Store drapery track in a clean dry area laid flat and blocked off ground to prevent sagging, twisting or warping.

E. Drapery shall not be delivered until the area is ready for installation.

F. Deliver drapery completely wrapped and protected against damage of every kind. Damaged fabrics will be rejected. Mark clearly with installation location.

G. Drapery shall be delivered free of loose threads or lint. Drapery shall not be delivered with horizontal creases.

1.05 JOB CONDITIONS

A. Examine substrate and conditions under which units are to be installed. Do not proceed until unsatisfactory conditions have been corrected by the [General Contractor, Owner].

B. Environmental controls shall be in operation forty-eight hours prior to, during, and continuously after installation of drapery fabric.

1.06 GUARANTEE

A. Promptly repair or replace drapery track and drapery showing defects of materials or workmanship at no cost to the Owner for a period of one (1) year after date of Substantial Completion.

Part 2 — PRODUCTS

The width of the specified items is indicated on the floor plan drawings. Information regarding length is included in the elevation and section drawings. These approximate lengths are considered adequate for bidding purposes. As with all items, site measurements are required for ordering and fabrication purposes.

2.01 DRAPERY HARDWARE

A. Track shall be [dual channel, single channel, C-shape] track as manufactured by [Manufacturer].
Size and weight:
Finish:

B. Track shall be equipped with the following components:
Master carriers: [ball bearing or slide, butt or overlap]
Carriers: [ball bearing or slide]
Pulley sets: [for dual channel or C-shape traverse]
Cord: [for dual channel or C-shape traverse]
Baton: [for hand operated]
Brackets: Use manufacturer's standard metal brackets of proper type, spacing and size for track system and installation indicated. Design brackets to support safely the weight of draperies and track assembly plus forces applied to operate draperies.
Accessories: Provide end stops, splicers, supports, installation anchorages, and other required accessories as recommended by manufacturer of track system.

2.02 TRACK FABRICATION

A. Prior to fabrication, verify actual opening dimensions by accurate site measurements. Adjust track components for proper fit at openings.

B. Fabricate window treatment components from non-corrosive, non-staining, non-fading materials which are completely compatible with each other.

2.03 DRAPERY

A. Drapery fabric shall be [Manufacturer, fabric name and product number]
Fiber content:
Weight:
Weave:

Width:

Color:

Approximate repeat size:

Soil-resistant treatment:

Shading coefficient:

B. Fabrics shall meet or exceed the following performance standards:
Flammability: [NFPA 701 small scale, NFPA 701 large scale, New York New Jersey Port Authority, New York City, Boston Fire Department, California Fire Marshall, Federal Method 5903]
Abrasion: [ASTM D 1175 64T]
Colorfastness: [AATCC 16E-1971]

2.04 DRAPERY FABRICATION

A. Draperies shall be [unlined, lined] custom made, fabricated to the highest industry standards and in accordance with the manufacturer's recommended standards and procedures.

B. Draperies are to extend the full length of the track with additional width for returns. For bi-parting draperies, center overlap shall be at least three inches (3").

C. Full-length draperies shall extend from the rod to one-half inch (1/2") above finished floor (AFF). Sill-length drapery shall be one-half inch (1/2") above sill when drapery falls within the window frame. Apron-length drapery shall be as shown on the drawings. Allowance shall be made for initial stretching or shrinking which may occur.

D. The drapery Contractor shall be responsible for positioning the drapery so that it does not rub on adjacent surfaces to cause premature wear.

E. Pleated draperies are to be fabricated as follows:

1. Place fabric on light table and examine for defects.

2. Cut along a weft or filling yarn of the fabric, avoiding any defects in the drapery lengths. Printed, textured and striped fabrics are to be properly matched. Patterns of all draperies are to be matched from the top down so at different length draperies will each have the same pattern at the top.

3. Join lengths of fabric on a sew and serge machine after removing selvedges. Stitching of seams shall align with warp threads of the fabric, be held to a true straight line and have no puckering. Use no less than half widths of fabric in each panel.

4. Form a 4" double, bottom hem using a blind stitch machine.

5. Form 1 1/4" double-side hems using a blind stitch machine. [For unlined draperies].

5. Fabricate lining in the same way as drapery. Attach lining to drapery fabric allowing for a 1" drapery fabric foldback on the lining side of the drapery [For lined draperies].
6. Table drapery to insure squareness. Adjust length from the top.
7. Fabricate for [folded, rolled, stitched, pinch pleat] draperies as described in paragraph 2.05. Heading fabrication must be carefully coordinated with track system.

F. Thread shall match the dominant color of the drapery fabric and shall be compatible with properties of the fabric. Monofilament nylon shall not be used except for stitching pleats.

G. Each drapery made of man-made yarns shall have a care label sewn into the bottom hem, detailing cleaning procedures to be used.

H. All draperies should be pressed, pleat folded when compatible with the heading system, and hung on individual hangers provided with large sleeves. Each drapery must be protected until installed.

2.05 HEADING FABRICATION

A. General
   1. Drapery fabric shall, for the full width, be sewn to [3", 3 1/2", 4"] permanent, non-woven heavy-weight buckram which shall then be folded under the fabric for a total of three complete fabric thicknesses plus the buckram to form the drapery heading.
   2. Drapery is to be [40%, 60%, 80%, 100%, 120%] fullness.

B. Pinch Pleat Fabrication
   1. All pleats are to be French style with three tines. The pleat is to be sewn in place using a double row of stitching the full height of the pleat beginning and ending in the center of the crinoline. Machine tack the pinched pleat in place, clipping all loose tacking threads from the pleat.

C. Stitched Pleat Fabrication
   1. To the heading attach Kirsch Accordia-fold [7 1/2", 8 1/2", 10"] snap tape. Follow instructions in the Kirsch Accordia-fold guide book.
   1. Use Graber Stack Pleat system, following the manufacturer's instructions.

D. Rolled Pleat Fabrication
   1. To the heading, attach Kirsch nylon snap tape with snaps on 4 1/4" centers. Follow instructions in the Kirsch Ripplefold guidebook.
   1. Use Graber Roll Fold system, following the manufacturer's instructions.

E. Folded Pleat Fabrication
    1. Finished drapery panels are to be fabricated per instructions in the Kirsch Archifold guidebook using [3 1/2", 4"] sew-on pleaters.
    1. Use Graber Neat Pleat system, following the manufacturer's instructions.

Part 3 — EXECUTION

3.01 INSPECTION

A. Drapery shall hang in natural draping conditions without creases.
B. Appearance of drapery shall indicate that it has been steamed and hand dressed at the job site.
C. All measurements shall conform to the drawings and to specification requirements.
D. Seams shall be flat. No puckering will be allowed.
E. All patterns shall be perfectly aligned, vertically and horizontally.
F. All items will be inspected to confirm compliance with respect to workmanship, materials, color and installation.

3.02 PREPARATION

A. The Contractor shall examine all room areas, surfaces, openings, and parts of the structure in which the drapery work is to be installed. Notify the Designer in writing if any conditions are detrimental to the proper and timely completion of the work. Do not proceed with the installation until such conditions have been corrected by the [General Contractor, Owner].
B. Once the Contractor commences the installation of a room or area under this specification, it shall be assumed that the condition of the window wall has been accepted and any repairs or further corrections in the window wall surfaces shall become the responsibility of the Contractor.
C. The Contractor shall be completely responsible for determining fabric requirements and fabrication details for the completion of this work. Before ordering materials or fabricating any work, verify all measurements and conditions at the job site. Field measure all window openings. Recheck all measurements after the installation of drapery hardware to insure proper fit of all draperies. No extra charge or compensation will be allowed on account of differences between field measurements and dimensions on the drawings.

3.03 INSTALLATION

A. The Contractor shall be responsible for monitoring the progress of the job in order to have all material ready to install at the proper time. Sufficient qualified personnel shall be employed in the installation to assure timely completion.

B. Installation of all items shall be by skilled mechanics and shall be of the highest degree of workmanship in accordance with the manufacturer's recommended standards and procedures.

C. Securely install specific tracks, accessories and hardware using manufacturer's recommended screws, brackets and other suitable fixtures applicable to substrate and finish. Cooperate with other trades in securing drapery track.

D. Drapery items shall be installed according to the drawings, except where unforeseen obstacles interfere. Should such be the case, the Designer will make the decision on alternate placement.

E. Set drapery track for one way or bi-parting draw as shown in the drawings.

F. When attaching drapery to track, add or decrease carriers as required for proper installation.

3.04 FIELD QUALITY CONTROL

A. The items will be inspected by the Designer to confirm compliance with the drawings and specifications with respect to workmanship, materials, color and installation.

B. All brackets shall be tested to withstand a pull commensurate with the weight of the draperies and track assembly, plus the forces applied in operating the system.

C. All cords and operational components shall operate without application of undue force.

3.05 ADJUST AND CLEAN

A. Keep the premises free and clear of all waste material in connection with the work, and at the completion of the work remove all waste and implements and leave the area clean.

B. Correct and repair all finger and tool marks and other blemishes.

C. Demonstrate the operation of all items installed to a designated representative of the Owner.

D. Adjust any inoperable conditions to the Owner's satisfaction throughout the guarantee period.

3.06 SCHEDULES

Attach window schedules here.

BIBLIOGRAPHY

General

Agranoff, Joan, editor: *Modern Plastics Encyclopedia.* NY, McGraw-Hill, 1983, *60:* 6-390.

Callender, John Hancock: *Time Saver Standards for Architectural Design Data,* 6th ed. NY, McGraw-Hill, 1982, pp. 3.277-3.310.

Dietz, Albert G.H.: *Plastics for Architects and Builders.* Cambridge, MA, MIT Press, 1969.

Huntington, Whitney Clark and Robert E. Mickadeit: *Building Construction.* NY, John Wiley and Sons, 1981.

Merritt, Frederick S.: *Building Design and Construction Handbook.* NY, McGraw-Hill, 1982, pp. 12-63.

Reznikoff, S.C.: *Specification for Commercial Interiors.* NY, Whitney, 1979.

Riggs, J. Rosemary: *Materials and Components of Interior Design.* Reston, VA, Reston, 1985.

Watson, Don A.: *Construction Materials and Processes.* NY, McGraw-Hill, 1978.

Floor Coverings

Allied Corporation; Fibers and Plastics Division, Judy Peters, editor: Carpet and Computers in Conflict; Electrostatic Disruption of Electronic Equipment. *Industry in Depth,* Chicago, Institute of Business Designers, vol. 8, April 1984.

Anderson, Roger L., Donald C. Mackel, Barry S. Stoller and George F. Mallison: Carpeting in Hospitals: An Epidemiological Evaluation. *Journal of Clinical Microbiology, 15:* 408-415, March 1982.

Antimicrobial Features of Commercial Carpeting. NY, Allied, n.d.

Armstrong Technical Data. Lancaster, PA, Armstrong, 1982.

Bakker, P.G.H. and J.L. Faoagali: The Effect of Carpet on the Number of Microbes in the Hospital Environment. *The New England Medical Journal,* pp. 88-92, Feb. 1977.

Bakker, P.G.H. and J.L. Faoagali: Antimicrobial Treatment for Hospital Carpets. *The New England Medical Journal,* pp. 132-135, Feb. 1977.

BASF Corporation: *Guidelines for Maintenance and Cleaning of Commercial Carpet.* Williamsburg, VA, BASF, n.d.

Benjamine, A. and S. Davis: *Flammability Testing for Carpet, Final Report.* Washington, D.C., U.S. Department of Commerce National Bureau of Standards, 1978.

Bodnar, James: Ceramic Tile Makes a Comeback. *The Construction Specifier,* pp. 58-63, Oct. 1985.

Carpet and Rug Institute: *Carpet Specifier's Handbook.* Dalton, GA, CRI, 1980 and 1987 editions, pp. 26-35, 40.

Case, R.K.: Carpeting: A Complex Spec. *The Construction Specifier,* pp. 64-68, Oct. 1985.

Chalmers, Ray: Selecting the Proper Tile Application Method. *Building Design and Construction,* pp. 118-120, Sept. 1985.

Chalmers, Ray: A Review of Related Products for Ceramic Tile. *Building Design and Construction,* pp. 124-125, Sept. 1985.

Chalmers, Ray and Margaret Doyle: Ceramic Tile Case Studies. *Building Design and Construction,* pp. 128-132, Sept. 1985.

The Designers Guide to Italian Tiles and Their Installation. NY, Italian Tile Center, 1983.

Doyle, Margaret: Ceramic Tile Suits a Variety of Uses. *Building Design and Construction,* pp. 114-117, Sept. 1985.

Dupont: *Maintenance Guide for Carpets of Dupont Antron®.* Wilmington, DE, Dupont, n.d.

Floor Covering Weekly, Specifier's Guide to Contract Floor Covering, 1983-84 Edition. NY, Hearst, pp. 9-52, 101-155.

Forman, Katherine: Olefin Carpets Serve High End Contract Needs. *Contract,* pp. 110-111, Feb. 1984.

Garner, Julia S. and Martin S. Ferraro: CDC Guidelines for Handwashing and Hospital Environmental Control, 1985, Revised. *Infection Control,* 7 (4): 231-243, 1986.

Graham, Gail and Richard Berkman: *Evaluation of Flooring in a Hospital.* Boston, Group Systems Engineering Program, Massachusettes Hospital Association, Sept. 1978.

Handbook For Ceramic Tile Installation. Princeton, NJ, Tile Council of America, Inc., 1984.

Joyner, William D: Carpeting. *Building Operation Management,* pp. 91-96, Feb. 1985.

Levine, George: Straight Answers to Ten Vexing Questions About Carpet Specifying. *Facilities Design and Management,* pp. 84-88, May 1983.

Maintenance of Vinyl Asbestos and Asphalt Tile Floors. Washington, D.C., Resilient Floor Covering Institute, 1975.

Mazzur, Richard P.: Choosing the Right Resilient Flooring. *The Construction Specifier,* pp. 70-82, March 1986.

Monsanto Contract Fibers: *Dataspec.* Atlanta, Monsanto, 1984.

National Tile Promotion Federation: *Ceramic Tile.* Alexandria, VA, CSI Monograph Series, Nov. 1984.

Recommended Installation Specifications for Vinyl Composition, Solid Vinyl and Asphalt Tile Floorings. Washington, D.C., Resilient Floor Covering Institute, 1982.

Rench, J.F.: Specifying Carpet Maintenance, A Fresh Approach. *The Construction Specifier,* pp. 70-73, Oct. 1985.

Snyder, William et al.: Facing Tile. *Progressive Architecture,* pp. 113-119, Oct. 1984.

The Specifier's Primer. *Tile and Decorative Surfaces,* pp. 56-64, June 1984.

Specification Guide for Carpets of Antron III Nylon®: Health Care. Wilmington, DE, Dupont, 1980.

Wall Finishes

Banov, Abel: *Paints and Coatings Handbook.* Farmington, MI, Structures Pub. Co., 1973.

B.F. Goodrich Wallcovering Could Save Your Life. Akron, B.F. Goodrich Company, 1986.

Guide for Specifications and Use of Vinyl Wallcovering. Columbus, Columbus Coated Fabrics, 1982.

Introducing Boltaflex® with Prefixx™. Toledo, DiversiTech General, 1986.

Introduction to Paint Technology. *Painting Systems for Specifiers and Applicators.* Cleveland, Sherwin Williams, 1983.

Martin, Robert et al.: A Prologue to Paint. *Progressive Architecture,* pp. 131-136, Nov. 1984.

Paints and Coatings: A Guide for Professional Performance. San Francisco, Fuller O'Brian, 1975.

Product and Painting Guide. Pittsburgh, Pittsburgh Paints, 1981.

Ray, Stacy: Vinyl Wall Covering. *Industry in Depth,* Chicago, Institute of Business Designers, vol. 1, Feb. 1982.

Test Results: Xorel Fabric Wallcoverings by Carnegie. NY, Rockville Center, Carnegie, 1982.

Zwers, Jim: Specifying Vinyl Wall Covering for Long Life. *The Construction Specifier,* pp. 70-75, April 1985.

Window Treatment

Architect's Guide to Kirsch Drapery Hardware. Sturgis, MI, Kirsch, 1983.

Architectural Alliance et al.: Through a Glass Brightly. *Progressive Architecture,* pp. 138-143, Nov. 1981.

Carrabino, Joseph D.: *Window Covering Cleaning: Ten Year Comparative Cost Study.* Santa Monica, Louver Drape, Inc., 1972.

Ferguson, James and Gerald D. Appel: Energy Efficiency at the Window. *Draperies and Window Coverings, 1* (6): 60-62, April/May 1982.

Shurcliff, William A.: *Thermal Shutters and Shades.* Andover, MA, Brick House, 1980.

Williams, Kathleen: Vertical Blinds: On Track for the 80's. *Draperies and Window Coverings, 1* (6): 26-30, 1982.

Williams, Kathleen: Interview with David F. Cooke. New Challenges for the Window Covering Industry. *Draperies and Window Coverings, 1* (6): 20-24, 1982.

Zoehrer, Richard: Energy Efficiency Can Be Improved With Good Window Management. *Contract,* pp. 66-69, Dec. 1980.

Upholstery Fabrics

BIFMA: Fact Finding Report on *A Study of Existing Flammability Tests and Requirements for Upholstered Furniture,* File R8044, Project 76NK5338. Chicago, Underwriters Laboratories, Inc., 1977.

CFFA Standard Test Methods: Chemical Coated Fabrics and Film. Cleveland, Chemical Fabrics and Film Association, 1984.

Cigarette Ignition Resistance of Upholstered Furniture Composites (NFPA 260B). Quincy, MA, NFPA, 1983.

Fabric Classification Test Method. High Point, NC, UFAC, 1983.

First Generation Voluntary Upholstered Furniture Flammability Standard for Business and Institutional Markets. Grand Rapids, BIFMA, 1980.

Guide to Man-made Fibers. Man-made Fibers Producers Association, Inc., Washington, D.C., 1977.

Harvie, Ashley: Helping to Put Out Fires. *Interiors,* pp. 74-80, Oct. 1983.

Joint-Industry Upholstery Fabric Standards Committee: *Woven Upholstery Fabric Standards and Guidelines.* Joint-Industry Committee, 1980.

Joint-Industry Knit Upholstery Fabric Standards Committee: *Knit Upholstery Fabric Standards and Guidelines.* Joint-Industry Committee, 1983.

Jackman, Dianne R. and Mary K. Dixon: *The Guide to Textiles.* Winnepeg, Peguis Pub. Ltd., 1983.

Larsen, Jack Lenor and Jeanne Weeks: *Fabrics For Interiors.* NY, Van Nostrand Reinhold, 1975.

Man-Made Fibers Fact Book. Man-made Fibers Products Association, Inc., Washington, D.C.; 1978.

Textile Handbook, 5th ed. Washington, D.C., American Home Economics Association, 1974.

Wool Information. NY, The Wool Bureau, Inc., 1983.

Thompson, Presley et al.: The Issue of Fire. *Progressive Architecture,* pp. 149-153, Sept. 1984.

Zoehrer, Richard: Confused by Fabric Flammability Ratings? *Facilities Design and Management,* pp. 70-72, Nov., Dec. 1982.

Furniture and Casework

Architectural Casework Details. Arlington, VA, Architectural Woodwork Institute, 1969.

Bocchi, Greg: Powder Coatings: A New Technology Takes Off. *The Construction Specifier,* pp. 102-105, Sept. 1986.

Duncan, Ed: High Pressure Decorative Laminates. *Industry in Depth,* Institute of Business Designers, June 1983.

High Pressure Plastic Laminate as an Architectural "Woodwork" Material. Arlington, VA, Architectural Woodwork Institute, 1981.

Performance, Application, Fabrication and Installation of High Pressure Decorative Laminates; Standards Publication/No. LD3.1. Washington, D.C., National Electrical Manufacturers Association (NEMA), 1986.

Specification Information Guide. Wayne, NJ, Formica Corporation, 1983.

Wilson Art Specifications Assistance. Temple, TX, Ralph Wilson Plastics Co., 1985.

Why Powder Coat? A Practical Guide to Powder Coating. Florence, KY, Volstatic, Inc., n.d.

INDEX

347

88.95